Dapr Unlocked
A Definitive Guide to Microservices and Cloud-Native Solutions

Nova Trex

© 2024 by Wang Press. All rights reserved.

No part of this publication may be reproduced, distributed, or transmitted in any form or by any means, including photocopying, recording, or other electronic or mechanical methods, without the prior written permission of the publisher, except in the case of brief quotations embodied in critical reviews and certain other noncommercial uses permitted by copyright law.

Published by Wang Press

For permissions and other inquiries, write to:
P.O. Box 3132, Framingham, MA 01701, USA

Contents

1 Introduction to Dapr and Microservices   9
    1.1 Understanding Microservices Architectures 10
    1.2 The Challenges of Microservices 14
    1.3 What is Dapr? 17
    1.4 Features and Benefits of Dapr 21
    1.5 Dapr vs. Traditional Approaches 25

2 Getting Started with Dapr: Installation and Setup   31
    2.1 System Requirements and Prerequisites 31
    2.2 Installing Dapr CLI 34
    2.3 Running Dapr in Self-hosted Mode 38
    2.4 Using Dapr in Kubernetes 43
    2.5 Dapr Dashboard Setup 48
    2.6 Verifying the Installation 53

3 Understanding Dapr Building Blocks   59
    3.1 Overview of Dapr Building Blocks 59
    3.2 Service-to-Service Invocation 64
    3.3 State Management 68

	3.4	Publish-Subscribe Pattern	73
	3.5	Resource Bindings	78
	3.6	Observability	83
	3.7	Actor Model	88

4 State Management with Dapr — 93

	4.1	Understanding State Management in Microservices	93
	4.2	Dapr's State Management Building Block	98
	4.3	Connecting to Different State Stores	102
	4.4	Using State APIs	107
	4.5	Consistency and Concurrency Models	112
	4.6	Transaction and Batch Operations	117
	4.7	Best Practices for Dapr State Management	121

5 Dapr Bindings and Pub/Sub — 127

	5.1	Exploring Dapr Bindings	127
	5.2	Configuring Input and Output Bindings	132
	5.3	Working with Event-Driven Architecture through Bindings	137
	5.4	Overview of Dapr Pub/Sub Mechanism	143
	5.5	Configuring Publishers and Subscribers	149
	5.6	Idempotent Subscriber Example	155
	5.7	Advantages and Use Cases of Dapr Bindings and Pub/Sub	158

6 Service Invocation and Resiliency — 165

	6.1	Service Invocation in Dapr	165
	6.2	Configuring Service Discovery	169
	6.3	Implementing Circuit Breaker Patterns	173
	6.4	Handling Retries and Timeouts	176

	6.5	Observability in Service Invocations	179
	6.6	Developing Fault-Tolerant Applications	183

7 Dapr's Role in Observability and Monitoring — 187

	7.1	Overview of Observability in Microservices	188
	7.2	Telemetry with Dapr	192
	7.3	Configuring Dapr for Monitoring	196
	7.4	Integrating with Monitoring Tools	201
	7.5	Tracing Requests with Dapr	206
	7.6	Custom Metrics and Logging	211
	7.7	Best Practices for Observability	216

8 Security and Dapr — 221

	8.1	Security Challenges in Microservices	221
	8.2	Dapr Security Model	225
	8.3	Transport Layer Security (TLS) in Dapr	228
	8.4	Component Security and Secret Management	232
	8.5	Access Control and Authentication	236
	8.6	Secure Communication with Dapr API	240
	8.7	Best Practices for Dapr Security	244

9 Advanced Dapr Features and Integrations — 249

	9.1	Integrating with External Systems	249
	9.2	Custom Components Development	254
	9.3	Multi-Cloud and Hybrid Deployments	259
	9.4	Advanced Actor Patterns	263
	9.5	Leveraging Dapr with Event-Driven Architectures	268
	9.6	Optimizing Performance with Dapr	273
	9.7	Case Studies and Real-World Integrations	279

10 Deploying Dapr in Cloud-Native Environments 285

    10.1 Understanding Cloud-Native Principles 285

    10.2 Preparing Your Environment for Dapr 289

    10.3 Deploying Dapr on Kubernetes 293

    10.4 Scaling Dapr Applications 298

    10.5 Managing Dapr in Production 303

    10.6 Leveraging Cloud Provider Services 308

    10.7 CI/CD for Dapr Applications 313

Introduction

In an era where digital transformation is not just an option but a necessity, software development methodologies have undergone significant shifts to accommodate rapidly changing demands. Microservices architecture has emerged at the forefront of this transformation, offering a modular and dynamic approach to building and scaling applications. These architectures are crucial for fostering business agility and resilience in today's competitive landscape. However, the complexity inherent in developing and managing microservices—particularly in ensuring effective service communication, state consistency, and seamless infrastructure integration—poses significant challenges.

"Dapr Unlocked: A Definitive Guide to Microservices and Cloud-Native Solutions" is crafted as an all-encompassing resource aimed at demystifying these complexities by delving into the robust capabilities of Dapr. Dapr, or Distributed Application Runtime, is an open-source project designed to streamline the development and lifecycle management of microservices applications. It achieves this by providing a set of essential building blocks which abstract away many of the difficult aspects inherent in distributed computing.

Dapr addresses common microservices challenges, such as service-to-service invocation, state persistence, publish-subscribe messaging, input/output bindings, and observability. By leveraging a sidecar architecture, Dapr seamlessly integrates with any service and abstracts the less visible but crucial infrastructural operations, empowering developers to focus on business logic and innovation.

This book provides a detailed examination of Dapr's core capabilities, ranging from getting started with installation to mastering its advanced features. We unravel the operational paradigms of Dapr, helping you harness it for efficient state management, secure and resilient communications, and adaptable scalability, crucial for cloud-native environments.

Our goal is to make Dapr an accessible tool for developers of all skill levels. This guide offers clear, step-by-step instructions and illustrative examples that facilitate the integration of Dapr into microservices projects, whether you are initiating a new application or enhancing an existing one. We begin with foundational concepts, ensuring you build a robust understanding before progressing to complex implementations and sophisticated user scenarios.

"Dapr Unlocked" seeks to be more than a manual; it is a companion in your journey to mastering microservices and cloud-native architectures. Whether you are aiming to craft robust digital solutions from scratch or refine and optimize existing platforms, this book provides the knowledge and insights necessary to harness Dapr's potential fully. In doing so, you position yourself and your organization to excel in an increasingly intricate and competitive technological ecosystem.

Chapter 1

Introduction to Dapr and Microservices

Microservices architecture has revolutionized how applications are developed and deployed, offering advantages like scalability and modularity. However, it introduces challenges such as managing distributed communications and maintaining system resilience. Dapr, the Distributed Application Runtime, emerges as a solution by providing developers with modular building blocks that abstract these complexities. With Dapr, the focus shifts back to business logic, easing the complexities of microservices implementation and accelerating the development of cloud-native applications. This chapter provides an analytic overview of microservices architecture, the inherent challenges it poses, and how Dapr offers a robust framework to address them efficiently.

1.1 Understanding Microservices Architectures

Microservices architecture represents a significant shift from traditional monolithic systems by providing a framework that allows for the development of more modular, scalable, and maintainable applications. This architectural style involves structuring an application as a collection of loosely coupled, independently deployable services. Each service in the microservices architecture is responsible for a distinct business capability and operates autonomously, allowing for decentralized governance and development processes.

The emergence of microservices architecture can be attributed to the need to address the limitations of monolithic systems, which often lead to issues such as tightly coupled components, difficulty in scaling, and challenges in implementing changes. Microservices architecture offers a solution by breaking down complex systems into manageable pieces, enabling teams to work on different services concurrently, implement changes more rapidly, and scale components independently.

One of the core principles of microservices architecture is the decomposition of a system based on business capabilities. Each microservice aligns with a specific business domain and contains the necessary logic and data management functionality to fulfill its designated role. This modularization facilitates an understanding of and reasoning about the application because it aligns system design with business goals.

Another key aspect of microservices architecture is autonomy. Each microservice operates in its own process and communicates with other services via lightweight mechanisms, often HTTP APIs or messaging queues. This autonomy allows for independent deployment and scaling of each service, promoting flexibility and resilience in the face of change or failure.

In a microservices architecture, decentralized governance is encouraged. Teams have the liberty to choose the most suitable technologies, tools, and programming languages for their services, aligning with the principle of using the "best tool for the job." This approach fosters innovation and allows services to evolve at their own pace without being constrained by a common technology stack.

1.1. UNDERSTANDING MICROSERVICES ARCHITECTURES

Below is a simple illustration of creating and deploying a basic microservice using a RESTful API. This example demonstrates the essentials of designing a microservice with clear endpoints and operations:

```python
from flask import Flask, jsonify, request

app = Flask(__name__)

# Sample data
users = [
    {'id': 1, 'name': 'Alice'},
    {'id': 2, 'name': 'Bob'},
]

# Endpoint to get all users
@app.route('/users', methods=['GET'])
def get_users():
    return jsonify(users)

# Endpoint to get a single user by id
@app.route('/users/<int:user_id>', methods=['GET'])
def get_user(user_id):
    user = next((user for user in users if user['id'] == user_id), None)
    return jsonify(user) if user else ('', 404)

# Endpoint to create a new user
@app.route('/users', methods=['POST'])
def create_user():
    new_user = request.get_json()
    users.append(new_user)
    return jsonify(new_user), 201

if __name__ == '__main__':
    app.run(debug=True)
```

This example underscores several characteristics of a microservice: statelessness, simple and well-defined APIs, and isolation from other system components. The service above independently handles requests, demonstrating the isolated nature of microservices. Further improvements would typically involve incorporating error handling, validation, and integration with persistent storage.

The benefits of adopting a microservices architecture are substantial. Notably, it supports enhanced scalability, allowing each service to scale independently to meet demand. This capability is especially crucial for applications experiencing varied loads across different modules. Additionally, microservices improve fault tolerance because the failure of one service does not necessarily bring down the entire system, allowing for graceful degradation of functionality.

However, while microservices offer these advantages, they also introduce new complexities. The need for managing inter-service communication poses significant challenges, particularly when considering network latency and data consistency. Developers must carefully orchestrate data exchange and manage state across distributed services to maintain reliability and performance.

Service discovery constitutes an essential component of the microservices infrastructure. In a dynamic environment where services can come and go, being able to locate services efficiently is crucial. Tools like Consul, Eureka, and others provide mechanisms for service registration and discovery, ensuring that microservices can communicate seamlessly.

Security is another complex aspect inherent in microservices. With multiple services communicating over the network, securing data exchange and access becomes critical. Implementing API gateways and adopting security protocols such as OAuth2 and JWT (JSON Web Tokens) are common practices to safeguard microservices and their interactions.

Below is an example illustrating how securing a microservice can be achieved using tokens in a Python-based REST API:

```python
from flask import Flask, jsonify, request, make_response
import jwt
import datetime

app = Flask(__name__)
app.config['SECRET_KEY'] = 'your_secret_key_here'

def token_required(f):
    def decorated(*args, **kwargs):
        token = request.headers.get('x-access-token')
        if not token:
            return jsonify({'message': 'Token is missing!'}), 403
        try:
            jwt.decode(token, app.config['SECRET_KEY'], algorithms=['HS256'])
        except:
            return jsonify({'message': 'Token is invalid!'}), 403
        return f(*args, **kwargs)
    return decorated

@app.route('/login', methods=['POST'])
def login():
    auth = request.authorization
    if auth and auth.password == 'password':
        token = jwt.encode({'user': auth.username, 'exp': datetime.datetime.utcnow() +
            datetime.timedelta(minutes=30)}, app.config['SECRET_KEY'])
        return jsonify({'token': token})
```

1.1. UNDERSTANDING MICROSERVICES ARCHITECTURES

```
    return make_response('Could not verify', 401, {'WWW-Authenticate': 'Basic realm
        ="Login required!"'})

@app.route('/secure-data', methods=['GET'])
@token_required
def secure_data():
    return jsonify({'message': 'This is secured data.'})

if __name__ == '__main__':
    app.run(debug=True)
```

This example highlights the implementation of JWT for authentication purposes, securing microservice endpoints. Token-based security ensures that only authenticated users with valid tokens can access protected resources, thereby adding a layer of protection against unauthorized access.

Building a robust microservices environment requires infrastructure to support the resilience and independence of microservices. Tools for monitoring, logging, and alerting are indispensable, providing insights into system health and facilitating prompt responses to issues. Tools like Prometheus, Grafana, and ELK stack (Elasticsearch, Logstash, Kibana) play a vital role in effectively managing these tasks.

Lastly, the deployment of microservices necessitates the adoption of continuous integration and continuous deployment (CI/CD) pipelines. These pipelines automate the process of testing, building, and deploying microservices, enabling rapid iteration and deployment while maintaining high-quality standards. Kubernetes has become a popular choice as an orchestration platform due to its comprehensive support for managing containerized applications, offering features like automated deployment, scaling, and rollback.

In essence, while microservices architectures provide a framework for modern application development that addresses many of the limitations inherent in monolithic applications, they also require careful planning and a robust ecosystem of tools to manage the complexity they introduce. The shift towards microservices architecture should be accompanied by a disciplined approach to system design, encompassing considerations for service granularity, communication, security, and deployment. Each of these elements contributes to building scalable, resilient, and maintainable software systems in the contemporary cloud-native landscape.

1.2 The Challenges of Microservices

While microservices architecture offers a plethora of benefits over monolithic systems, it introduces a new set of complexities and challenges that need to be addressed to harness its full potential. These challenges primarily arise from the distributed nature of microservices, the necessity for efficient inter-service communication, effective state management, and the ability to scale seamlessly.

One of the primary challenges in microservices is service communication. In a distributed system, services must interact to fulfill business functions, typically through network-based protocols. Communication in microservices can be synchronous, using RESTful APIs or gRPC, or asynchronous, utilizing message brokers like Apache Kafka or RabbitMQ. Each communication strategy has its pros and cons.

- **Synchronous Communication:** This type involves direct, real-time interaction between services through APIs. Although synchronous communication can simplify the implementation of certain transactional patterns, it ties the availability of the whole system to the availability of involved services. The inherent latency of network calls and the potential for cascading failures if one service goes down are significant concerns.

  ```
  import requests

  def get_user(user_id):
      response = requests.get(f'http://example.com/api/users/{user_id}')
      if response.status_code == 200:
          return response.json()
      else:
          return None
  ```

  The example demonstrates a synchronous pattern where a service depends on the response of another service to proceed, potentially introducing latency, especially with remote or heavyweight operations.

- **Asynchronous Communication:** This design employs messaging queues to decouple services spatially and temporally, leading to more resilient systems. However, it requires additional infrastructure and complexity, such as message schema evolution,

1.2. THE CHALLENGES OF MICROSERVICES

handling travel time for messages, and ensuring delivery guarantees.

```
import pika

connection = pika.BlockingConnection(pika.ConnectionParameters('localhost'))
channel = connection.channel()

channel.queue_declare(queue='task_queue', durable=True)

message = 'Task message'
channel.basic_publish(
    exchange='',
    routing_key='task_queue',
    body=message,
    properties=pika.BasicProperties(
        delivery_mode=2, # make message persistent
    ))

connection.close()
```

Another significant challenge in microservices architectures is **distributed data management**. Unlike monolithic applications where data consistency can be maintained within a single database transaction, microservices often require a distributed approach, leading to the complexities of eventual consistency. Implementing a distributed data management strategy involves balancing consistency, availability, and partition tolerance as per the CAP theorem. Eventual consistency models must be understood and alternatives for data replication and transaction compensation need to be designed.

Service Choreography vs. Orchestration presents further complexity. Choreography allows services to make decisions independently, coordinating indirectly through events. In contrast, orchestration uses a central service to direct the workflow. The choice between these models significantly impacts the architecture's manageability, debuggability, and adaptability to change.

Managing **state** across microservices demands techniques like event sourcing or leveraging cloud-based data management systems, both requiring additional layers of infrastructure and design planning.

Scaling Microservices efficiently creates another layer of difficulty. Although one of the major benefits of microservices is scalable infrastructure, achieving optimal scaling involves rigorous monitoring, maintaining that scaling is correctly matched with demand, and preventing over-provisioning.

```
apiVersion: autoscaling/v1
kind: HorizontalPodAutoscaler
metadata:
  name: user-service-autoscaler
spec:
  maxReplicas: 10
  minReplicas: 1
  scaleTargetRef:
    apiVersion: apps/v1
    kind: Deployment
    name: user-service
  targetCPUUtilizationPercentage: 80
```

This Kubernetes example showcases configuring autoscaling for a microservice based on CPU utilization, which requires a deep understanding of load patterns and monitoring techniques.

Observability and Monitoring become paramount with many distributed services. Tools and practices like distributed tracing (e.g., using OpenTelemetry), comprehensive logging, and metrics aggregation are crucial to understanding the health and performance of the services. However, setting up such infrastructure is sophisticated and demands an investment in proper tooling and team training.

Security presents yet another substantial challenge. The distributed nature of microservices increases the attack surface. Different points of interaction necessitate robust authorization, authentication, and encryption measures. Implementing zero-trust architectures, API gateways, and implementing security best practices are necessary yet complex tasks.

```
http {
    ...
    limit_req_zone $binary_remote_addr zone=mylimit:10m rate=1r/s;
    server {
        ...
        location /api/ {
            limit_req zone=mylimit burst=5;
        }
    }
}
```

Deploying microservices in production involves **management overhead**, requiring operations teams to manage a more significant number of services, deployments, and instances. These operations necessitate proficient automatic deployment pipelines, versioning, and rollback mechanisms to ensure seamless integration and delivery.

The challenges with microservices architectures—while numerous and complex—do not diminish their allure or efficacy. Instead, they require dedicated strategies, tools, and managerial oversight to implement and operate effectively. Balancing these complex requirements and successfully mitigating risks often involves building a robust ecosystem of support, leveraging modern infrastructure, and continuing to innovate technical and process solutions. Through thoughtful application governance, skillful use of technology, and targeted investments in operational support, organizations can achieve success with microservices while overcoming the intricate challenges they present.

1.3 What is Dapr?

Dapr, short for Distributed Application Runtime, is an open-source runtime designed to facilitate the development of microservices and cloud-native applications. It abstracts complex distributed system challenges by providing a set of building blocks that simplify common tasks such as service invocation, state management, and resource binding. Dapr seamlessly integrates into existing applications, allowing developers to focus on business logic rather than infrastructure concerns.

The foundational goal of Dapr is to enhance the microservices development experience by reducing the cognitive load associated with managing the interactions and dependencies of distributed systems. Dapr proposes a new model to build microservices applications by providing capabilities that are standardized, vendor-agnostic, and pluggable.

One of Dapr's primary features is its ability to manage **service-to-service communication**. By using Dapr's service invocation API, microservices can easily communicate with each other through HTTP or gRPC protocols without embedding specific implementation details in the application code. Dapr guarantees secure, reliable, and fault-tolerant communication between services, leaving the intricacies of protocols and routing to the runtime.

```
POST http://localhost:<dapr-port>/v1.0/invoke/<app-id>/method/<method>
Content-Type: application/json

{
```

```
"key": "value"
}
```

This HTTP POST request demonstrates service invocation, where <app-id> is the target application ID and <method> is the method name Dapr uses to facilitate RPC-like behavior.

The **state management** capabilities of Dapr allow developers to handle state efficiently across distributed applications. Dapr supports stateful services by allowing them to store and retrieve state seamlessly with a simple key-value API. It abstracts the underlying storage technology, providing flexibility to plug in various storage backends like Redis, Azure Cosmos DB, or AWS DynamoDB without necessitating a change in application code.

```
import requests

# Save state
state_data = [{"key": "order_1", "value": {"id": 1, "item": "book", "quantity": 3}}]
requests.post("http://localhost:<dapr-port>/v1.0/state/<store-name>", json=
    state_data)

# Retrieve state
response = requests.get("http://localhost:<dapr-port>/v1.0/state/<store-name>/
    order_1")
order = response.json()
```

In the above example, Dapr's state API is utilized to store and retrieve an order's state, thus abstracting the underlying state store details from the business logic.

Dapr's Actor Model is another component that simplifies handling distributed objects with lifecycle management. The actor pattern is widely used for building distributed, stateful objects with single-threaded execution. Dapr provides a built-in actor runtime with features such as timers, reminders, persistent state, and actor distribution. This makes actor management significantly simpler and allows developers to efficiently separate business logic into individually manageable components.

```
# Actor configuration is linked via Dapr CLI or configuration file
dapr run --app-id myapp --app-port 3000 python3 app.py

# Actuation of actor system
POST http://localhost:<dapr-port>/v1.0/actors/<actor-type>/<actor-id>/method
    /<method>
```

1.3. WHAT IS DAPR?

```
{
  "data": 10
}
```

In this configuration, Dapr handles the lifecycle and state of actors, making complex concurrency structures and state replication between actors more manageable.

When developing microservices, **resource binding** and triggered bindings are crucial. Dapr's binding API offers seamless integration with various external systems such as messaging systems, databases, and trigger-based cloud services. By defining input and output bindings, developers can interact with external systems in a standard, vendor-neutral way.

Observability is a major challenge in any microservices-based system, and Dapr aims to mitigate this through a comprehensive set of observability features. It provides logs, metrics, and tracing out of the box, helping developers to understand the system's behavior and diagnose issues efficiently. Each Dapr service can output metrics to monitoring systems such as Prometheus, enabling enhanced visibility into service health and performance.

Security is another critical feature incorporated into Dapr's design. It provides secure communication between services through mutual TLS encryption. This ensures data in transit is protected, fulfilling a vital role in securing microservices. Dapr includes authentication of microservice requests and supports the use of secret stores for securely accessing sensitive data, like keys or credentials.

```
apiVersion: dapr.io/v1alpha1
kind: Configuration
metadata:
  name: appconfig
spec:
  mtls:
    enabled: true
    workLoadCertTTL: "24h"
    allowedClockSkew: "15m"
```

By using the above configuration, Dapr automatically manages certificates and their renewal, simplifying the security management significantly.

Dapr can be extended to run on a range of environments from local development to cloud hosting providers like Azure, AWS, or on any Kubernetes cluster. Dapr supports both **self-hosted mode** for local development and a Kubernetes-hosted mode for production deployments. This flexibility allows developers to start small and scale as needed, leveraging the same toolset throughout development and production.

Dapr's **extensibility** offers significant advantages by allowing developers to bring additional components into the runtime, customizing or extending default behaviors to meet specific use cases. It maintains modularity and encourages community-contributed components and libraries, enhancing the ecosystem around microservices development practices.

Below is an example illustrating how Dapr seamlessly integrates a pub-/sub messaging system with minimal configuration or code changes:

```
apiVersion: dapr.io/v1alpha1
kind: Component
metadata:
  name: pubsub
  namespace: default
spec:
  type: pubsub.redis
  version: v1
  metadata:
  - name: redisHost
    value: redis-master.redis.svc.cluster.local:6379
  - name: redisPassword
    value: ""
```

```
# Publishing to a topic
event = {'data': 'Sample data'}
requests.post('http://localhost:<dapr-port>/v1.0/publish/<pubsub-name>/<topic>',
    json=event)
```

The provided example indicates how Dapr's definition format allows clean and manageable integrations into external systems like Redis without deeply embedding these tools into application code.

In essence, Dapr significantly reduces the complexity involved in developing microservices applications by providing a set of consistent and portable APIs. Using Dapr can lead to increased development speed, greater architectural flexibility, and enhanced runtime features. It provides a pragmatic balance between adhering to microservices best practices and allowing developers to avoid complex infrastructure issues through rich, abstracted service capabilities. By integrating these capabilities into the development process, organizations can more effectively deploy and manage scalable, resilient, and secure microservices applications in a cloud-first world.

1.4 Features and Benefits of Dapr

Dapr, or Distributed Application Runtime, stands out as a versatile and efficient tool designed to ease the complexities inherent in crafting modern cloud-native applications and microservices. By abstracting common concerns and leveraging a set of modular building blocks, Dapr provides developers with a powerful toolkit that brings consistency, security, and flexibility to application development and deployment. This section delves into the features and benefits of Dapr, highlighting how it enhances development efficiency and operational effectiveness.

Building Block Architecture: At the heart of Dapr is its building block architecture, offering a collection of independent, pluggable components that developers can mix and match. These building blocks address common requirements across microservices, such as service invocation, state management, pub/sub messaging, and resource binding. The modularity of Dapr allows developers to harness only the components they need, resulting in streamlined and focused application design.

- **Service Invocation:** This enables seamless, fault-tolerant communication across services. Dapr abstracts the networking complexities through HTTP or gRPC, automatically handling retries and error handling, which would otherwise require intricate custom code implementations.

```
package main

import (
    "bytes"
    "fmt"
    "io/ioutil"
    "net/http"
)

func invokeService(appID, method string, payload []byte) {
```

```go
        url := fmt.Sprintf("http://localhost:3500/v1.0/invoke/%s/method/%s",
            appID, method)
        req, err := http.NewRequest("POST", url, bytes.NewBuffer(payload))
        if err != nil {
            fmt.Println("Error creating request:", err)
            return
        }

        req.Header.Set("Content-Type", "application/json")
        client := &http.Client{}
        resp, err := client.Do(req)
        if err != nil {
            fmt.Println("Error executing request:", err)
            return
        }
        defer resp.Body.Close()

        body, _ := ioutil.ReadAll(resp.Body)
        fmt.Println("Response:", string(body))
}
```

- **State Management:** With Dapr, persisting and retrieving state becomes straightforward, regardless of the backend. Dapr supports key-value state stores and transactions, making it easy to implement reliable stateful applications. The abstraction provided here means cloud or self-hosted state stores can be used interchangeably without altering the business logic.

- **Pub/Sub Messaging:** This feature abstracts and simplifies the integration with different message brokers, allowing for robust event-driven architectures. Developers can leverage various pub-/sub components like Kafka, Redis, or MQTT, without needing to modify message publish and subscription code.

```java
import io.dapr.client.DaprClient;
import io.dapr.client.DaprClientBuilder;
import io.dapr.client.domain.CloudEvent;

public class Publisher {
    public static void main(String[] args) {
        DaprClient client = new DaprClientBuilder().build();

        String topicName = "example-topic";
        CloudEvent cloudEvent = new CloudEvent<>("unique-id", "
            example-source", "example-type", "example-subject", "Example
            data.");

        client.publishEvent("pubsub", topicName, cloudEvent).block();

        System.out.println("Event published.");
    }
}
```

1.4. FEATURES AND BENEFITS OF DAPR

- **Bindings:** Resource bindings are instrumental in connecting services to external resources. With output bindings, results from microservices can easily be sent to any supported service like Azure Blob Storage or AWS Kinesis with minimal configuration changes.

Interoperability and Pluggability: One of Dapr's distinct advantages is its interoperability across different environments and languages. Developers can bind Dapr to practically any language or framework, thanks to its use of standardized protocols like HTTP/gRPC. This ensures a minimal learning curve and simplified integration into existing technology stacks. Furthermore, Dapr components can be swapped in and out based on the application's or infrastructure's changing needs, promoting agility and responsiveness to new challenges or opportunities.

Enhanced Observability: As applications grow in complexity, observability becomes critical. Dapr includes built-in support for observability through open standards. Applications can automatically emit logs, traces, and metrics, which can be forwarded to monitoring suites like Prometheus, Grafana, or the ELK stack. Distributed tracing enables developers to trace through the entire call flow of complex applications, helping identify performance bottlenecks and reliability issues.

```
apiVersion: dapr.io/v1alpha1
kind: Configuration
metadata:
  name: metricconfig
spec:
  tracing:
    samplingRate: "1"
    exporterType: "zipkin"
    exporterAddress: "http://localhost:9411/api/v2/spans"
```

The configuration provided above enables applications to export trace data to Zipkin, a well-known distributed tracing tool.

Cross-Platform Operation: Dapr excels in its flexibility, running seamlessly in local, Kubernetes, or cloud-based environments. This allows developers to maintain consistent workflows and testing processes across development, staging, and production environments. Moreover, Dapr can operate both in self-hosted modes for simplicity during development and in advanced configurations on Kubernetes for production-grade applications.

Security Built-In: As security continues to be a paramount concern, Dapr integrates essential security features out of the box. Dapr automatically ensures secure connections between services through mutual TLS (mTLS). Secrets management is also supported, facilitating secure and standardized ways to access sensitive data across different cloud providers or on-premises setups.

Simplified Microservices Design: Dapr abstracts the complexity of microservices design, mitigating challenges related to maintaining telemetry, service discovery, fault handling, and more. By utilizing Dapr, architects and developers can invest more of their cognitive resources into developing differentiated, value-centric functionalities instead of focusing on identical infrastructure problem-solving.

Cloud-Native and Portable: Being cloud-native, Dapr takes advantage of emerging technologies and deployment patterns. Dapr is designed to be independent of specific cloud vendors, offering portable applications that can be easily moved between different cloud providers or on-premises environments with minimal alterations.

The following code snippets illustrate how Dapr injects application configurations and environment variables that ease the running of polyglot services:

```
FROM openjdk:11-jre-slim
WORKDIR /app
COPY target/myservice-0.0.1-SNAPSHOT.jar myservice.jar
CMD ["java", "-jar", "myservice.jar"]

# Dapr sidecar
dapr run --app-id myservice --app-port 8080 --dapr-http-port 3500 -- java -jar
    myservice.jar
```

Ease of Deployment and Operation: Dapr's ease of deployment is bolstered by an active community and comprehensive documentation. Developers have access to a range of examples, tutorials, and best practices that enable rapid familiarization with the tool and integration into existing projects. Built-in observed patterns reflect industry-leading architectural values, distributing a ready-made set of practices that skills teams in scalable, reliable application delivery.

Dapr's rich set of features and inherent benefits carve out a compelling case for its adoption in the sphere of microservice-based application development. Through its simplification of the foundational aspects of distributed systems, Dapr empowers developers to focus on business value, accelerate innovation, and deploy resilient services that are both scalable and secure. Whether an organization is embarking on its first microservices project or refining a seasoned multi-service environment, Dapr delivers the robustness and flexibility required to excel in today's digital landscape.

1.5 Dapr vs. Traditional Approaches

The evolution of microservices has been driven by the need for flexible, modular, and efficient software architectures. Traditional approaches to building microservices often involve manually integrating various systems and components, each with their individual configuration and management requirements. Dapr (Distributed Application Runtime) introduces a paradigm shift by simplifying and standardizing these processes. This section compares Dapr with traditional microservices approaches, emphasizing its distinct advantages and the modern development efficiencies it introduces.

Traditional architectures often require developers to manually connect and configure the components necessary for service discovery, message-based communication, state management, and more. These components, while powerful, can impose steep learning curves and significant maintenance overheads. For example, service discovery traditionally might be managed with systems like Consul or Eureka, requiring developers to explicitly configure, manage, and monitor these services to ensure reliability. In contrast, Dapr abstracts these complexities, offering a more seamless integration through service invocation and registries without the need for extensive configuration.

Service Invocation:

Traditional approaches to service invocation typically rely on REST or gRPC for inter-service communication. In traditional systems, establishing secure, reliable service calls can involve laborious error handling, such as manual retry logic, circuit breakers (such as Netflix Hystrix or Resilience4j), and client-side load balancers configured in the code or system settings.

Dapr simplifies these operations through its built-in service invocation APIs, which inherently support service discovery, load balancing, and fault resolution. For instance, invoking a service in Dapr can be as straightforward as sending an HTTP or gRPC request to the Dapr sidecar, which will manage service discovery and load balancing under the hood.

Example of a Dapr service invocation call in Python:

```python
import requests

try:
    # Invoking another service via Dapr
    response = requests.post('http://localhost:3500/v1.0/invoke/service-to-call/method/endpoint', json={"input": "data"})
    response.raise_for_status()
    print(response.json())
except requests.exceptions.RequestException as e:
    print("Service invocation error:", e)
```

Dapr takes care of retries and implements automatic service discovery, drastically reducing implementation time and complexity.

State Management:

Traditional microservices might depend directly on specific databases or state management systems, needing integration code that ties application logic tightly to storage mechanics. This tight coupling can hinder portability and agility as applications evolve or infrastructure changes, such as migrating from a SQL-based database to a NoSQL solution for scalability.

Dapr decouples applications from specific databases through its state management building block, allowing state stores to be switched or reconfigured with minimal code changes. This capability denotes a significant shift from traditional methods where application code dictates dependencies.

Example of Dapr state management API use:

```javascript
const fetch = require('node-fetch');

// Save state
async function saveState(storeName, key, value) {
    await fetch(`http://localhost:3500/v1.0/state/${storeName}`, {
        method: 'POST',
        headers: {'Content-Type': 'application/json'},
        body: JSON.stringify([{ key: key, value: value }])
    });
```

1.5. DAPR VS. TRADITIONAL APPROACHES

```
}
// Get state
async function getState(storeName, key) {
    const response = await fetch('http://localhost:3500/v1.0/state/${storeName}/${
        key}');
    return await response.json();
}

saveState('statestore', 'user1', { name: 'Alice' });
getState('statestore', 'user1').then(user => console.log(user));
```

With the above example, changes to the state backend configuration require no changes to the business logic, enhancing adaptability.

Pub/Sub Messaging:

Traditional systems may require intricate integration with specific messaging technologies like RabbitMQ, Apache Kafka, or AWS SNS/SQS, each introducing their own configuration, operating concerns, and failure modes.

Dapr simplifies pub/sub processing by enabling you to publish and subscribe to topics using any supported message broker, abstracted through its pub/sub building block. This flexibility is critical for dynamic architectures that evolve over time or need to interoperate with legacy systems.

Example of publishing to a Dapr pub/sub topic in Java:

```
import io.dapr.client.DaprClient;
import io.dapr.client.DaprClientBuilder;

public class EventPublisher {
    public static void main(String[] args) {
        try (DaprClient client = new DaprClientBuilder().build()) {
            String message = "Hello from Dapr!";
            client.publishEvent("pubsub", "mytopic", message).block();
            System.out.println("Message published successfully");
        }
    }
}
```

This code exemplifies how Dapr decouples the application from the choice of message broker.

Bindings:

Traditional bindings to cloud services or third-party APIs often involve extensive custom coding, with each binding implemented differently according to service-specific APIs and access patterns. Dapr alleviates this by letting developers define bindings declaratively via YAML configurations. This uniformity supports faster development and alignment with DevOps practices, such as Infrastructure-as-Code.

Example Dapr output binding configuration for Azure Blob storage:

```
apiVersion: dapr.io/v1alpha1
kind: Component
metadata:
  name: bloboutput
spec:
  type: bindings.azure.blobstorage
  metadata:
  - name: connectionString
    value: "<AZURE_STORAGE_CONNECTION_STRING>"
  - name: storageAccount
    value: "<STORAGE_ACCOUNT>"
  - name: container
    value: "output-container"
```

Observability and Security:

Traditional monitoring of microservices typically requires integrating various tools for logging, security monitoring, tracing, and metrics collection, often compounding system complexity. Each service would need a separate instrumentation logic, complicating service development and introduction of redundancies.

Dapr's inherent observability features provide centralized logging, metrics, and tracing capabilities out-of-the-box. Dapr is designed to work with industry-standard tools, including OpenTelemetry, Prometheus, and more, offering effortless integration. Moreover, mTLS and secret management features in Dapr augment traditional security models, providing strong inter-service encryption and a secure store for application secrets without bespoke implementations.

```
apiVersion: dapr.io/v1alpha1
kind: Configuration
metadata:
  name: tracingconfig
spec:
  tracing:
    enabled: true
    samplingRate: "1"
    exporterType: "zipkin"
    exporterAddress: "http://localhost:9411/api/v2/spans"
```

Dapr offers a robust and flexible framework that abstracts the complexities associated with traditional microservices approaches. It empowers developers by handling infrastructure concerns and enabling faster iteration, reduced complexity, and enhanced productivity in building cloud-native applications. By fostering a separation of concerns, Dapr offloads much of the responsibility from developers, allowing them to concentrate more acutely on business logic and innovation. As businesses strive to keep pace with evolving technological landscapes, Dapr serves as an enabling technology that balances cutting-edge capabilities with pragmatic simplicity, making it an attractive complement or alternative to traditional microservice architectures.

Chapter 2

Getting Started with Dapr: Installation and Setup

This chapter guides you through the essential steps to begin your journey with Dapr, from understanding the system requirements to installing and setting up your development environment. It covers the installation of the Dapr CLI, key configurations for running Dapr in both self-hosted and Kubernetes modes, and setting up the Dapr Dashboard. With clear instructions on verifying your setup, you'll ensure that your environment is properly configured, ready to harness Dapr's capabilities in building distributed applications efficiently.

2.1 System Requirements and Prerequisites

The preliminary phase of engaging with Dapr involves ensuring that your system meets the necessary requirements and that all prerequisites are established. This section is pivotal to setting the groundwork for a smooth installation and configuration of the Distributed Application Runtime (Dapr). It covers the essential software, hardware specifications, system configurations, and prior knowledge essential for operating the Dapr environment efficiently.

The following is a comprehensive outline of the prerequisites to ensure system readiness for Dapr:

- **Operating System Compatibility:** Dapr is designed to be cross-platform, supporting major operating systems including Windows, macOS, and Linux distributions. Ensuring compatibility with your specific OS version is crucial.

    - **Windows:** Dapr supports Windows 10 (version 1809 and above), Windows Server 2016, and later versions. Ensure that Windows Subsystem for Linux (WSL) 2 is installed for an optimized development experience, particularly when interacting with Docker.
    - **macOS:** System versions beginning from macOS Mojave (10.14) are supported, leveraging Homebrew for efficient package management.
    - **Linux:** Dapr is compatible with various distributions, including Ubuntu 18.04 or later, Fedora 29 or later, Debian 10, and compatible distributions. Verify compatibility with package manager versions such as apt or yum.

- **Hardware Specifications:** The hardware requirements for running Dapr are modest; however, they depend on the complexity and scale of your applications.

    - **Processor:** Multi-core processors are recommended to handle parallel computations efficiently.
    - **Memory:** A minimum of 4 GB RAM is required, with 8 GB or more recommended for environments running multiple services.
    - **Disk Space:** At least 10 GB of free space is necessary to accommodate Dapr CLI, its dependencies, and additional toolsets.

2.1. SYSTEM REQUIREMENTS AND PREREQUISITES

- **Software Dependencies:** Before installing Dapr, ensure that the following software dependencies are properly configured:
  - **Docker:** Docker is essential for containerization, a central aspect of Dapr's self-hosted mode. Install Docker Desktop on Windows and macOS, or Docker Engine on Linux. Ensure Docker is running and accessible from the command line.
  - **Node.js:** It is advisable to have Node.js installed, as Dapr offers Node.js SDK support. Use the Long-Term Support (LTS) version.
  - **Package Manager:** Utilize package managers like Homebrew on macOS or Chocolatey on Windows for streamlined installation processes.

- **Network Configuration:** Proper network configuration is integral to the seamless operation of Dapr, especially when interacting with cloud services and external APIs.
  - **Firewall Settings:** Adjust firewall settings to permit access on ports 3500, 61000, and others used by Dapr sidecars and services.
  - **Network Bandwidth:** A stable internet connection with adequate bandwidth is essential, particularly when deploying applications in cloud environments.

- **Development and Runtime Environment:** Configuring an appropriate development environment improves productivity and facilitates efficient interaction with Dapr.
  - **IDE:** Integrated Development Environments like VSCode or JetBrains IntelliJ IDEA are recommended for their robust support for multiple programming languages and debugging capabilities.
  - **Runtime Languages:** Familiarity and installation of runtime environments for languages such as Go, Python, Java, and .NET are crucial as they form the basis of application development with Dapr. These should match the SDKs you plan to utilize.

- **Cloud Service Integrations (Optional):** For those intending to leverage cloud services as part of their Dapr workflows:
    - **Cloud Accounts:** Set up and configure cloud accounts for services like Microsoft Azure, AWS, or Google Cloud Platform (GCP) as Dapr facilitates seamless integration with these services.
    - **SDKs and CLI Tools:** Install SDKs and command-line tools specific to your cloud provider, such as Azure CLI or AWS CLI. Ensure these tools are authenticated and configured correctly.
- **Prior Technical Knowledge:** Proficiency in distributed systems, microservices architecture, and familiarity with containerization concepts enhance the effectiveness of interacting with Dapr.
    - **Microservices Architecture:** Understanding how microservices operate, including inter-service communication and state management, provides a solid foundation for using Dapr.
    - **Containerization:** Comprehending how containers work, including Docker fundamentals, is crucial as Dapr relies on container mechanisms for environment abstraction.

With these system requirements and prerequisites in order, you are poised to embark on the installation process for Dapr, refining your setup for a conducive development environment that capitalizes on Dapr's capabilities in creating efficient distributed applications.

2.2 Installing Dapr CLI

The installation of Dapr Command-Line Interface (CLI) is a crucial step in setting up the environment for Dapr's use. The Dapr CLI facilitates the management and deployment of Dapr applications, providing a straightforward way to interface with Dapr's services and components. This section details the comprehensive steps for installing the

Dapr CLI across various platforms, while providing insights into configuration and troubleshooting. Each platform requires slightly different steps, so precise adherence is key.

Installation on Windows

To install the Dapr CLI on Windows, it is recommended to utilize the PowerShell command environment for its robust command execution capabilities, providing a seamless process to automate and script the installation effectively. The steps are outlined below:

1. **Launch PowerShell as Administrator:** This ensures the necessary privileges for the installation process.

2. **Execute the Installation Script:**
   Navigate to the PowerShell window and execute the following command to download and install Dapr:
   ```
   iwr -Uri https://raw.githubusercontent.com/dapr/cli/master/install/install.ps1 -UseBasicParsing | iex
   ```

3. **Verify the Installation:**
   Confirm the successful installation of the Dapr CLI by running:
   ```
   dapr --version
   ```

   ```
   CLI version: 1.x.x
   Runtime version: 1.x.x
   ```

   Ensure the version displayed matches the latest release, reflecting a correctly executed installation.

Installation on macOS

For macOS users, Homebrew is a widely-used package manager that simplifies the process of installing the Dapr CLI. Follow these steps:

1. **Open Terminal:** Key to executing command-line instructions efficiently.

2. **Install Homebrew (if not already installed):**
   Use the following command to install Homebrew:

```
/bin/bash -c "$(curl -fsSL https://raw.githubusercontent.com/Homebrew/
        install/HEAD/install.sh)"
```

3. **Install Dapr CLI:**
   With Homebrew ready, execute:
   ```
   brew install dapr/tap/dapr-cli
   ```

4. **Verify the Installation:**
   Check the installation status by entering:
   ```
   dapr --version
   ```

   CLI version: 1.x.x
   Runtime version: 1.x.x

Installation on Linux

For Linux systems, the installation can be performed using a script or via package managers such as apt (for Debian-based systems) or yum (for Fedora-based systems).

Using Installation Script:

1. **Open Terminal**

2. **Execute Installation Script:**
   Download and execute the installation script using:
   ```
   wget -q https://raw.githubusercontent.com/dapr/cli/master/install/install.
         sh -O - | /bin/bash
   ```

3. **Verify Installation:**
   Confirm setup by executing:
   ```
   dapr --version
   ```

   CLI version: 1.x.x
   Runtime version: 1.x.x

Using Package Manager:

On Debian-based systems:

2.2. INSTALLING DAPR CLI

```
sudo apt install dapr-cli
```

And for Fedora-based systems:

```
sudo dnf install dapr-cli
```

Both commands will need sufficient privileges (admin access).

Configuring the Dapr CLI

Post-installation, configuring the Dapr CLI for optimal usability can enhance the development experience. Configurations typically involve environmental setups and, occasionally, proxy settings depending on your network context.

Environment Variables

Environment variables help in defining configurations globally across sessions:

- **DAPR_CONFIG:** Defines the default configuration path for the Dapr CLI.
- **DAPR_PLATFORM:** Specifies the platform (such as Kubernetes or self-hosted) to be targeted by the Dapr CLI.

To configure, add the following to your shell profile (.bashrc or .zshrc):

```
export DAPR_CONFIG=~/.dapr/config.yaml
export DAPR_PLATFORM=self-hosted
```

Proxy Configuration

For environments behind a proxy, defining proxy variables ensures seamless CLI operations:

- HTTP_PROXY and HTTPS_PROXY: Required for establishing outbound connections through a proxy.
- NO_PROXY: Lists domains and IPs that should bypass the proxy.

Example commands to set up these variables in your terminal session or profile file:

```
export HTTP_PROXY=http://proxy.example.com:8080
export HTTPS_PROXY=https://secureproxy.example.com:443
export NO_PROXY=localhost,.example.com
```

Troubleshooting Installation Issues

Installation could sometimes encounter errors due to network restrictions, incorrect permissions, or conflicting software. Below are guidelines to troubleshoot common issues:

- **Permission Errors:** Ensure you have administrative rights. Use sudo in Linux if facing permission denied errors.

- **Network Issues:** Verify network connectivity and DNS settings. If behind a firewall, check if the required ports are open.

- **Path Configuration:** Confirm that the installation directory is included in your PATH variable:
  ```
  export PATH=$PATH:/usr/local/bin/dapr
  ```

Through the above detailed instructions and insights into configuring and troubleshooting the Dapr CLI installation, users are prepared to leverage the robust features of Dapr effectively in their development environments. This provides a solid foundation for further integration of Dapr into dynamic and distributed application systems.

2.3 Running Dapr in Self-hosted Mode

Running Dapr in self-hosted mode provides a flexible and straightforward method for application development. This mode is particularly advantageous for local development, testing, and environments where leveraging full Kubernetes orchestration is not necessary or feasible. This section deeply explores setting up and operating Dapr in a self-hosted environment, offering insights into configuration, running applications, and managing Dapr components effectively.

Introduction to Self-hosted Mode

In self-hosted mode, Dapr runs as a sidecar to your application processes. Each Dapr instance operates in its own process container

2.3. RUNNING DAPR IN SELF-HOSTED MODE

across different environments, creating a lightweight infrastructure setup. This section provides an exhaustive guide on how to deploy Dapr in this fashion with various use-case scenarios.

Initialization of Dapr in Self-hosted Mode

The initialization process ensures the deployment of the Dapr runtime environment suitable for your application setup:

1. **Start Dapr:** The basic command to initiate Dapr in self-hosted mode is executed via the CLI:

   ```
   dapr init
   ```

   This command downloads necessary binaries and sets up the system environment required for Dapr runtime.

2. **Verify Initialization:** To ensure that the Dapr services are running correctly, use:

   ```
   dapr status
   ```

   ```
   SUCCESS: dapr-operator running.
   SUCCESS: dapr-placement running.
   SUCCESS: dapr-sentry running.
   ```

The aforementioned status command confirms the successful deployment and operation of Dapr's core components including dapr-operator, dapr-sentry, and dapr-placement.

Running a Dapr-enabled Application

To run an application using Dapr in self-hosted mode, follow these steps. Assume a simple application demo to illustrate the setup:

Create a Simple Application Here's a simple Python HTTP server application that echoes the input:

```python
from flask import Flask, request

app = Flask(__name__)

@app.route('/echo', methods=['GET'])
def echo():
    return {'message': request.args.get('msg', '')}, 200
```

CHAPTER 2. GETTING STARTED WITH DAPR: INSTALLATION AND SETUP

```
if __name__ == '__main__':
    app.run(port=5000)
```

Running the Application with Dapr

To run this Python application with Dapr, follow the procedure below:

1. **Start Dapr Sidecar:**

   Execute the following command to run your application with a Dapr sidecar, providing intermediation services and features such as service invocation:

   ```
   dapr run --app-id echo-app --app-port 5000 python3 app.py
   ```

   The above command specifies 'echo-app' as the application ID and binds Dapr to port 5000, the port on which the application is accessible.

2. **Verify Application Run:**

   Upon successful initiation, Dapr will output logs indicating it's using specified configuration and component files, reporting:

   ```
   Starting Dapr with id echo-app. HTTP Port: 3500. gRPC Port: 50001
   You're up and running! Dapr logs will appear below:
   ```

Exploring Service Invocation

One of Dapr's primary capabilities is service invocation — allowing secure and straightforward method calls between different services running across your infrastructure.

Invoking a Service:

Using Dapr's HTTP API, we can make a call to the "echo-app" using the following example targeting the already described service.

```
curl -X GET http://localhost:3500/v1.0/invoke/echo-app/method/echo?msg=hello
```

```
{
    "message": "hello"
}
```

2.3. RUNNING DAPR IN SELF-HOSTED MODE

This command sends a GET request to the Dapr sidecar via HTTP, invoking the "/echo" endpoint with a message parameter of "hello."

State Management and Pub/Sub

Dapr simplifies implementations for operations such as state management and publish/subscribe pattern, solidifying distributed application scenarios.

State Management:

Dapr provides robust APIs for interacting with key/value stores to manage state persistency. Here is an example of storing and retrieving state using Dapr.

```
# Save state command
curl -X POST \
    http://localhost:3500/v1.0/state/statestore \
    -H "Content-Type: application/json" \
    -d '[{ "key": "order_id", "value": "12345" }]'

# Retrieve state command
curl -X GET http://localhost:3500/v1.0/state/statestore/order_id
```

"12345"

The example illustrates storing and retrieving an "order_id" using a state store component configured within Dapr.

Pub/Sub Interaction:

Publishing a message to a topic and subscribing a service can be straightforwardly managed as shown below:

```
# Publish a message
curl -X POST \
    http://localhost:3500/v1.0/publish/pubsub/topic \
    -H "Content-Type: application/json" \
    -d '{ "message": "Hello, World!" }'
```

Here, the service subscribes to and processes the payload from the "topic" using Dapr components such as Redis or Kafka.

Observability and Metrics

Observability in Dapr involves logs, metrics collection, and tracing which are essential for debugging and optimizing applications.

Viewing Logs:

Dapr's CLI allows you to view logs with the command.

```
dapr logs --app-id echo-app
```

Logs provide insights into application and Dapr sidecar interactions.

Monitoring Metrics:

Use tools like Prometheus to scrape and visualize Dapr metrics by configuring a metrics server endpoint exposed by Dapr.

```
scrape_configs:
  - job_name: 'dapr'
    static_configs:
      - targets: ['localhost:9090']
```

Grafana can be used alongside Prometheus for rich dashboard visualizations.

Managing Dapr Components and Configuration

Dapr's architecture utilizes components defined in YAML files for various operations like Pub/Sub, state management, etc. Configuration management is vital to ensure desired microservice operations.

```
# Sample component configuration file
apiVersion: dapr.io/v1alpha1
kind: Component
metadata:
  name: statestore
spec:
  type: state.redis
  version: v1
  metadata:
    - name: redisHost
      value: localhost:6379
    - name: redisPassword
      value: ""
```

These files define the component type and metadata necessary for connecting services.

Running Dapr in a self-hosted mode provides a powerful, flexible environment for developing, testing, and exploring distributed application paradigms. Understanding and utilizing Dapr's extensive features here prepares developers to handle complex distributed architectures smoothly. This provides a baseline from which transitioning to more scaled-up environments, such as Kubernetes-hosted settings, becomes natural and intuitive.

2.4 Using Dapr in Kubernetes

Deploying Dapr in a Kubernetes environment takes advantage of Kubernetes' robust orchestration capabilities, providing scalability, self-healing, and seamless integration into cloud-native applications. Managing distributed systems through Dapr in Kubernetes allows developers to handle microservice challenges efficiently with minimal configuration overhead. This section explores the steps to deploy Dapr in a Kubernetes cluster, detailing configuration, operation, and the symbiotic relationship between Kubernetes and Dapr's feature sets.

Overview of Kubernetes and Dapr Integration

Within Kubernetes, Dapr operates via sidecar injection into Kubernetes pods, managing service invocation, state persistence, and pub/sub, among other distributed application features. The powerful synergies of Kubernetes' container orchestration combined with Dapr's application-level capabilities form a formidable platform for modern application development.

Prerequisites for Dapr on Kubernetes

Prior to deploying Dapr in a Kubernetes environment, ensure that your setup meets the following prerequisites:

- **Kubernetes Cluster:** A properly configured Kubernetes cluster. This can be a local development cluster such as Minikube or a cloud-managed service like Amazon EKS, Google Kubernetes Engine (GKE), or Azure Kubernetes Service (AKS).

- **kubectl CLI:** The Kubernetes command-line tool `kubectl` must be installed and configured to interact with your cluster.

- **Helm (v3+):** Helm is recommended for managing Kubernetes applications and is integral to deploying Dapr efficiently.

- **Docker:** Required for building and managing container images.

Installing Dapr in Kubernetes

Deploying Dapr into your Kubernetes cluster is streamlined using Helm. Follow these steps:

Step 1: Add Dapr Helm Repository

Begin by ensuring Helm is updated and adding the Dapr repository:

```
helm repo add dapr https://dapr.github.io/helm-charts
helm repo update
```

Step 2: Install Dapr on the Cluster

Deploy Dapr using the Helm chart:

```
helm install dapr dapr/dapr --namespace dapr-system --create-namespace
```

The above command installs Dapr into a dedicated namespace dapr-system, isolating it from other application deployments.

Step 3: Verify Installation

To check the installed Dapr components, execute:

```
kubectl get pods --namespace dapr-system
```

Visible pods such as dapr-operator and dapr-sidecar-injector should be in a running state, confirming the correct deployment of Dapr in the cluster.

Deploying a Dapr-enabled Application

With Dapr running in your Kubernetes cluster, deploying a Dapr-enabled application involves creating Kubernetes resources like Deployments and Services while including necessary Dapr annotations to enable sidecar injection.

Sample Application Deployment

Assume deploying a simple Node.js application in Kubernetes. Begin by creating a deployment.yaml file:

```yaml
apiVersion: apps/v1
kind: Deployment
metadata:
  name: nodeapp
spec:
  replicas: 1
  selector:
    matchLabels:
      app: nodeapp
  template:
    metadata:
      labels:
        app: nodeapp
```

2.4. USING DAPR IN KUBERNETES

```
  annotations:
    dapr.io/enabled: "true"
    dapr.io/app-id: "nodeapp"
    dapr.io/app-port: "3000"
spec:
  containers:
  - name: nodeapp
    image: myregistry/nodeapp:latest
    ports:
    - containerPort: 3000
```

The key annotations include dapr.io/enabled: "true" for sidecar injection, dapr.io/app-id: "nodeapp" for application identity, and dapr.io/app-port: "3000" for interaction with the service.

Create Kubernetes Service

Define a service for the application:

```
apiVersion: v1
kind: Service
metadata:
  name: nodeapp
spec:
  ports:
  - port: 80
    targetPort: 3000
  selector:
    app: nodeapp
```

This YAML file describes a Service that forwards traffic to the application deployed in the previous step.

Apply Deployment and Service Files

Deploy the application by running:

```
kubectl apply -f deployment.yaml
kubectl apply -f service.yaml
```

Advanced Dapr Features on Kubernetes

Dapr provides advanced features that enhance the microservices architecture when deployed on Kubernetes.

State Management

Implement state management through configuration:

```
apiVersion: dapr.io/v1alpha1
kind: Component
metadata:
```

```
name: statestore
namespace: default
spec:
  type: state.inmemory
  version: v1
  metadata:
  - name: key
    value: "value"
```

Apply this configuration across your Kubernetes cluster:

```
kubectl apply -f statestore.yaml
```

Pub/Sub Application

Implementing pub/sub with Dapr-managed messaging services in Kubernetes requires a well-defined component YAML file. Here's an example using Redis:

```
apiVersion: dapr.io/v1alpha1
kind: Component
metadata:
  name: redis-pubsub
  namespace: default
spec:
  type: pubsub.redis
  version: v1
  metadata:
  - name: redisHost
    value: redis-master:6379
  - name: redisPassword
    value: ""
```

Deploy this configuration:

```
kubectl apply -f pubsub.yaml
```

Publish and subscribe commands are then executed using Dapr's HTTP or gRPC API interfaces.

Observability and Scaling in Kubernetes with Dapr

Observability and the ability to scale are inherent strengths of Kubernetes enhanced by Dapr features.

Metrics Collection

Integrate tools such as Prometheus to collect and analyze metrics. Modify the Prometheus configuration to scrape Dapr pods in the cluster:

2.4. USING DAPR IN KUBERNETES

```
scrape_configs:
 - job_name: 'dapr'
   kubernetes_sd_configs:
    - role: pod
```

Tracing

Dapr supports distributed tracing tools such as Zipkin and Jaeger. This setup enables deeper insight into request pathways and latency tracking across microservices.

Scaling

Kubernetes' horizontal pod autoscaler (HPA) can be configured for Dapr-enabled applications to ensure elasticity and resilience under varying load conditions.

```
apiVersion: autoscaling/v1
kind: HorizontalPodAutoscaler
metadata:
  name: nodeapp
spec:
  scaleTargetRef:
    apiVersion: apps/v1
    kind: Deployment
    name: nodeapp
  minReplicas: 1
  maxReplicas: 10
  targetCPUUtilizationPercentage: 50
```

This file illustrates maintaining optimal CPU utilization across replicated pod instances.

Utilizing Dapr within a Kubernetes cluster offers scalable and manageable solutions for distributed systems. This setup leverages Kubernetes' orchestration strengths while employing Dapr's service-mediation capabilities to enhance microservice architectures. The efficient deployment, management, and scaling of Dapr applications in such environments ensure that development and operational processes remain robust and flexible to meet modern application demands. This seamless integration stands as a testament to the symbiotic potential of harnessing both platforms, providing developers with a comprehensive toolkit for successful cloud-native applications.

2.5 Dapr Dashboard Setup

Setting up the Dapr Dashboard offers a powerful way to monitor and manage Dapr applications and infrastructure effectively. The dashboard provides real-time visibility into service health, component states, and logs, enhancing operational oversight and aiding in troubleshooting efforts. Through this section, we delve into the detailed process of setting up the Dapr Dashboard, exploring its features, usage, and the benefits it brings to managing distributed applications. This exploration will include step-by-step configuration instructions, insights into handling metrics and logs, and troubleshooting common problems evident in modern cloud environments.

Introduction to Dapr Dashboard

The Dapr Dashboard is a comprehensive web-based user interface designed to provide visual insights into the operations of Dapr systems. It is instrumental for developers and operators to gain a deeper understanding of the running services, their interconnections, and the internal state of Dapr components.

This interface intuitively correlates log data, metrics, and telemetry from Dapr-managed applications, allowing for instant diagnosis of performance bottlenecks and architectural anomalies. Its integration with out-of-the-box observability stacks further enhances the capability to maintain high availability and reliability of distributed systems.

Installing Dapr Dashboard

Installing the Dapr Dashboard is a straightforward process but requires ensuring that the Dapr runtime is already set up and running in your chosen environment whether self-hosted, Kubernetes, or within a different orchestration tool.

2.5. DAPR DASHBOARD SETUP

Pre-Installation Requirements

- **Dapr CLI:** Ensure that the Dapr CLI is installed. The CLI is essential for running, updating, and interfacing with the Dapr Dashboard.

- **Browser:** A modern web browser such as Chrome, Firefox, or Edge is required to access the dashboard.

Launching the Dashboard Locally

On a local environment with the Dapr CLI set up, initiate the Dapr Dashboard using the following steps:

```
dapr dashboard
```

Running this command starts the server for the Dashboard, typically accessible by default at http://localhost:8080. The CLI returns an explicit URL which can be accessed using any supported web browser.

```
Starting Dapr dashboard on http://localhost:8080
```

This URL leads to the home view of the Dapr Dashboard, where all runtime instances are visually represented alongside relevant metadata.

Deploying the Dashboard in Kubernetes

For environments orchestrated by Kubernetes, the Dapr Dashboard can be managed as a service within the cluster. Follow these installation steps:

Step 1: Access Dapr CLI in Kubernetes In the context of a Kubernetes setup, use your configured terminal to access the Kubernetes cluster using the Dapr CLI:

```
kubectl port-forward service/dapr-dashboard 8080:8080 --namespace dapr-system
```

Executing the above command permits remote access to the Dashboard service hosted within the Kubernetes cluster on port 8080, allowing complex and large-scale deployments to be visualized and managed efficiently.

Step 2: Secure Dashboard Options Security constraints specific to Kubernetes ensure resource-access integrity:

- **Service Account Control:** Restrict access using Kubernetes role-based access control (RBAC), defining permissible operations for the Dapr Dashboard application.

- **Ingress and Egress Policies:** Use network policies within Kubernetes to limit data flow into and out of the Dashboard service if it's externally exposed within the network.

Features of the Dapr Dashboard

Real-time Service View

Upon accessing the Dapr Dashboard, users are met with a comprehensive real-time service map. This visualization shows active applications, their service IDs, and endpoints currently managed within the Dapr network model. Enabling operators to identify service statuses at a glance supports seamless monitoring.

Component Inspection

Dapr's component architecture allows diversified configurations such as state stores, bindings, and pub/sub systems. The Dashboard provides detailed insights into each component's operational health, state changes, and configuration metadata.

Examples of actionable insights include detecting misconfigured endpoint URLs, observing state store latency issues, and monitoring pub/sub message flow bottlenecks directly from the Dashboard.

2.5. DAPR DASHBOARD SETUP

Observability and Log Analysis

Dapr Dashboard furnishes logs from applications and sidecar interactions. By integrating with tools like Prometheus and Grafana, the Dashboard offers synchronized telemetry data and time-series metrics, providing:

- **Log Traceability:** Enables filtering based on service ID, error codes, and timestamps to pinpoint specific event sequences or service failures.

- **Performance Metrics:** CPU and memory utilization panel, afforded through enabled Metrics Server in Kubernetes or monitored resource limits in other hosting configurations.

Troubleshooting the Dashboard

While Dapr Dashboard eases observability, certain operational obstacles may arise. Below are common issues and respective troubleshooting approaches:

Access Issues

If unable to reach the Dashboard, affirm the port-forwarding configuration or hosting route setup. For locally self-hosted systems, reexamine host firewall directives potentially blocking access. Kubernetes setups require confirmation of service exposure policies.

Lag and Performance Concerns

For dashboards experiencing sluggish operation, increase internal data refresh intervals or allocate additional CPU/memory resources to the Dashboard pod. The performance intricacies are frequently aligned with resource provisioning managed by underlying orchestration layers, like the Kubernetes Vertical Pod Autoscaler.

Data Mismatch and Lagging Logs

Inconsistent service status information or delay-laden logs often trace back to divergent synchronization cycles or incomplete integration with telemetry systems. Validation of component alignment to telemetry agents and configured refresh cycles within Kubernetes offers clarity.

Enhancing Usability with Automation

Automation facilitates streamlined dashboard operations. Declare deployment files for your Dashboard interface, implementing CI/CD pipelines to cover staging, deployment, and updating of dashboard resources. Casual automation additions include:

```
apiVersion: batch/v1
kind: CronJob
metadata:
  name: dapr-dashboard-maintenance
spec:
  schedule: "0 3 * * *"
  jobTemplate:
    spec:
      template:
        spec:
          containers:
          - name: dapr-dashboard-cleanup
            image: myrepo/cleanup-script:latest
          restartPolicy: OnFailure
```

This CronJob automatically maintains housekeeping functions, ensuring logs are rotated or outdated cache is purged to maintain optimal performance.

The Dapr Dashboard emerges as a vital tool for observing, managing, and maintaining distributed applications within both development and production scenarios. It offers capabilities that streamline complex service orchestrations by leveraging unique cloud-native patterns, critical for scalable and resilient deployments. Embracing this tool within DevOps pipelines augments microservice efficiency, accelerates troubleshooting, and enhances cross-team collaboration, forming a balanced ecosystem capable of supporting contemporary development demands.

2.6 Verifying the Installation

Ensuring the accurate installation of Dapr is critical for its stable operation within any environment, be it a local development setup, a self-hosted deployment, or a Kubernetes cluster. Verifying the installation involves confirming the presence and functionality of core components and addressing any discrepancies before they impact system performance. This section describes a comprehensive approach to verify Dapr installations, with methods tailored to suit different environments and deployment contexts. It encompasses verification procedures, troubleshooting common challenges, and offers insights into leveraging Dapr's diagnostic utilities effectively.

- **General Verification Procedures**

- **Verifying Dapr CLI Installation**

After installing the Dapr CLI, verify its correct installation and accessibility using:

```
dapr --version
```

```
CLI version: 1.x.x
Runtime version: 1.x.x
```

The output presents CLI and runtime versions, which should correspond to the latest or intended versions installed. Address discrepancies by reviewing installation logs or re-running setup scripts, ensuring necessary environment paths like /usr/local/bin are correctly set.

- **Checking System Dependencies**

Confirm all system dependencies are met using diagnostic utilities built into the CLI, verifying that Docker and container runtime permissions are correctly configured:

```
docker --version
```

Output should reflect Docker's version, confirming its presence and readiness for Dapr's functionalities.

```
docker run hello-world
```

This command checks Docker's operational status by executing a simple container, validating the containerization components.

- **Verifying Self-hosted Mode Installation**

When using a self-hosted mode installation, Dapr utilizes local system resources. Verification procedures assist in ensuring component availability and functionality.

- **Local Environment Setup Validation**

Ensure Dapr's initialization completed successfully; re-run initialization if necessary:

```
dapr init
```

Run the Dapr status command to check runtime services:

```
dapr status -k
```

```
NAME             STATUS   AGE
dapr-dashboard   Running  10m
dapr-placement   Running  10m
dapr-operator    Running  10m
dapr-sentry      Running  10m
```

The above output should indicate that all components are in a running state.

- **Running a Local Application**

Next, test with a local sample application to ensure interaction with Dapr components:

A simple Python application designed to echo input verifies operational health:

```
from flask import Flask
app = Flask(__name__)
```

2.6. VERIFYING THE INSTALLATION

```python
@app.route('/echo', methods=['GET'])
def echo():
    return {"status": "Running"}, 200

if __name__ == '__main__':
    app.run(port=5000)
```

Run the application under Dapr:

```
dapr run --app-id echo-service --app-port 5000 python3 app.py
```

Confirm connectivity by invoking the service:

```
curl -X GET http://localhost:3500/v1.0/invoke/echo-service/method/echo
```

The expected response validates the operational status of Dapr and interaction readiness.

- **Verifying Kubernetes Installation**

For installations on Kubernetes, components and services require deeper integration and a broader verification scope, leveraging Kubernetes' orchestration and resource management.

- **Kubernetes Environment Check**

Ensure the kubectl command-line tool operates correctly:

```
kubectl version
```

This command confirms access rights and Kubernetes API server connectivity.

- **Checking Dapr Components in Kubernetes**

Deploy Dapr components should be verified through detailed pod status views:

```
kubectl get pods -n dapr-system
```

NAME   READY   STATUS   RESTARTS   AGE

CHAPTER 2. GETTING STARTED WITH DAPR: INSTALLATION AND SETUP

```
dapr-dashboard-5d6459c966-78c9b              1/1    Running  0    15m
dapr-operator-8485875c86-w7q5p               1/1    Running  0    15m
dapr-placement-68756987b-j5pwp               1/1    Running  0    15m
dapr-sentry-b664f8d8d-cbnf2                  1/1    Running  0    15m
dapr-sidecar-injector-584c64c984-f6jhh       1/1    Running  0    15m
```

Pods should appear in a "Running" status confirming successful deployment.

- **Service Functionality Verification**

Testing service invocation and monitoring components ensures runtime efficiency. Apply a deployment using tools like Helm:

```
helm install myapp ./myapp
```

Verify deployment:

```
kubectl get deployment myapp
```

Confirm response capabilities of the service through Dapr's API:

```
curl -X POST http://<LoadBalancer-IP>/v1.0/invoke/myapp/method
```

- **Log Inspection and Configuration Review**

Logs are vital for diagnosing issue locations across distributed setups; ensure comprehensive logging using `kubectl logs`:

```
kubectl logs <pod_name> -n dapr-system
```

This extracts pod logs, indicating common API errors or misconfigurations.

Proper configuration files (`yaml` files) must be correct at a component level; review configurations to spot consistencies and misalignments in deployments.

- **Troubleshooting Common Issues**

Proper troubleshooting remediates installation missteps and optimizes setup validation:

2.6. VERIFYING THE INSTALLATION

- **Common Install Errors and Resolutions**

  - **API Server Connectivity:** Ensure network paths to the Kubernetes API are open and viable; check both internal and external network paths.
  - **Configuration Discrepancies:** Validate YAML configurations through Dapr control plane components, and introspect metadata for type correctness.
  - **Pod Lifecycle Status:** Examine pod logs if lifecycle transitions (CrashLoopBackOff) indicate dependency startup failures.

- **Diagnostic and Observability Tools**

Utilize diagnostic commands to identify performance issues:

```
dapr metrics -k
```

Stack integration with observability tools such as Prometheus or Grafana further extends insights into microservice states and end-to-end process diagnostics.

- **Performance Optimization Post-Installation**

Performance metrics gathered guide optimization steps:

- **Resource Allocation:** Reassess allocation for CPU and memory limits set within Kubernetes resource conventions to reduce bottlenecks.

- **Horizontal Scaling:** Utilize horizontal pod autoscalers (HPA) based on insights from monitoring tools. Implement intelligently with minimum and maximum threshold strategy plans.

Verification extends beyond initial installation into continuous monitoring to uphold system vitality over time. Be alert to platform updates that alter feature configurations or fiscal compliance, maintaining agility through up-to-date integrations.

Automate verification steps in CI/CD pipelines and document troubleshooting strategies directly related to architecture variations, maintaining robust setup resilience against expanding workloads. The configuration correctness derived from these steps assures system architects and developers of the engineered reliability and enduring integrity required by complex cloud-native applications augmented by Dapr's distributed architecture.

Chapter 3

Understanding Dapr Building Blocks

This chapter delves into the foundational components that constitute Dapr, known as building blocks, which simplify the development of microservices by abstracting complex infrastructure tasks. It provides a detailed exploration of service invocation, state management, publish-subscribe messaging, resource bindings, observability, and the actor model. Each building block is designed to enhance developer productivity by reducing the intricacy of coding necessary for distributed applications, thereby allowing for a deeper focus on delivering business value.

3.1 Overview of Dapr Building Blocks

Dapr, the Distributed Application Runtime, is a portable, event-driven runtime that simplifies the challenges associated with building resilient, microservice-based, stateful applications. The primary intention of Dapr is to abstract the intricacies of building microservices, thereby promoting a seamless development experience. The cornerstone of Dapr is its collection of modular building blocks that provide essential capabilities required for cloud-native applications. These building blocks consist of service invocation, state management, publish-subscribe messaging, resource bindings, observability, and the actor model. Each block is intended to address a discrete concern, enabling developers to compose these elements to suit specific application needs effectively.

Dapr's value lies in its ability to act as a middleware layer, abstracting the underlying complexities of infrastructure. Traditionally, developers faced significant challenges when building distributed systems, including handling communication between services, managing application state, integrating with external systems, and ensuring effective observability. By utilizing Dapr's building blocks, developers are relieved from the burden of boilerplate code, error handling loops, and managing diverse protocols. The approach fosters greater focus on business logic and reduces time-to-market, thereby enhancing productivity.

The architecture of Dapr is based on sidecar pattern deployment, where a Dapr sidecar runs alongside each application instance. This design facilitates communication and provides functionalities central to Dapr's offerings in a language-agnostic way, as the sidecar interacts with the application over standard HTTP or gRPC APIs. Such an architecture not only simplifies the task of building resilient applications but also aligns well with popular container orchestration platforms like Kubernetes.

To further elucidate the practical implementations of Dapr's building blocks, the following sections will describe each block in detail. These insights help in understanding how they integrate seamlessly within applications and offer real-world code examples that demonstrate their utilities.

1. **Service Invocation**: This building block addresses the challenge of direct communication between different services. Using HTTP or gRPC, Dapr allows one service to invoke another in a distributed environment where such interactions are not natively supported. The invocation mechanism supports reliable request handling, automatic retries, and latency-aware load balancing. It ensures that inter-service calls can be made as simple as ordinary function calls, abstracting network complexities from the developer.

3.1. OVERVIEW OF DAPR BUILDING BLOCKS

```
# Dapr invocation HTTP request example
POST http://localhost:3500/v1.0/invoke/<service-name>/method/<
    method-name>
Content-Type: application/json

{
    "parameter": "value"
}
```

This invocation technique supports both synchronous and asynchronous communication, empowering developers to choose the appropriate mode based on their application's need.

2. **State Management**: Dapr's state management building block allows developers to create, read, update, and delete (CRUD) state across services with simplified APIs. It provides consistency guarantees and durability by abstracting common concerns involved with stateful applications. The state management component supports different state stores such as Redis, Azure Cosmos DB, and others. Developers can configure the state store using Dapr's configuration mechanism, ensuring flexibility and scalability.

```
# Example for saving state using Dapr HTTP API
POST http://localhost:3500/v1.0/state/<store-name>
Content-Type: application/json

[
    {
        "key": "order_id",
        "value": 12345
    }
]
```

Using Dapr, state management is simplified with automated features such as state versioning and linearizability guarantees for high consistency. Additionally, Dapr provides mechanisms to manage transient, standard, and critical state operations depending on the specific use case requirements.

3. **Publish-Subscribe Pattern**: Enabling real-world event-driven architectures, the publish-subscribe (pub/sub) pattern supports decoupled interaction between services. Dapr abstracts complex messaging systems using a consistent API that communicates with underlying message brokers like Kafka, RabbitMQ, and Azure Service Bus. The building block allows

publishing messages on topics, with other services subscribing to these topics for further processing.

```
# Publish a message to a topic using Dapr
POST http://localhost:3500/v1.0/publish/<pubsub-name>/<topic>
Content-Type: application/json

{
    "order": 12345
}
```

The pub/sub model implemented by Dapr offers several advantages, such as scalability, fault tolerance, and loose coupling. These qualities are essential for modern microservice architectures that demand high flexibility and resilience.

4. **Resource Bindings**: This building block allows applications to interact with external systems such as databases, message queues, and file systems without tightly coupling with platform-specific SDKs. Input bindings allow the application to respond to events and data inputs from external sources, whereas output bindings facilitate event emission. These interactions provide a cloud-native interface to various resources, enhancing interoperability across heterogeneous environments.

```
# Define a binding to receive events from storage
POST http://localhost:3500/v1.0/bindings/<binding-name>
Content-Type: application/json

{
    "operation": "create",
    "data": {
        "filename": "example.txt",
        "content": "Hello, Dapr!"
    }
}
```

The resource bindings simplify interacting with external services by providing pluggable components. Support for dynamic runtime configuration through metadata attributes empowers developers to adapt their applications to evolving needs rapidly.

5. **Observability**: To maintain comprehensive observability in distributed applications, Dapr offers built-in telemetry, tracing, and logging capabilities. By integrating with popular tools like Prometheus and Zipkin, developers can achieve detailed insights

3.1. OVERVIEW OF DAPR BUILDING BLOCKS

into system performance and health metrics. Dapr's observability features help diagnose and troubleshoot issues effectively, ensuring applications are resilient and performant.

```
# Example code snippet using Dapr observability API
import logging
from dapr.clients import DataClient

logging.basicConfig(level=logging.INFO)

def log_example_operation():
    client = DataClient()
    client.increment_counter("example-counter")
    logging.info("Counter increment operation logged.")
```

Effective observability with Dapr enables end-to-end tracing and log management, contributing to a sophisticated approach to managing applications across diverse environments.

6. **Actor Model**: Leveraging the actor model pattern, Dapr supports building highly concurrent, stateful applications using actors. This model simplifies concurrency and state management complexities by encapsulating state and behavior within individual, isolated actors. Each actor operates independently, processing messages sequentially, thus preventing deadlocks and race conditions.

```
# Example for invoking an actor using Dapr API
POST http://localhost:3500/v1.0/actors/<actor-type>/<actor-id>/method/<method-name>
Content-Type: application/json

{
    "data": 7890
}
```

Actors offer powerful paradigms for applications with fine-grained requirements for state management, ensuring robust actor lifecycle management and state persistence. This characteristic is pivotal where modular and component-oriented system designs are prioritized.

Dapr represents a significant advancement in the management and deployment of distributed systems, addressing core challenges with modular solutions. Its building blocks consolidate years of best practices and lessons learned in developing microservices, thus empowering developers to focus on enhancing core business functionalities rather than peripheral technical concerns. Through Dapr's diverse building blocks, each tailored for specific needs, developers can build applications that are not only rich in functionality but also robust in resilience, efficiency, and maintainability.

3.2 Service-to-Service Invocation

Service-to-service invocation is a fundamental building block offered by Dapr that enables seamless communication between microservices. In a microservice architecture, individual services often need to communicate or invoke functionalities of other services, sometimes referred to as Remote Procedure Calls (RPC). This communication can become complex due to the need for network address resolution, load balancing, error handling, and securing endpoints. Dapr alleviates these challenges by providing a simple, language-agnostic API for service invocation.

The service invocation building block utilizes HTTP or gRPC protocols to facilitate communication. This choice allows for high compatibility with modern cloud-native applications and ensures that service interactions are fast, reliable, and secure. The mechanism abstracts network-related complexities, allowing developers to focus on business logic without worrying about infrastructure concerns.

Dapr implements service invocation using a sidecar architecture, where each application instance runs alongside a Dapr sidecar. This sidecar provides the necessary APIs for invocation, acting as a proxy that manages service discovery and communication under the hood. When a service wants to invoke another, it makes a request to its own Dapr sidecar, which then locates and calls the target service's sidecar. This model guarantees a high level of abstraction and decoupling, essential for scalable and maintainable system design.

- **Key Components of Service-to-Service Invocation**
    - **Service Discovery and Naming**: Dapr employs a simple naming mechanism for service discovery. Each service is identified by a unique name, which is used as a reference for communication. This removes the need for hardcoding

network addresses and allows dynamic service location in distributed environments.

- **Load Balancing**: Dapr offers built-in client-side load balancing, routing requests to instances of a service based on the lowest response time, ensuring efficient utilization of resources and quick response times even during high load scenarios.
- **Resiliency and Fault Tolerance**: By incorporating retry policies, timeouts, and circuit breakers, Dapr enhances the reliability of service communications. These policies ensure that transient errors do not disrupt service operations, thereby maintaining robust inter-service communication.
- **Security**: Secure communication is a priority within Dapr, which supports mutual TLS (mTLS) to authenticate and encrypt messages. This ensures that sensitive data remains protected across services.
- **Protocol Abstraction**: Dapr abstracts away the differences between HTTP and gRPC, allowing services to communicate regardless of the protocol choice. This flexibility means services can evolve independently without requiring changes to the whole system.

- **Service Invocation API** The primary mode of interacting with the service invocation building block is through well-defined APIs that integrate seamlessly with HTTP/gRPC protocols. This approach minimizes the need for complex integrations and allows developers to focus on implementing business logic. Below is an example of invoking a service using Dapr.

- **HTTP Example** The following example demonstrates how to invoke a remote method through an HTTP-based service invocation request:

```
POST http://localhost:3500/v1.0/invoke/orders-service/method/
    createOrder
Content-Type: application/json

{
    "orderId": 7891,
    "customerName": "John Doe"
}
```

In this example, the service named orders-service provides a method named createOrder, which can be called by issuing a POST request to the local Dapr sidecar, specifying the service's unique name and method.

- **gRPC Example** For applications utilizing gRPC, the service invocation can benefit from lower latency due to compact binary encoding and robust stream support:

```
service Invocation {
    rpc InvokeServiceMethod(InvocationRequest) returns (InvocationResponse
    ) {}
}

message InvocationRequest {
    string service_name = 1;
    string method_name = 2;
    google.protobuf.Any data = 3;
}

message InvocationResponse {
    google.protobuf.Any response = 1;
}
```

- **Resiliency Patterns** Dapr incorporates standard resiliency patterns such as retries, timeouts, and circuit breakers. By setting these attributes within the Dapr configuration, developers can tailor the invocation behavior to match their application's tolerance to communication failures.

```
# Configuration for retry policy
apiVersion: dapr.io/v1alpha1
kind: Configuration
metadata:
  name: retry-config
spec:
  httpPipeline:
    handlers:
      - name: retry
        spec:
          policy:
            retries: 3
            interval: 200ms
            maxInterval: 1s
            timeout: 5s
```

The above configuration demonstrates setting a retry policy, where failed requests are attempted again with specific intervals, enhancing the availability and resilience of service communications.

- **Security Considerations** Security is paramount in service-to-service communication. Dapr's support for mutual TLS ensures that only authorized and authenticated services can communicate with each other. This layer of encryption and authentication ensures robust protection of data integrity and confidentiality in transit. Setting up mTLS in Dapr involves configuring the TLS settings, trusted roots, and certificates to provide a seamless secure communication environment.

```
apiVersion: dapr.io/v1alpha1
kind: Component
metadata:
  name: tls-config
spec:
  type: api.tls
  version: v1
  metadata:
    - name: trustDomain
      value: mycluster.local
    - name: rootCA
      value: /etc/dapr/certs/ca.crt
```

- **Performance and Scalability** Service invocation plays a critical role in the performance and scalability of microservice architectures. Dapr's client-side load balancing, combined with efficient service discovery, ensures that requests are routed optimally, distributing load evenly across service instances and preventing bottlenecks.

  Scaling services horizontally by adding more instances allows Dapr to continue balancing traffic, supporting high-throughput applications. It enables auto-scaling mechanisms, enhancing system responsiveness to varying workloads.

- **Advantages and Use Cases** Utilizing Dapr's service-to-service invocation offers several advantages:

  - **Simplified Communication**: The reduced complexity of inter-service calls allows developers to integrate services with minimal effort.
  - **Flexible Integration**: Supports a variety of interaction paradigms, making it suitable for synchronous or asynchronous communication.

- **Enhanced Resilience**: Built-in resiliency patterns ensure continuity of service in unpredictable network conditions.
- **Agility**: Services can change without impacting others, promoting evolutionary architecture designs.
- **Security**: Ensures data protection through encryption, safeguarding sensitive business transactions.

This building block is particularly beneficial for applications that require high decoupling and robust communication mechanisms, such as online transactional systems, real-time data processing, and complex business workflows.

The service-to-service invocation building block is integral to Dapr's offering, enabling clean, efficient, and secure communication between services. With its wide range of support spanning across different protocols, security measures, and resiliency mechanisms, it lays the groundwork for developing next-generation distributed systems. By abstracting unwieldy infrastructure tasks, developers can lead on innovation and high-level application logic, ensuring quality and robustness in their service architectures.

3.3 State Management

State management is a critical aspect of developing reliable and robust microservices, especially when building applications that require data persistence across service interactions. Dapr's state management building block facilitates hassle-free development by handling complexities such as data consistency, persistence, and scalability. This component is principally designed to abstract away the intricacies of managing data state, enabling developers to focus more exhaustively on crafting the underlying business logic rather than dealing with stateful operations' technical challenges.

Dapr provides an API for applications to save, read, and query state, allowing developers to manage both transient and durable state across distributed systems effortlessly. It supports a variety of state stores like Redis, Azure Cosmos DB, AWS DynamoDB, and others, providing flexibility in storage backends. The choice of a state store depends on use-case specific requirements, such as latency, consistency, size, and cost considerations.

- **Core Concepts**: The state management functionality in Dapr can be dissected into several core areas that highlight its capabilities and benefits:

    1. **Key-Value State Management**: At its core, Dapr provides a key-value storage model that supports quick access to data using a unique key. This model simplifies state interactions, making it easy for developers to perform Create, Read, Update, and Delete (CRUD) operations on application data.
    2. **State Consistency**[1]: Dapr supports different consistency levels to match application needs:
        - Strong Consistency ensures reads return the most recent write for a given item of data.
        - Eventual Consistency offers better performance by allowing reads to return out-of-date values but ensures that, eventually, all replicas converge to the most recent state.
    3. **State Persistence**: Persisting state across sessions is pivotal for stateful applications. Dapr's architecture facilitates durable storage, ensuring that application state survives restarts and failures, imperative for maintaining reliability in long-running operations.
    4. **Concurrency Resolution**: Managing concurrent access to shared state is essential in distributed systems. Dapr provides version control mechanisms, preventing conflicts from simultaneous attempts to update the same piece of data. This helps avert inconsistencies or data corruption within applications.
    5. **State Management APIs**: Dapr comes with a robust REST and gRPC API that enables state operations through

---

[1]Consistency modes are critical to align with the application requirements for correctness and performance.

simple HTTP calls or through gRPC for environments where lower latency and efficiency are paramount.

- **State Management Operations**: The Dapr state management API supports several operations that allow fine-grained control over how state is handled:

  1. **Save State**: This operation is used to persist data with a specified key. The payload typically consists of the state object and its associated metadata.

     ```
     POST http://localhost:3500/v1.0/state/<state-store>
     Content-Type: application/json

     [
       {
         "key": "user123",
         "value": {
           "name": "Alice",
           "balance": 350.00
         }
       }
     ]
     ```

     Here, a user state is saved under a unique key "user123". This state can be easily retrieved or modified later.

  2. **Get State**: To read data stored in the state store, a 'GET' request is made specifying the key.

     ```
     # Python example using Dapr's SDK
     import dapr.clients

     client = dapr.clients.DaprClient()

     user_data = client.get_state(store_name="statestore", key="user123")
     print(user_data)
     ```

     The command above retrieves the state corresponding to "user123" and outputs the stored information, ensuring easy access to persistent data.

  3. **Delete State**: Removing data is as straightforward as saving it; a 'DELETE' request results in state removal.

     ```
     DELETE http://localhost:3500/v1.0/state/<state-store>/user123
     ```

     This operation would remove the state associated with the "user123" key if it exists.

4. **Transactional State Operations**: Dapr supports executing multiple state operations atomically. In complex scenarios, this ensures that either all operations complete or none, maintaining system integrity.

```
POST http://localhost:3500/v1.0/state/<state-store>/transaction
Content-Type: application/json

{
    "operations": [
        {
            "operation": "upsert",
            "request": {
                "key": "order456",
                "value": "confirmed"
            }
        },
        {
            "operation": "delete",
            "request": {
                "key": "cart789"
            }
        }
    ]
}
```

This feature is invaluable when maintaining relational data consistency or orchestrating related operations.

- **Scalability and Performance**: The scalability of state management in distributed systems is crucial. Dapr leverages its backends' capabilities to manage state effectively, using distributed state stores like AWS DynamoDB or Azure CosmosDB which are designed for elastic scaling. These stores handle enormous data volumes and concurrent requests, ensuring that application performance scales in tandem with business needs.

  When choosing state stores, considerations such as available read/write IOPS, latency requirements, global replication, and data security are crucial. Dapr abstracts the complexity of accessing these details while allowing configurational flexibility to meet various scaling demands.

- **Consistency Models**: Dapr offers selectable consistency models. For applications requiring the latest data state on every read, such as in financial systems, the strong consistency model ensures that what is read or modified reflects the most recent write. This comes with a potential cost in operations latency due to distributed system synchronization overhead.

On the other hand, eventual consistency is advantageous for applications focused on high throughput and minimal latencies, such as analytics platforms, where it's acceptable that reads may not reflect the most current state immediately, thus favoring performance over precision.

- **Concurrency Handling**: Distributed systems often struggle with concurrency as multiple services might access shared state simultaneously, risking conflict. Dapr addresses this through ETag-based concurrency controls, providing optimistic concurrency support. The ETag value represents the state version, and any updates require matching this version to succeed. If the ETag does not match due to an intermediate update, the transaction will fail, prompting the client to retry, thus preventing lost updates or inconsistencies.

```
# Example of ETag usage
POST http://localhost:3500/v1.0/state/<state-store>
Content-Type: application/json

[
    {
        "key": "session-lock",
        "value": "active",
        "etag": "d677d4f2",
        "options": {"concurrency": "first-write"}
    }
]
```

- **Best Practices in State Management**: Effective state management is key to building resilient distributed applications. Here are some best practices when utilizing Dapr state management:

    – Choose the appropriate consistency level based on the application's requirements for correctness and performance.

    – Utilize transactional operations judiciously to maintain consistency across composite operations, especially in financial domains.

- Implement ETag-based concurrency control to handle overlaps in state accesses and prevent data corruption.
- Optimize the choice of state store based on latency, data model compatibility, and cost metrics to ensure the right balance between performance and operational cost.

- **Real-World Use Cases**:
    1. **E-commerce Platforms**: Track sessions, manage user profiles, and preserve shopping cart state across interactions and devices, ensuring seamless user experience without loss of data.
    2. **IoT Solutions**: Maintain device states and telemetry data, enabling real-time system status monitoring and updates while balancing latency and consistency across globally distributed instances.
    3. **Financial Services**: Implement account transactions with strict consistency requirements, leveraging Dapr's transactional capabilities for atomic state changes across distributed environments.
    4. **Gaming**: Store player progress and scores reliably in a scalable manner, allowing real-time updates and interactions that enhance gameplay experience.

Dapr's state management building block provides an intuitive, robust framework for handling state in microservices, encapsulating crucial features that allow developers to concentrate on solving business challenges rather than wrestling with complex low-level infrastructure issues. This abstraction layer serves as a facilitator of innovative, scalable applications, paving the way for aspiring cloud-native systems that showcase resilience and adaptability in today's dynamically advancing technological landscape.

3.4 Publish-Subscribe Pattern

The publish-subscribe (pub/sub) pattern is a widely adopted messaging paradigm within distributed systems that facilitates asynchronous communication among components. It ensures that producers of messages, known as publishers, communicate with consumers, termed subscribers, via a message broker that handles message distribution and delivery. This architectural pattern, offered by Dapr, is pivotal in constructing loosely coupled, event-driven applications where components can operate independently yet respond to dynamic system events.

Dapr's publish-subscribe building block introduces a seamless, platform-agnostic approach for implementing pub/sub semantics over different underlying message brokers. With this abstraction, developers can integrate various cloud-native messaging systems such as Kafka, RabbitMQ, and Azure Service Bus without worrying about the specifics of each technology. This facilitates the adoption of best-of-breed tools and strategies while maintaining easy, consistent interactions in application lifecycles.

Core Advantages of Pub/Sub Pattern

The pub/sub pattern's advantages in distributed systems and microservices architectures include:

- **Decoupling**: Publishers and subscribers are independent components, which only interact through the message broker. This decoupling fosters modular system architectures where services can be developed, deployed, and scaled independently.

- **Scalability**: This pattern supports horizontal scaling. Detaching publishers from subscribers ensures that load increases can be distributed across multiple service instances without modifying system design.

- **Resilience and Flexibility**: Pub/sub systems are decentralized, meaning that service components can fail or be updated without affecting the overall message flow, enhancing system resilience.

- **Event-Driven Architecture Support**: By supporting asynchronous event processing, the pub/sub mechanism aids in designing reactive systems that more readily support use cases like notifications, streaming data pipelines, and integrating microservices seamlessly.

3.4. PUBLISH-SUBSCRIBE PATTERN

Pub/Sub in Dapr

Dapr abstracted pub/sub APIs promote high portability across cloud service providers and local installations, enabling uniform application development irrespective of deployment context. Below are core aspects of how Dapr implements pub/sub within distributed systems.

Pub/Sub Architecture

The Dapr pub/sub component consists of publishers, subscribers, and a message broker. Publishers send messages to a broker identified by topics, while subscribers inform the broker of their interest in specific topics. The broker then ensures message delivery to subscribed services based on topics of interest.

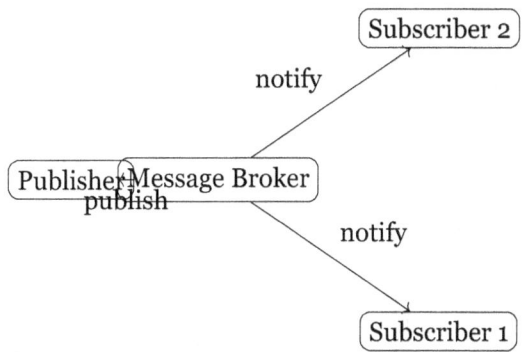

Publishing Messages

To publish messages onto a topic using Dapr, developers utilize HTTP or gRPC endpoints exposed by the Dapr sidecar. The following HTTP request demonstrates this process:

```
POST http://localhost:3500/v1.0/publish/<pubsub-name>/<topic>
Content-Type: application/json

{
    "eventId": 12345,
    "message": "New Order Created"
}
```

In this instance, the '<pubsub-name>' refers to the configured message broker, and '<topic>' represents the topic to which the message is published. This abstraction ensures that developers can switch underlying messaging systems without impacting code.

Subscribing to Messages

Subscribers are configured to listen for specific events or topics. A typical subscriber service defines its topics of interest and uses HTTP endpoints to handle incoming messages.

Here is a Python example demonstrating how a subscription is handled using the Dapr SDK:

```
import dapr.clients
import flask

app = flask.Flask(__name__)

@app.route('/dapr/subscribe', methods=['GET'])
def subscribe():
    return flask.jsonify([{"pubsubname": "pubsub", "topic": "orders", "route": "
        neworder"}])

@app.route('/neworder', methods=['POST'])
def new_order():
    message = flask.request.json
    print(f"Received order: {message['eventId']}")
    return '', 204

if __name__ == '__main__':
    app.run(port=5001)
```

In this code, the '/dapr/subscribe' endpoint registers the service as a subscriber for the 'orders' topic. The 'new_order' endpoint processes messages received on this topic, enabling the subscriber to take action based on the event payload.

Message Brokers and Configuration

Dapr supports several message brokers, each suited to different use cases. The configuration of a pub/sub component typically involves specifying broker type, connection details, and options for fault tolerance, persistence, and routing.

An example configuration for a pub/sub component using Kafka:

```
apiVersion: dapr.io/v1alpha1
kind: Component
metadata:
  name: pubsub
spec:
  type: pubsub.kafka
  version: v1
  metadata:
```

```
- name: brokers
  value: "kafka-broker:9092"
- name: consumerGroup
  value: "order-consumers"
- name: authType
  value: "plain"
```

Scaling and Load Balancing

The decoupled nature of pub/sub systems inherently supports scalability. By adding more instances of publishers and subscribers and utilizing load balancers, systems can seamlessly manage higher loads and ensure messages are processed efficiently.

Ensuring Message Delivery

Dapr provides guarantees related to message delivery patterns. Common models like at-least-once and at-most-once are supported, allowing developers to tune broker configurations for delivery semantics that best meet application needs. Leveraging dead-letter queues allows for handling messages that cannot be processed, enhancing robustness in failure scenarios.

Use Cases and Pattern Applicability

The publish-subscribe pattern offers extensibility and flexibility across a variety of application scenarios:

- **Microservices Orchestration**: Coordinate services through event-driven triggers, enabling workflows where events in one service can initiate operations in another.

- **Data Pipeline Construction**: Facilitate complex event processing and aggregation, such as streaming analytics that require real-time, scalable data processing.

- **Device Communication in IoT**: Distribute messages to device networks, supporting scalable systems that react to sensor inputs and status updates.

- **User Interaction Systems**: Maintain real-time notifications messages for chat applications, alert systems, and social media updates.

Best Practices for Pub/Sub Systems

Harnessing the full potential of the pub/sub pattern with Dapr involves:

- **Topic Design**: Design topics to reflect business domains, which promotes a clearer separation of concerns and improves manageability.

- **Broker Selection and Configuration**: Choose a broker based on message throughput, persistence needs, and infrastructure compatibilities.

- **Monitoring and Logging**: Continuously monitor the health and performance of pub/sub systems to diagnose bottlenecks and optimize message flow.

- **Broker Security**: Secure message brokers through authentication and encryption, safeguarding communication channels from unauthorized access.

- **Eventual Consistency and Idempotency**: Architect systems to handle message redelivery gracefully by being idempotent to prevent unintended state transitions.

Implementing the publish-subscribe pattern with Dapr empowers developers to create modular applications that are easier to scale, manage, and evolve. This design not only enhances modern distributed architectures by abstracting integration complexities but also aligns with cloud-native best practices, ensuring the creation of future-proof, resilient systems capable of handling dynamic demands and growth. Through effective use of pub/sub mechanisms, organizations can harness the benefits of event-driven design, resulting in a substantially improved capacity for rapid innovation and high responsiveness in application development.

3.5 Resource Bindings

In the evolving landscape of distributed systems and cloud-native applications, integrating with external services and resources is a fundamental requirement. Dapr's resource bindings component provides a

3.5. RESOURCE BINDINGS

powerful abstraction for enabling easy interactions with external systems such as databases, message queues, cloud services, file systems, and more. The need for seamless integration with external services is paramount for the real-world functionality of applications, and Dapr addresses this with a comprehensive, flexible approach.

The concept of bindings in Dapr allows applications to react to external events or execute operations on external resources without the boilerplate code typically associated with such tasks. This abstraction is implemented in a language-agnostic manner, allowing developers to utilize bindings via HTTP/gRPC calls, which are translated into various operations understood by the external system.

- **Core Features of Resource Bindings**: Dapr offers two primary types of bindings: input and output bindings.
  - **Input Bindings**: These are used to trigger application logic in response to events from external systems, such as when a file is uploaded to cloud storage or a message is queued.
  - **Output Bindings**: These allow applications to initiate operations in external systems, such as writing data to a database or sending a message to a queue.

- **Advantages of Using Resource Bindings**: Resource bindings provide several key advantages which simplify and enhance the development of complex applications:
  - **Code Abstraction and Reuse**: By abstracting the connectivity and protocol-specific code required for integrating with external resources, bindings promote reuse and modularity in application logic.
  - **Decoupling**: They facilitate a clear separation between application logic and resource interaction, making codebases cleaner and easier to maintain.
  - **Simplified Configuration Management**: Alternate resource configurations can be easily managed using Dapr components without modifying application code, thus enhancing flexibility in dynamic environments.

- **Cross-Platform Compatibility**: The language-agnostic nature of Dapr's bindings provides a consistent, cross-platform API for interacting with diverse resource types, reducing the learning curve and complexity.

- **Configuring Resource Bindings**: Bindings in Dapr are configured using components, which define details on how Dapr should connect to the specified resources.

Example Configuration for an Azure Blob Storage Input Binding

```
apiVersion: dapr.io/v1alpha1
kind: Component
metadata:
  name: myblobinput
spec:
  type: bindings.azure.blobstorage
  version: v1
  metadata:
    - name: storageAccount
      value: myAccount
    - name: storageAccessKey
      value: xxxx-xxxx-xxxx-xxxx
    - name: container
      value: mycontainer
    - name: blob
      value: example.txt
```

In this configuration, an input binding listens for changes or new blob creations in an Azure Blob Storage account. When a blob is created or modified, Dapr triggers a defined endpoint in the application, enhancing automation workflows.

- **Input Bindings in Action**: Input bindings enable applications to react to events through endpoint invocations. Here, when an event fires, the Dapr runtime invokes the configured URL in the application with event data.

Example: Processing a Queue Message

Consider the scenario where an application needs to process messages from an external queue service such as AWS SQS. The following configuration harnesses input bindings to achieve this:

3.5. RESOURCE BINDINGS

```
apiVersion: dapr.io/v1alpha1
kind: Component
metadata:
  name: my-sqs-input
spec:
  type: bindings.aws.sqs
  version: v1
  metadata:
    - name: queueName
      value: myQueue
    - name: region
      value: us-west-2
    - name: accessKey
      value: XXXXXXXXXXXXXXXXX
    - name: secretKey
      value: XXXXXXXXXXXXXXXXX
```

The application then specifies an endpoint, '/messages', to handle incoming messages from the configured SQS queue:

```
@app.route('/messages', methods=['POST'])
def handle_message():
    data = flask.request.json
    print(f"Received message: {data}")
    return '', 204
```

This setup decouples the application logic from the underlying messaging platform specifics, streamlining the process of extending and maintaining the application.

- **Output Bindings in Detail**: Output bindings allow applications to send data to or invoke methods in external services. This includes operations such as updating a cloud service's state, queuing messages, or interacting with APIs.

Example: Sending Data to an HTTP Endpoint

Consider a scenario where your application needs to send data to a third-party HTTP endpoint. Dapr makes this seamless through output bindings:

```
apiVersion: dapr.io/v1alpha1
kind: Component
metadata:
  name: webhook
spec:
  type: bindings.http
  version: v1
  metadata:
```

```
- name: url
  value: https://example.com/webhook
- name: method
  value: POST
```

To trigger the binding:

```
import requests

def send_webhook():
    data = {"event": "user_signed_up", "detail": {"user_id": "1234"}}
    response = requests.post('http://localhost:3500/v1.0/bindings/webhook', json=
        data)
    print(f"Webhook delivered: {response.status_code}")
```

This utilization of Dapr bindings abstracts the delivery method and manages communication with the external system efficiently.

- **Best Practices for Using Resource Bindings**: To maximize the effectiveness of Dapr's resource bindings, adhere to the following best practices:

    - **Modular Design**: Structure applications to leverage inclusive binding configurations for modularity, enhancing scalability and maintainability.

    - **Secure Secrets Management**: Always manage secrets such as API tokens and keys using secure storage solutions like Kubernetes secrets or parameter stores, referenced within bindings through metadata attributes.

    - **Efficient Error Handling**: Design applications with robust error handling and retries for binding operations, accommodating network variations or service downtimes.

    - **Comprehensive Logging and Monitoring**: Implement comprehensive logging to monitor the effectiveness and performance of bindings, quickly addressing and troubleshooting any discrepancies.

    - **Version Control for Component Definitions**: Apply version control to component definitions to easily track changes and manage deployment configurations across environments.

- **Real-World Applications and Examples**: In various industries, the effective use of bindings offers tremendous benefits, enabling complex use cases:
    - **Data Synchronization and ETL Workflows**: Bindings streamline the integration of data sources to perform extract-transform-load operations, keeping datasets accurate and up-to-date across large-scale enterprise systems.
    - **IoT Device Management**: Enable triggering and feedback mechanisms on device events such as firmware updates, using bindings with storage, functions, or notifications.
    - **Financial Services Transaction Processing**: Manage secure transactions by utilizing bindings to process payments, update ledgers, and notify users through seamless integration with financial service APIs.
    - **CRM and Enterprise Integration**: Wide-reaching CRM systems benefit from bindings with real-time connectors to synchronize user interactions and customers' data across disparate enterprise resources.

Dapr's resource bindings eliminate integration friction by providing a standardized mechanism to interact with external systems and services. Through abstractions, it promotes a design that prioritizes code simplicity, reusability, and operational efficiency. This makes it a cornerstone for applications that leverage the cloud, third-party APIs, and complex multi-service orchestrations. The flexibility offered by Dapr through bindings makes it a powerful enabler in the landscape of distributed systems, supporting a wide range of real-world applications while simplifying development processes and enhancing system reliability.

3.6 Observability

Observability within distributed systems is crucial for understanding, monitoring, and maintaining the health and performance of applications. In microservices architectures, with numerous services interacting across a network, capturing metrics, logs, and traces is pivotal for diagnosing issues and ensuring optimal functionality. Dapr's observability building block offers a comprehensive suite of tools to enhance visibility into microservice interactions and system behavior.

Dapr provides built-in observability features that seamlessly integrate into applications, without requiring extensive configuration. These capabilities are designed to capture a wide range of telemetry data, automatically instrumenting applications with minimal user effort. Key elements of Dapr observability include metrics, distributed tracing, and logging. Each of these elements is crucial for building resilient cloud-native applications that can adapt to dynamic workloads and environments.

- **Observability Framework Components:** The observability framework within Dapr focuses on three main components:
    - **Metrics**: Metrics provide quantitative data points that describe the performance characteristics of a service. These data points can include statistics such as request counts, response times, CPU usage, and error rates, enabling real-time operational insights and performance benchmarking.
    - **Distributed Tracing**: Tracing tracks the flow of requests through your system, recording how requests traverse different services. Distributed tracing offers a holistic view of a request's lifecycle, helping developers pinpoint latency bottlenecks and errors across service boundaries.
    - **Logging**: Logs capture detailed information about application events, allowing for historic debugging, error tracking, and system auditing. Logs provide narrative details that complement the quantitative analysis of metrics and traces.

- **Metrics Collection and Analysis:** Dapr provides metrics out-of-the-box, collected from both the Dapr runtime and the application. These metrics are accessible via the '/metrics' endpoint in Prometheus format, making integration with monitoring systems straightforward.

- **Key Metrics:** Some of the primary metrics Dapr emits include:

3.6. OBSERVABILITY

- **HTTP Request/Response Count and Latency:** Measures the number of incoming and outgoing HTTP requests and the average time taken to handle these requests.
- **gRPC Request Statistics:** Captures similar metrics for gRPC-based communications.
- **State Store Operations:** Stats related to state management operations such as reads, writes, and errors.
- **Pub/Sub Messaging:** Tracks message publishing and delivery success rates.

- **Example Prometheus Configuration:** To leverage Prometheus for monitoring Dapr metrics, ensure a configuration such as:

```
scrape_configs:
 - job_name: 'dapr'
   static_configs:
     - targets: ['localhost:3500']
```

Here, Prometheus scrapes data from the specified endpoint where Dapr metrics are exposed, enabling detailed performance monitoring and alerting based on real-time conditions.

- **Distributed Tracing:** Distributed tracing provides visibility into how requests flow through a system composed of numerous microservices, helping identify where delays or failures occur across services. Dapr integrates with popular distributed tracing systems including Zipkin and OpenTelemetry.

- **Setting Up Tracing:** Configuring tracing involves setting up a tracing provider:

```
apiVersion: dapr.io/v1alpha1
kind: Configuration
metadata:
  name: daprConfig
spec:
  tracing:
    samplingRate: "1.0"
    zipkin:
      endpointAddress: "http://<zipkin-server>:9411/api/v2/spans"
```

This YAML configuration specifies the trace sampling rate and the endpoint address of the Zipkin server where spans are reported.

- **Tracing Usage:** Once configured, traces can be visualized to understand the flow of requests through distinct services. This visualization enables developers to identify latency issues and understand service dependencies, effectively tracing issues that impact experience and performance:

    - **Tracing Request Flow:** Analyze the entire flow from entry point through all involved services.
    - **Identifying Bottlenecks:** Highlight services that introduce undue processing time or resource constraints.
    - **Failure Diagnosis:** Trace back errors to understand failure points and their context, simplifying root cause analysis.

- **Log Management:** Logs offer crucial context around events in microservices. Dapr logs both the runtime events and logs can be extended to include application-level logs.

- **Logging Integration:** Dapr integrates with logging solutions to centralize log management, ensuring consistency and easy access:

    - **Elastic Stack (ELK):** Integrate with Elasticsearch, Logstash, and Kibana to aggregate logs and provide a detailed, searchable log repository.
    - **Fluent Bit and Fluentd:** Use these log forwarding agents to route logs from Dapr services to a desired backend, ensuring robustness and reliability in log data handling.

- **Observability Best Practices:** Effective observability within Dapr applications involves several best practices:

    - **Comprehensive Instrumentation:** Employ both metrics, tracing, and logs to gather a full-spectrum view of your system.

- **Centralized Monitoring:** Utilize centralized solutions like Prometheus and Grafana to visualize metrics and configure alerts for critical threshold breaches.
- **Active Trace Analysis:** Consistently review trace data to align capacity planning with application demands, ensuring resources are proportionally scaled.
- **Efficient Log Management:** Rotate and archive logs appropriately to maintain optimal disk usage while preserving essential data for post-incident analysis.
- **Security and Privacy:** Ensure that logged information complies with privacy standards, masking or avoiding sensitive data where necessary.

- **Real-World Use Cases:**
    - **E-commerce Platforms:** Monitor request latency, transaction throughput, and inventory updates for high-performance, reliable user experiences.
    - **Financial Systems:** Trace request journeys to meet audit requirements and conduct thorough end-to-end transaction analysis.
    - **Healthcare Applications:** Ensure data integrity and fault tolerance while managing sensitive patient data, using metrics to maintain high service reliability.
    - **IoT Networks:** Continuously monitor the flow of device-generated data, capturing both large-scale trends and local anomalies for proactive system management.

Dapr's observability suite empowers developers to achieve unparalleled insights into distributed applications, enabling them to tackle diverse use cases with assurance of system performance and reliability. By making metrics, tracing, and log management fundamental components, Dapr fosters the development of highly observable and resilient systems. The ease of integration with industry-standard tools further simplifies the diagnostic and optimization processes, ensuring that applications are robust, agile, and capable of meeting the stringent demands of today's technology landscape.

3.7 Actor Model

The actor model is a computational framework designed for managing concurrent computations in distributed systems. Originating in the 1970s, the actor model presents an abstraction where each actor encapsulates state and behavior, interacting with other actors solely through message passing. This paradigm allows for the construction of systems with high concurrency and isolation levels, managing scalable, stateful entities with minimal lock contention or shared state complications.

Dapr's implementation of the actor model builds upon these foundational principles, providing a robust method for developers to orchestrate stateful object interactions across microservices and cloud environments. The actor pattern is especially beneficial in scenarios requiring complex state management, like gaming sessions, IoT device communications, and user session handling.

- **Core Features and Principles of the Actor Model**: Dapr enhances the actor model with essential features that align with contemporary requirements in distributed computing, providing scalable, manageable, and reliable solutions:

    - **Encapsulation of State and Behavior**: Each actor in Dapr manages its state privately and manipulates this state only through defined methods. This encapsulation ensures actors operate independently, allowing for scripting complex business logic that remains isolated from others.

    - **Concurrency and Isolation**: By handling interactions exclusively through message passing, the actor model naturally sidesteps issues related to concurrency, like deadlocks or race conditions. Each actor processes a single message at a time, guaranteeing sequential execution within the actor and eliminating shared state pitfalls.

    - **Dynamic Actor Management**: Dapr supports both statically defined and dynamically created actors, providing agility in managing actors as demanded by application conditions. This allows for seamless scaling, crucial in applications that experience volatile load conditions.

3.7. ACTOR MODEL

- **Persistence and Resiliency**: Actor state persistence ensures that critical state data survives failures and restarts, significantly enhancing system reliability. Dapr facilitates this through its state management abstractions, tying actor state effortlessly to preferred storage backends.

- **Setting Up the Actor Model in Dapr**: The implementation of actors within Dapr is straightforward yet versatile, promoting integration with various microservice environments and programming languages.

- **Actor Definition**: Define actors by encapsulating state along with behavioral methods. Consider an example where we define a user session actor:

```
from dapr.actor import Actor, actor_method

class UserSessionActor(Actor):

    def __init__(self, actor_id):
        super(UserSessionActor, self).__init__(actor_id)

    @actor_method
    async def login(self, user_info):
        # Actor state initialization/update
        return f"User {user_info['username']} logged in."

    @actor_method
    async def logout(self):
        # Clear state or update transition details
        return f"User session {self.actor_id} terminated."

    @actor_method
    async def get_session_data(self):
        # Retrieve state data
        return {"actor_id": self.actor_id, "status": "active"}
```

In this example, the session-related state is maintained within the actor, and methods are used to perform state manipulations relevant to the user session lifecycle.

- **Actor Activation**: Actors are activated on-demand in Dapr, meaning they are initialized upon receiving their first message. This lazy instantiation helps optimize resource usage while allowing easy scalability:

- **Instancing Actors**: Each actor is identified by a unique ID, and communication with the actor is routed based on this identifier. An HTTP or gRPC interface then manages these communications.

* **Actor Communication and Messaging**: Actors communicate by message passing, which simplifies the conceptual model compared to shared-state concurrency. This involves dispatching messages to actor instances where each request is encapsulated in a form of serialized data.

* **Example HTTP-based Actor Invocation**: Below is how you would typically invoke actor methods using HTTP with the Dapr runtime:

```
POST http://localhost:3500/v1.0/actors/UserSession/1234/method/login
Content-Type: application/json

{
  "username": "alice",
  "lastLogin": "2023-10-12T09:30:00Z"
}
```

In the above request, the actor ID is '1234', and a 'login' method call is being made to the 'UserSession' actor type to update the login details of the user.

* **State Persistence and Recovery**: Dapr's actor model benefits significantly from integrated state management services, allowing state persistence across actor instances. This feature is vital for ensuring that actor states can recover reliably following application restarts or failures:

  - **Configuring State Persistence**: Define a state store and configure actor states to persist using Dapr's State Management API such as through Redis or Cosmos DB.

    ```
    apiVersion: dapr.io/v1alpha1
    kind: Component
    metadata:
      name: actorStateStore
    spec:
      type: state.redis
    ```

```
version: v1
metadata:
- name: redisHost
  value: redis.master.svc.cluster.local:6379
```

This configuration snippet sets up state storage with a Redis backend, ensuring persistent and resilient actor state management.

- **Scenarios and Use Cases**: The actor model is suited for a variety of applications that require high concurrency, state encapsulation, and autonomous operation:

    1. **Game Development**: Manage highly stateful and interactive player sessions, tracking game statistics, inventories, and other dynamic data individually for each player.
    2. **IoT Device Management**: Oversee stateful interactions for devices in IoT networks, facilitating updates, commands, and telemetry for thousands of devices with isolated state.
    3. **Financial Transactions**: Track sequences of financial transactions as stateful processes ensuring secure, idempotent, and consistent state transitions, especially in payments.
    4. **User Profiles and Preferences**: Maintain personalized settings and session data on a per-user basis, enhancing customization and session continuity across devices and platforms.

- **Challenges and Considerations**: Despite its benefits, adopting the actor model requires consideration of several factors:

    - **Serialization Overhead**: As actors primarily interact through message-passing, attention must be given to serialization protocols and data formats to avoid performance bottlenecks.
    - **Finite State and Actor Count**: Designing actor systems needs careful planning in terms of actor lifecycle, avoiding unlimited growth in actors or indefinite state accrual.

- **Partial State Failures**: While actors individually process messages sequentially, guaranteeing consistency across multiple actors needs higher-level patterns like sagas or workflow engines.

Dapr's implementation of the actor model furnishes developers with a powerful toolkit for creating highly parallelized and fault-tolerant distributed applications. By focusing on simplicity, isolation, and concurrency, the actor model aligns well with microservices architectures that demand scalability and resilience. As distributed systems continue to gain prominence, leveraging actors through Dapr heralds opportunities for creating more intuitive, scalable, and maintainable applications that meet diverse business needs in a rapidly evolving technological environment.

Chapter 4

State Management with Dapr

This chapter focuses on Dapr's approach to state management, a critical aspect of building reliable microservices. It covers the mechanisms Dapr provides to handle stateful services, including the integration with various state stores and the use of state APIs for data handling. Additionally, the chapter explains consistency and concurrency models, transaction and batch operations, and best practices for efficient state management. These tools and guidelines empower developers to build applications that maintain consistency and resilience in distributed environments.

4.1 Understanding State Management in Microservices

In modern software architecture, microservices have emerged as a prominent paradigm due to their ability to decompose large systems into smaller, more manageable pieces. Each microservice can independently manage its lifecycle, scaling, deployment, and technology stack.

An essential aspect of this architecture, which often dictates its performance and reliability, is state management. Understanding how state is managed within microservices is crucial for achieving consistency and reliability in distributed systems. This section delves into the concept of state within microservices, exploring its definitions, challenges, and the mechanisms employed to address these challenges.

Microservices are inherently distributed systems, meaning that they run across different processes and often on different physical or logical machines. In such systems, the notion of a "state" becomes complex. Here, the state refers to any data that the system needs to remember between processing requests, which can be the data from a user session, transaction data, or any intermediate processing data. Survival of this data is critical for ensuring the integrity of processing, user interaction, and system monitoring.

The first step in understanding state management in microservices is recognizing the types of state that exist. Broadly, state can be categorized into two types: stateless and stateful.

Stateless Microservices: In stateless services, each request from a client is treated as an independent transaction, unrelated to any previous requests. The server does not store any client state between requests, which implies there is no session data stored on the server. This characteristic allows stateless microservices to handle more requests simultaneously, as each request can be routed to any instance of the service. An example of a stateless service is a RESTful web service where all the required information must be included in each request.

The merits of this design include scalability and simplicity, as horizontal scaling can be achieved by simply adding more instances without a need for session data coordination. However, for scenarios where state is essential, stateless services alone are inadequate.

Stateful Microservices: These services retain session information or state between client requests. Managing state becomes more complex as it requires ensuring consistency and availability amidst failures or network partitions. Stateful services might utilize in-memory data structures for faster access, or they may leverage external state stores such as databases, caches, or distributed file systems to persist data.

A stateful service would be an online shopping cart where the application caches a user's shopping list across sessions. Here, the service needs to manage this stateful interaction either by storing it in the client's browser, server-side, or in a shared database.

The determination of whether a service is stateless or stateful depends largely on the necessity of storing data over the interaction period.

Challenges in State Management: As microservices architectures lean towards distributing components, several challenges in state management arise:

- **Data Integrity and Consistency:** Maintaining consistent state across distributed systems is a non-trivial task. Various consistency models, such as eventual consistency, causal consistency, and strong consistency, present trade-offs between performance and the temporal guarantees of state synchronization.

- **Scalability:** State management solutions must be scalable, allowing for increased load handling without degradation of system performance. Accommodating scaling properly often involves distributed databases or data grids.

- **Fault Tolerance:** System components will inevitably fail. State management solutions must provide resilience against such failures, ensuring no data loss or corruption. Techniques include using redundant backups or implementing state checkpointing.

- **Latency:** Minimizing the time taken to access state data while ensuring prompt responses to client interactions is crucial. This often necessitates the use of in-memory caches which are positioned strategically within the architecture.

- **Security:** Protecting the state from unauthorized access or loss is essential. This encompasses encryption of sensitive data, strict access controls, and audit mechanisms.

We can delve deeper into how these challenges are navigated in a microservices architecture.

```
import java.io.IOException;
import javax.servlet.http.HttpServlet;
import javax.servlet.http.HttpServletRequest;
import javax.servlet.http.HttpServletResponse;
```

```java
public class StatelessHttpService extends HttpServlet {
    protected void doGet(HttpServletRequest request, HttpServletResponse response)
            throws IOException {
        String clientData = request.getParameter("data");
        // Process the request without any stored state
        String processingResult = computeResult(clientData);
        response.getWriter().write(processingResult);
    }

    private String computeResult(String data) {
        // Stateless logic here processing the input
        return "Processed " + data;
    }
}
```

This Java service demonstrates a stateless service, where the processing result depends solely on the input parameters provided in each HTTP request. It avoids any need for shared in-memory state or session storage, promoting easy scalability.

```java
import java.util.HashMap;
import java.util.Map;
import javax.servlet.http.HttpServlet;
import javax.servlet.http.HttpServletRequest;
import javax.servlet.http.HttpServletResponse;
import javax.servlet.http.HttpSession;

public class StatefulHttpService extends HttpServlet {
    private Map<String, String> sessionData = new HashMap<>();

    protected void doPost(HttpServletRequest request, HttpServletResponse response)
            throws IOException {
        HttpSession session = request.getSession(true);
        String sessionId = session.getId();
        String newData = request.getParameter("data");
        sessionData.put(sessionId, newData);
        response.getWriter().write("Stored data in session: " + newData);
    }

    protected void doGet(HttpServletRequest request, HttpServletResponse response)
            throws IOException {
        HttpSession session = request.getSession();
        String sessionId = session.getId();
        String storedData = sessionData.getOrDefault(sessionId, "No data found");
        response.getWriter().write("Retrieved data from session: " + storedData);
    }
}
```

This Java service example uses HttpSession to store and retrieve session data, highlighting a basic stateful service approach. In a real-world implementation, such data would likely be stored in a database or cache for enhanced persistence and resilience.

4.1. UNDERSTANDING STATE MANAGEMENT IN MICROSERVICES

Effective state management within microservices often leverages external services designed to manage complexity inherent in maintaining state.

Distributed Databases: Systems such as Apache Cassandra, Amazon DynamoDB, or Google Cloud Spanner offer distributed database solutions, providing high availability and fault tolerance. These systems use consistent hashing and replication strategies to distribute state across nodes, ensuring no single point of failure.

Distributed Caching Solutions: Products like Redis, Memcached, and Hazelcast offer fast access to state data. They act as in-memory data stores, delivering quicker state retrieval to microservices, thus reducing reliance on slower, traditional databases. They also provide features such as distributed patterns and automatic sharding to accommodate state scaling and distribution.

Stateful Stream Processing: Stream processing frameworks such as Apache Kafka support stateful processing of incoming data streams. They store intermediate processing states, allowing stateful transformations and aggregations to be performed on data streams. Kafka's Streams API, for example, interacts with distributed state stores to maintain state consistency throughout stream processing.

Microservices may also adopt event sourcing and Command Query Responsibility Segregation (CQRS) patterns to address state consistency. Event sourcing involves capturing all changes as a sequence of events that anyone can replay to determine the current state. CQRS handles update commands and query requests differently, optimizing for distinct use cases.

The strategic use of state management methodologies will vary based on application requirements. Understanding these approaches aids developers in designing microservices that are robust, scalable, and performant, thereby ensuring system reliability and integrity across distributed architectures. As developers approach state management in microservice architectures, considering the outlined principles and technologies is imperative to construct efficient, consistent, and reliable systems.

4.2 Dapr's State Management Building Block

In the ever-evolving landscape of microservices architecture, managing state uniformly and efficiently across distributed components remains a significant challenge. The Distributed Application Runtime (Dapr) emerges as a powerful abstraction layer that simplifies complex state management tasks without forcing developers to grapple with the intricacies of different state store implementations. By centralizing state management functionality via a platform-agnostic layer, Dapr ensures that developers can focus more on business logic rather than the complications of back-end state stores.

At the core of Dapr's offering is the concept of building blocks. One such building block dedicated to state management is Dapr's State Management, which facilitates storing, retrieving, and managing state across diverse state stores seamlessly. This section explores the design principles, functionality, and implementation details of Dapr's state management capabilities, providing insights that help streamline stateful service development within microservices environments.

Dapr's architectural design revolves around providing standardized APIs for state management. The state management building block, specifically, focuses on abstracting stateful operations, enabling application developers to effectively work with state data through a series of well-defined REST or gRPC APIs.

State Abstraction Layer: Dapr provides a consistent and simple interface for interacting with state data, abstracting the underlying intricacies of individual state stores. By using this abstraction, developers interact with a unified API, regardless of whether the backend state store is Redis, Amazon DynamoDB, Azure Cosmos DB, or any other supported storage system.

This abstraction layer consists of three primary operations:

- **State Saving** - Persists key-value pairs within a configured state store.
- **State Retrieval** - Guides the fetching of saved state data via key identifiers.

4.2. DAPR'S STATE MANAGEMENT BUILDING BLOCK

- **State Deletion** - Removes the persisted state for specific keys, ensuring data lifecycle management.

Here's an example illustrating the simplicity of using Dapr's HTTP API for these operations. Each example assumes a running Dapr sidecar that communicates with the configured state store.

```
# Save state data to a store
POST /v1.0/state/store
Content-Type: application/json

[
  {
    "key": "userProfile",
    "value": {
      "name": "Alice",
      "email": "alice@example.com"
    }
  }
]

# Get state data from a store
GET /v1.0/state/store/userProfile

# Delete state data
DELETE /v1.0/state/store/userProfile
```

In this example, the operations are executed against an HTTP endpoint exposed by a Dapr sidecar, demonstrating how straightforward it is to save, retrieve, and delete state. The sidecar abstracts state store differences, allowing for scalable and resilient stateful solutions.

State Store Providers: Dapr supports a range of state store providers, expanding developer choices and flexibility. Default state stores include Redis and Azure Cosmos DB, among others. Each store is associated with specific properties, configurable via Dapr's components mechanism, ensuring compatibility and adaptability based on specific operational needs.

A typical configuration for a Redis state store with Dapr might look like the following:

```
apiVersion: dapr.io/v1alpha1
kind: Component
metadata:
  name: statestore
  namespace: default
spec:
  type: state.redis
  version: v1
```

```
metadata:
  - name: redisHost
    value: "redis-master:6379"
  - name: redisPassword
    value: ""
```

This YAML configuration file defines a state store component for Redis, including necessary metadata like host and password. It illustrates how straightforward configuring different backends with Dapr can be, highlighting Dapr's extensibility across state providers.

Programming Model and Integration: One of Dapr's strengths is how seamlessly it integrates with existing applications, regardless of the programming model used. Whether a service executes its logic in Node.js, Python, Java, or .NET, Dapr's state management API remains accessible through the same consistent API signature. Services merely authenticate with their local Dapr sidecar, which grants them access to state management functionality.

Initializing a Dapr client in a Python application might appear as follows:

```
from dapr.clients import DaprClient

with DaprClient() as d:
    # Save state with key-value pair
    d.save_state(store_name='statestore', key='user', value='{"name": "Alice"}')

    # Retrieve state by key
    resp = d.get_state(store_name='statestore', key='user')
    print(f"Retrieved state: {resp.data}")

    # Delete state by key
    d.delete_state(store_name='statestore', key='user')
```

The pythonic example encapsulates save, retrieve, and delete operations within a high-level client library, simplifying interaction with Dapr's state API. This enables the construction of application logic that remains independent of underlying store technologies, facilitating easy swapping or scaling of state store solutions as the system architecture evolves.

Advanced State Management Concepts:

- **ETags for Concurrency Control:** Dapr employs ETags to manage concurrency, minimizing potential conflicts that emerge in distributed systems. Each piece of state data is associated with an ETag. When updates occur, this ETag must match the current state, ensuring that simultaneous conflicting writes are adequately handled, thus maintaining data consistency across distributed systems.

- **Transactional State Operations:** Dapr supports transactional capabilities within state operations, allowing batched state changes that occur in a single atomic transaction. This feature delivers consistency within processes, reducing the complexity of managing multi-step state modifications which are common in business logic operations.

- **State TTL (Time-to-Live):** Implementing TTLs helps in managing the lifespan of state data, automatically purging outdated state data. This functionality can be particularly advantageous in controlling memory utilization and performance within rapidly changing state environments.

- **Bulk Operations:** Dapr provides efficient APIs to fetch and save multiple states in a single operation, optimizing performance particularly on large data sets or batch processing tasks. This is exemplified in Dapr's 'bulk-get', 'bulk-save', and 'bulk-delete' state endpoints which reduce the number of network hops and overhead associated with multiple individual transactions.

By leveraging these advanced constructs, Dapr significantly elevates the level of sophistication with which state management can be handled in applications, ensuring robustness and ease of use.

The Deployment and Operational Benefits:

Dapr's sidecar architecture, which attaches a sidecar container to each service in a Kubernetes deployment, provides operational benefits such as easy monitoring, distributed tracing, and unified metrics for state operations. The sidecar approach isolates state management workloads from main application logic, encouraging a separation of concerns that ensures better maintainability and observability.

Moreover, Dapr enhances elasticity by enabling dynamic scaling of microservices - an essential characteristic when dealing with variable load scenarios in production environments. This capability is underpinned by its state management block that can be extended in tandem with the systems' scaling requirements, allowing horizontal and vertical adjustments across different state management components.

Dapr's state management building block seamlessly integrates into the microservices landscape, abstracting complexities associated with state manipulation. Through its comprehensive API, configurable state stores, and innate scalability, Dapr revolutionizes state management, ensuring that developers maintain a focus on business logic implementations. By harmonizing the intricacies of state operations across heterogeneous systems, Dapr supports the construction of robust, responsive, and high-performance microservice applications, all while keeping architecture flexibly agile.

4.3 Connecting to Different State Stores

In the context of microservices architecture, state management's effectiveness and efficiency are significantly influenced by the underlying state stores. Dapr, with its flexible architecture, facilitates seamless connectivity to an array of state stores, aiding developers in selecting solutions that align with specific application requirements and organizational infrastructure. This section explores the intricacies of connecting to different state stores using Dapr, highlighting supported stores, configuration nuances, and illustration through comprehensive examples.

At its core, Dapr is designed to abstract the complexities associated with interfacing multiple state store technologies. By providing a consistent API, Dapr enables developers to effortlessly switch between state store implementations, thus aiding in achieving high availability, fault tolerance, and the fulfillment of application-specific data persistence needs.

Supported State Store Providers:

Dapr supports a diverse suite of state store providers, each serving distinct use cases that cater to a wide range of scalability, consistency, and performance needs. Some of the prominent state stores supported by Dapr include:

4.3. CONNECTING TO DIFFERENT STATE STORES

- **Redis:** Redis is an open-source, in-memory key-value store known for its speed and flexibility. It supports a wide variety of data structures, making it suitable for caching and transient data storage where low latency is crucial. Redis's implementation in Dapr persists state across microservices via its state-redis component.

- **Azure Cosmos DB:** As a globally distributed, multi-model database service, Azure Cosmos DB offers turnkey global distribution across Azure regions, elastic scalability of throughput and storage, and a broad consistency model spectrum. Dapr enhances application resilience by providing this as a state store.

- **Amazon DynamoDB:** DynamoDB is a fully managed, serverless, key-value NoSQL database designed to run high-performance applications. Through Dapr, its integration abstracts complexities around scaling and offers a cost-effective storage solution.

- **Firebase:** The integration with Firebase's real-time NoSQL database allows Dapr to provide real-time data synchronization and offline support, making it apt for mobile applications and collaborative applications.

- **PostgreSQL and MySQL:** Both relational databases are supported as state stores within Dapr. This enables leveraging the extensive features of traditional SQL databases, such as ACID transactions and complex query capabilities, for microservices state persistence.

These state stores cater to divergent architectural needs, allowing applications to balance between speed, reliability, and cost. Connecting to each store with Dapr involves a straightforward configuration process that abstracts underlying implementation details.

Configuration of State Store Components:

Dapr employs a consistent component configuration model that uses declarative YAML files. These files detail the connection specifics such as endpoints, authentication credentials, and other necessary metadata for interfacing with the state store.

The following example shows the configuration for a Redis state store:

CHAPTER 4. STATE MANAGEMENT WITH DAPR

```
apiVersion: dapr.io/v1alpha1
kind: Component
metadata:
  name: statestore
  namespace: default
spec:
  type: state.redis
  version: v1
  metadata:
  - name: redisHost
    value: "redis-master:6379"
  - name: redisPassword # Optional, secured separately
    value: ""
```

This YAML file specifies the location and credentials to connect to a Redis instance. Similar configurations apply for other supported state stores, with specific metadata parameters tailored to each store's requirements.

For Azure Cosmos DB, a configuration might include:

```
apiVersion: dapr.io/v1alpha1
kind: Component
metadata:
  name: statestore
  namespace: default
spec:
  type: state.azure.cosmosdb
  version: v1
  metadata:
  - name: url
    value: "<your-cosmos-db-url>"
  - name: masterKey
    value: "<your-master-key>"
  - name: database
    value: "<your-database-name>"
  - name: collection
    value: "<your-collection-name>"
```

This configuration defines connection specifics such as the database endpoint, authentication key, and database/collection identifiers. The typical setup requires careful handling of credentials, stored securely in a manner compliant with security best practices.

Connecting to PostgreSQL/MySQL as a State Store:

To use relational databases like PostgreSQL or MySQL as state stores, Dapr requires users to define a relevant component configuration. The example below outlines a PostgreSQL configuration:

```
apiVersion: dapr.io/v1alpha1
```

4.3. CONNECTING TO DIFFERENT STATE STORES

```
kind: Component
metadata:
  name: statestore
  namespace: default
spec:
  type: state.postgresql
  version: v1
  metadata:
  - name: connectionString
    value: "user=username password=password host=localhost dbname=dapr sslmode
      =disable"
```

The connection to the database is detailed in the connection string, encapsulating credentials and database identifiers. The versatile nature of PostgreSQL, supporting ACID transactions, makes it favorable for scenarios requiring strict data consistency and relational operations.

Connecting Dapr with Amazon DynamoDB:

DynamoDB's integration delivers fault-tolerant, horizontally scalable storage that can serve applications with ultra-low-latency data access needs. A typical DynamoDB configuration with Dapr might look like:

```
apiVersion: dapr.io/v1alpha1
kind: Component
metadata:
  name: statestore
  namespace: default
spec:
  type: state.aws.dynamodb
  version: v1
  metadata:
  - name: region
    value: "us-west-2"
  - name: table
    value: "<your-table-name>"
  - name: accessKey
    value: "<your-access-key>"
  - name: secretKey
    value: "<your-secret-key>"
```

These configurations direct Dapr to the correct AWS region, DynamoDB table, and necessitate valid AWS credentials with appropriate access permissions. Complemented by DynamoDB's flexible scalability, this offers a robust state management solution suitable for read-heavy workloads.

Advantages of Dapr's Multi-cloud, Multi-backend Approach:

The Dapr state store model simplifies application design by abstracting store deployment and connectivity concerns. This is particularly beneficial in hybrid cloud strategies or migration scenarios, where application state needs portability across environments.

1. **Interchangeability of Stores:** One exceptional capability of Dapr is its ability to interchange state stores effortlessly. Suppose the application scaling demands suddenly necessitate a transition from Redis to Azure Cosmos DB; Dapr facilitates this transition without requiring a comprehensive application code rewrite due to its uniform API layer.

2. **Redundancy and Resilience:** By supporting multiple state stores, Dapr enables redundancy. Developers can implement fallback mechanisms, configuring multiple stores in tandem, thus enhancing system resilience against single-point failures.

3. **Effortless Security Management:** Dapr secures sensitive information, such as credentials, with integration into secret stores like Kubernetes secrets, ensuring credentials remain encrypted and inaccessible directly from source code or configuration files.

4. **Operational Efficiency:** By using a consistent configuration model, Dapr reduces the cognitive and operational load associated with deploying new state stores. It enables DevOps teams to concentrate on deployment logistics and performance tuning rather than operational nuances of individual stores.

Considerations for State Store Selection:

When choosing a state store, developers need to assess several considerations for optimal performance:

- **Scalability Requirements:** High-scale applications may lean toward databases like DynamoDB or Cosmos DB with dynamic scaling capabilities.

- **Latency Sensitivity:** For applications with real-time constraints, in-memory data stores like Redis or Firebase may offer superior performance.

- **Consistent Data Handling:** If transactions and relational data manipulation are fundamental, PostgreSQL or MySQL provide strong consistency guarantees.

- **Cost Effectiveness:** The cost of state storage over time and predicted application traffic should guide the selection of a cost-efficient provider.

Dapr equips developers with the tools necessary to address each of these considerations, ensuring the chosen state store aligns perfectly with service-level objectives, business constraints, and user expectations.

Dapr presents a comprehensive model for interfacing with various state stores, each with unique benefits and configurable through a consistent interface. By harmonizing these interactions, Dapr aids in constructing agile, robust microservice systems that can pivot responsively to evolving business and technological landscapes.

4.4 Using State APIs

State management within microservices introduces complexities that often require sophisticated solutions to ensure data integrity across distributed systems. Within the framework of the Distributed Application Runtime (Dapr), the state management building block is accessed through its robust State APIs. These APIs provide a uniform interface to access, manipulate, and manage state across a variety of underlying data stores, including both ephemeral and persistent storage solutions.

This section dives deep into the use cases, functions, and intricacies involved in using Dapr's State APIs. We will explore examples and scenarios depicting exemplary practices in state management using diverse programming models and delve into performance-oriented considerations facilitated by Dapr's state abstraction.

Overview of State APIs:

Dapr's State APIs revolve around simplicity and efficacy in state manipulation. The operations can primarily be classified as saving, retrieving, deleting state data, and performing bulk operations. These functions ensure that regardless of the store's complexity or the deployment's geographic dispersion, the interface to interact with the state remains elegantly simple and consistent.

These APIs are accessible through both REST and gRPC, offering flexibility in application design depending on desired communication protocols and performance considerations.

State API Operations:

- **Save State:**

    This operation persists key-value pairs to a state store. The simplicity of saving operations underlies its immense utility; it encapsulates underlying complexities from serialization to store communication.

    ```
    POST /v1.0/state/statestore
    Content-Type: application/json

    [
      {
        "key": "userData",
        "value": {
          "id": "user123",
          "name": "John Doe",
          "email": "john.doe@example.com"
        }
      }
    ]
    ```

    In the above HTTP POST request, a JSON payload is sent to the Dapr sidecar, which subsequently stores the data in the designated state store. This abstracted interaction allows applications to manipulate state efficiently.

- **Retrieve State:**

    The fetching of a stored state is handled through a straightforward API call, ensuring that data retrieval is consistent with expectations of low-latency within distributed environments.

    ```
    GET /v1.0/state/statestore/userData
    ```

    The GET request retrieves data associated with the specified key. Dapr ensures this operation respects store-specific attributes like consistency models, secreting these details away from the application developer.

4.4. USING STATE APIS

In a Python application, using Dapr's client library, code to achieve similar functionality might resemble:

```
from dapr.clients import DaprClient

with DaprClient() as client:
    response = client.get_state(store_name='statestore', key='userData')
    print("Retrieved state:", response.data)
```

This demonstrates how Pythonic interfaces can compactly exploit the power of Dapr's State APIs while maintaining code clarity and conciseness.

- **Delete State:**

  Removing unnecessary state data ensures efficient resource usage and eliminates data that is no longer valuable.

  ```
  DELETE /v1.0/state/statestore/userData
  ```

  The deletion ensures the configured state store ceases to hold specified data, promoting systematic data management and archiving processes.

- **Bulk Operations:**

  These operations, including bulk saving and retrieval, are crucial for applications needing to process large datasets efficiently by reducing network overhead and latency through consolidated API interactions.

  ```
  POST /v1.0/state/statestore
  Content-Type: application/json

  [
    { "key": "item123", "value": {"description": "Item Desc 1", "price": 10.99} },
    { "key": "item456", "value": {"description": "Item Desc 2", "price": 5.49} }
  ]
  ```

  Through bulk operations, Dapr facilitates efficient batch processing, vital for applications dealing with high throughput scenarios. This minimizes bottlenecks associated with sequential processing models.

- **Transactional State Operations:**

  The provision for transactional operations allows multiple actions within a single atomic burst, preserving data integrity during interconnected state manipulations.

```
POST /v1.0/state/statestore/transaction
Content-Type: application/json

{
  "operations": [
    {
      "operation": "upsert",
      "request": {
        "key": "user123",
        "value": {"name": "John Doe"}
      }
    },
    {
      "operation": "delete",
      "request": {
        "key": "session456"
      }
    }
  ]
}
```

This unification of multiple operations addresses scenarios where database consistency via atomic updates is crucial, akin to financial transactions or complex state updates.

Achieving Concurrency and Consistency:

Dapr leverages ETags to manage concurrent data modifications, preventing race conditions and ensuring state integrity across distributed procedures. When a state write occurs, an ETag is included, which synchronizes when alterations are confirmed as non-conflicting.

Transactional states bring about heightened assurance against hazards typically encountered in distributed systems, such as network partitions or node failures. Through meticulous ETag-based conflict resolution, state alterations remain mutually consistent.

Design Strategies for Efficient Use of State APIs:

Efficient application and architect design can greatly enhance the state performance and resilience using the following strategies:

- **State Segmentation:** By categorizing keys and values based on access patterns or lifecycle stages, applications can optimize retrieval through distilling state stores to their essentials, reducing unnecessary I/O operations.

- **Securing API Interactions:** Utilize API keys or OAuth mechanisms to secure state API endpoints. Guard API flows with requisite identity checks.

- **Latency Considerations:** Avoid tight coupling of business logic with immediate state fetches. Instead, utilize asynchronous patterns wherever possible to minimize user-facing latency impacts.

- **Monitoring and Metrics:** Instrument metrics for state API operations, logging latencies, and capturing metadata to monitor state access patterns, enabling systematic diagnostic and optimization efforts.

Concurrency Management and Resilience:

In practical applications, concurrency control is critical in maintaining accurate state across instances. Dapr naturally aids this through practical constructs like optimistic concurrency achieved via ETags, bolstering consistency, especially in write-heavy environments. Dapr's concurrency offerings abstract collision handling allowing developers to gracefully handle simultaneous state alterations with retry patterns integrated.

A robust monitoring setup can further augment this architecture, using solutions such as Prometheus for metrics and Grafana dashboards for visualization of state access patterns, spotting anomalies, and tuning APIs for peak performance efficiency.

Cross-platform Compatibility:

Dapr's APIs cater indiscriminately to multiple development environments, ensuring compatibility across diverse languages and frameworks. Whether microservices are designed in Node.js, Java, Go, or C#, developers can embrace the consistent functionality delivered through Dapr's uniform API interface. Toolkits enabling readiness across languages amplify Dapr's state APIs usability.

Real-world Application and Advanced Use Cases:

Consider an e-commerce platform where session information, customer preferences, and shopping carts need persistent state storage yet require dynamic scalability under fluctuating user loads. Dapr's State APIs seamlessly allow such a system to manage session consistency, whether it scales across continents with distributed data across multiple regions leveraging Azure Cosmos DB or Firebase's real-time database solution.

For cloud-native applications leveraging Kubernetes, Dapr abstracts the complexities involved in state persistence to cloud-provider databases, automating configurations and providing resilient state management across distributed application instances. For example, automating Redis failover configurations or adjusting to Cosmos DB's consistency levels through templated deployments simplifies operational demands.

By unraveling API complexities and taming infrastructural challenges, Dapr's State APIs empower developers to construct microservices that maintain data accuracy, support seamless scalability, and foster exceptional application responsiveness efficiently within varied cloud ecosystems.

4.5 Consistency and Concurrency Models

In microservices architectures, managing consistency and concurrency becomes critical due to the distributed nature of components across networks and nodes. As microservices, often stateless themselves, interact with external state stores to retain necessary data, understanding and implementing the appropriate consistency and concurrency models is paramount. Within the Dapr framework, these models are carefully designed to ensure data integrity and coherence across services while maintaining scalability and high performance.

This section will explore the intricacies of consistency and concurrency models available in Dapr, focusing on concepts, use cases, and their significance in distributed state management. Additionally, pragmatic code examples will illustrate how to leverage these models within a Dapr-enhanced microservices architecture. The discussion will extend to broader architectural considerations, elucidating how Dapr's features harmonize stability with operational efficiency.

Defining Consistency and Concurrency:

4.5. CONSISTENCY AND CONCURRENCY MODELS

Consistency within distributed systems refers to the guarantee that all nodes or services reflect the same data state, even amidst updates. It tackles the challenge of ensuring conflicting updates do not result in divergent data views, which could derail data accuracy and integrity in applications reliant upon consistent data access.

Concurrency, however, encompasses managing multiple operations and ensuring they do not interfere with each other in ways that produce inconsistent results. Concurrency controls prevent situations where simultaneous operations compromise data correctness, a scenario common in high-throughput applications.

Consistency Models in Dapr:

Dapr offers multiple consistency levels for interaction with state stores, providing developers with the flexibility to choose according to specific application requirements:

- **Strong Consistency:** This model ensures that once a write operation completes, all subsequent reads reflect that write. Thus, all components working with the database observe the same order of writes, providing a seamless and consistent view across distributed systems. Strong consistency is crucial where transactional integrity is non-negotiable, such as in financial applications.

- **Eventual Consistency:** Eventual consistency relaxes immediate data consistency guarantees, allowing temporary divergences in data views across services. However, the system guarantees convergence towards consistency after some time. This model is advantageous for applications where immediate consistency is non-critical, allowing enhanced write throughput and system availability.

- **Causal Consistency:** Providing a middle ground, causal consistency ensures that operations observed to be causally related maintain that order across services, while unrelated operations may appear out of sequence. This model is advantageous in collaborative applications or systems capturing causally linked actions.

Ensuring appropriate consistency in systems often means selecting a model aligned with the business logic and performance trade-offs characteristic of each application domain.

Implementing Consistency with Dapr:

Configuring consistency models in Dapr typically involves specifying options in the state action parameters, embedding decisions within your code or configuration files reliant on the consistency needs of application actions.

For example, enabling strong consistency in a state update operation might involve setting corresponding metadata parameters:

```
POST /v1.0/state/store
Content-Type: application/json

[
  {
    "key": "order123",
    "value": { "product": "widget", "amount": 10 },
    "metadata": {
      "consistency": "strong"
    }
  }
]
```

The above JSON payload demonstrates how consistency settings integrated into data interaction commands ensure desired model compliance. With consistency specified explicitly, developers can effectively manage state even under simultaneous write conditions.

The clarity that Dapr brings in decoupling application logic from underlying state management intricacies through intuitive metadata configuration provides a platform that scales effortlessly across diverse consistency requirements.

Concurrency Management in Dapr:

Concurrency control strategies in Dapr lean heavily on optimistic concurrency, a method preferred over more lock-centric approaches due to its suitability for distributed systems with high contention and latency sensitivities. Optimistic concurrency encompasses mechanisms allowing transactions to proceed without locking but performing conflict checks before finalizing updates.

Central to optimistic concurrency within Dapr is the use of ETags (Entity Tags). ETags operate as version identifiers unique to a state entry.

4.5. CONSISTENCY AND CONCURRENCY MODELS

In practice, they enhance concurrent operation safety through verification mechanisms; updating operations include the current ETag, and successful commits happen if the presented ETag matches the store's latest, ensuring changes apply only to unmodified versions of data.

An optimistic concurrency control operation with ETags typically follows this sequence:

- **Retrieve State with ETag:**

```
from dapr.clients import DaprClient

with DaprClient() as client:
    response = client.get_state(store_name='statestore', key='profile', etag
        =True)
    profile_data = response.data
    etag = response.etag
```

- **Conditional Update:**

```
POST /v1.0/state/store
Content-Type: application/json

[
  {
    "key": "profile",
    "value": { "name": "Jane Doe" },
    "etag": etag,
    "options": {
      "concurrency": "first-write"
    }
  }
]
```

If the ETag matches, the operation succeeds; otherwise, the system would reject it, indicating a concurrent modification elsewhere.

This style of concurrency checks significantly reduces latency overheads and contention issues typical of locking mechanisms, scaffolding scalable and robust execution structures.

Designing for Consistency and Concurrency:

Effective design around these models involves an alignment between application objectives and consistency/concurrency requirements:

- **Frictionless State Access:** Where strong consistency is crucial, design components to access fewer but essential data requests, avoiding unnecessary contention.

- **Deferred Resolution:** Embrace eventual consistency where suitable, particularly in systems with geographically distributed users, leveraging user experience cues to mask latencies.

- **Conflict Detection and Resolution:** Design interfaces that accommodate conflict notifications, enabling end-user or automatic workflow-based resolutions.

Dapr further fosters observability into consistency and concurrency operations, offering developers insights into stability and facilitating strategic adaptation for performance tuning through structured logging and monitoring.

Practical Use Cases and Examples:

A real-world distributed shopping cart scenario:

- **Strong Consistency for Order Processing:** Ensures each customer maintains unique instance state integrity during checkout. Order changes must instantaneously reflect across services to prevent overselling.

- **Eventual Consistency for Inventory Views:** Separate services caching inventory statuses may operate under eventual consistency, syncing updates in batches rather than instantaneously, thus relieving real-time pressure.

- **Causal Operations for Customer Activity Logs:** Causal consistency allows user activities logged in sequence based on action correlation, balancing user operation fluidity with record accuracy.

Through applicable use case design, Dapr's capabilities enable microservice developers to robustly architect vibrant and adaptable systems, pairing agility with steadfast assurance against data inconsistencies that could otherwise hamstring application processes.

Dapr simplifies microservices' consistency and concurrency management demands, rendering capabilities approachable and empowering developers to cultivate sophisticated, dynamically scalable, and robust applications in various distributed contexts.

4.6 Transaction and Batch Operations

Transaction and batch operations are foundational for maintaining data integrity and efficiency in microservices architectures. Dapr brings robust support for both, ensuring complex state manipulations are executed reliably and efficiently across distributed services. Understanding and utilizing transaction and batch operations in Dapr can significantly simplify the management of business processes, improve application performance, and guarantee data consistency.

This section examines the concepts of transaction handling and batch processing within Dapr's framework, exploring the principles behind these operations, the technical execution, and the practical implications for developing and managing microservices architectures. Examples illustrate the implementation and strategic considerations when leveraging these capabilities in real-world applications.

Understanding Transactions in Dapr:

In distributed systems, transactions refer to a sequence of operations that are treated as a single unit. These operations should maintain the ACID (Atomicity, Consistency, Isolation, Durability) properties to ensure robustness in execution. Transactions encompass multiple state changes spanning different state stores or within a single store, but they must execute such that either all changes commit or none do.

Dapr supports this by allowing atomic state transactions, enabling developers to perform multi-operation transactions that either fully succeed or fail without partial application.

```
POST /v1.0/state/statestore/transaction
Content-Type: application/json

{
  "operations": [
    {
      "operation": "upsert",
      "request": {
        "key": "order123",
        "value": { "product": "Widget A", "quantity": 5 }
      }
    },
    {
      "operation": "delete",
      "request": {
        "key": "obsoleteItem123"
      }
```

```
    }
  ]
}
```

The example demonstrates a transaction wherein an item is added and another removed atomically. This prevents scenarios where only part of a transaction might go through, leading to inconsistent states across services that expect tight consistency.

Principles of Batch Operations:

Batch processing involves the execution of a series of jobs concurrently, thus optimizing resource use by reducing the overhead associated with repeated execution of similar tasks. This is particularly advantageous when working with large datasets or when the same operation must be applied across numerous state entries concurrently.

Dapr enhances batch processing by providing APIs that handle bulk state uploads, retrievals, and deletions, minimizing API call overhead and improving systemic throughput. Let's explore an example of batch insertion:

```
POST /v1.0/state/statestore
Content-Type: application/json

[
  { "key": "itemBatch1", "value": { "name": "Product X", "price": 29.99 } },
  { "key": "itemBatch2", "value": { "name": "Product Y", "price": 39.99 } },
  { "key": "itemBatch3", "value": { "name": "Product Z", "price": 59.99 } }
]
```

In this batch operation, multiple state entries are persisted simultaneously, enhancing efficiency by consolidating network requests and lowering transaction processing times.

Implementation and Strategic Use Cases:

Implementing transaction and batch operations optimally requires understanding their role within specific business contexts:

- **Financial Services:** Transactions ensure atomicity during financial operations, necessary for tasks like debiting multiple accounts simultaneously or updating multiple ledger entries, ensuring balance integrity.

- **Inventory Management:** Batch processes update stock lev-

4.6. TRANSACTION AND BATCH OPERATIONS

els or refresh product catalog data, key during high-volume sales events or inventory replenishment operations, helping avoid outdated stock levels.

Technical Execution of Transactions and Batches:

1. **Atomic Transactions:**

   - Ensure all-or-nothing principles hold.
   - Useful in operations where a failure triggers a rollback.

2. **Batch Processing:**

   - Reduce transaction overhead across data processing operations.
   - Perform read or write operations that span multiple entries simultaneously to maintain system efficiency.

```
from dapr.clients import DaprClient

with DaprClient() as d:
    d.save_bulk_state(store_name='statestore', states=[
        StateItem(key='item1', value={'name': 'Product1', 'price': 100}),
        StateItem(key='item2', value={'name': 'Product2', 'price': 200}),
        StateItem(key='item3', value={'name': 'Product3', 'price': 300})
    ])
```

Mastery of these concepts means understanding when to leverage transactional integrity versus batch efficiencies. For instance, instances involving non-essential data precision, like data aggregation tasks, could prioritize batch operations. However, user-account-related updates may center on transaction-driven assurances due to their precision demands.

Performance Implications and Best Practices:

While utilizing these operations enhances robustness and efficiency, certain considerations guide effective deployment:

- **Data Partitioning:** Strategically partitioning data can enhance batch operation performance by aligning with underlying state store partitioning, reducing lock contention and improving transaction speeds.

- **Load Balancing:** Consider distributing transaction loads evenly across services to avoid bottlenecks caused by high-concentration simultaneous requests.

- **Circuit Breaker Patterns:** Implement circuit breaker patterns around transaction endpoints to enhance fault tolerance, avoiding systemic failures due to congestion or transient errors.

- **Timeout Management:** Mitigate indefinite waits through timeout configurations, protecting system resources and triggering appropriate fail-safe mechanisms during prolonged transaction waits.

In terms of architecture, intertwining Dapr's transaction and batch operations with established patterns such as event sourcing or CQRS complements their utility, allowing strategic segregation of write-heavy operations from read operations, often seen in complex, user-centric applications.

Advanced Scenarios:

Consider an e-commerce platform navigating a flash sale:

- Transactions handle order confirmation processes, updating stock levels and customer details in tandem, ensuring no downside impact resulting from concurrent order placements.

- Batches refresh promotional pricing across thousands of inventory items instantaneously, maintaining competitive responsiveness.

A transportation network leveraging Dapr might:

- Use transactions to synchronize ride-booking slots between drivers and passengers, atomicity ensuring no double-booking scenarios.

- Implement batch processing to assimilate traffic data updates across several areas, maintaining navigation accuracy and predictive routing responses.

Such scenarios illuminate the breadth of Dapr's technological contributions in catering to complex, dynamic operational demands inherent in modern microservices systems.

Resilience and Error Handling:

Beyond transactional atomicity and batch performance optimization, resilience in operation entails gracefully managing errors and proactively handling fluctuations in transactional workloads:

- Integrate idempotency into transaction design, preventing redundant operations from unfavorable re-try contexts.

- Use logging frameworks to capture transaction states and monitor batch performance dynamically, providing insights conducive to debugging and optimizing operational flow.

Through these facets, Dapr empowers developers and architects to sculpt resilient, high-performance microservices ecosystems, adept at maintaining data integrity and operational excellence in the face of profound concurrent demands and diverse processing tasks.

4.7 Best Practices for Dapr State Management

Effective state management within microservices architectures is critical for achieving scalability, performance, and resilience. The Distributed Application Runtime (Dapr) simplifies state management by abstracting underlying complexities and providing a uniform API for developers. However, despite these simplifications, adhering to best practices is crucial for leveraging Dapr's full potential in state management. This section outlines strategies, techniques, and considerations for optimizing Dapr state management, ensuring microservices applications remain robust, maintainable, and scalable.

1. Aligning State Management with Business Requirements:

The choice of state store and management practices should align with the application's business goals and requirements. Whether the focus is on high-throughput transactions, real-time analytics, or extensive data persistence, selecting an appropriate state store type (e.g., in-memory, NoSQL, SQL) and consistency model that align with these goals is crucial.

- **Evaluate Consistency Requirements:** Determine whether strong consistency, eventual consistency, or causal consistency is appropriate for your application scenarios. Strong consistency may offer more reliability at the cost of latency, while eventual consistency offers better performance in distributed settings.

- **State Store Selection:** Choose a state store that matches performance, cost, and availability needs. For instance, Redis offers low-latency access for caching, while Azure Cosmos DB provides global distribution and high availability.

2. Designing for Scalability and Performance:

To ensure that state management scales along with your microservices, consider the following practices:

- **Partitioning and Sharding:** Use partitioning strategies that distribute data effectively across clusters to avoid bottlenecks. This technique is particularly useful in large-scale applications that handle high transaction volumes.

- **Encapsulate State Access:** Encapsulate your state access logic using Dapr's state management APIs. This design not only simplifies code but also ensures that performance optimizations can be applied at a single point, making the overall system more maintainable.

```
from dapr.clients import DaprClient

class StateManager:
    def __init__(self, store_name):
        self.store_name = store_name

    def save_state(self, key, value):
        with DaprClient() as client:
            client.save_state(store_name=self.store_name, key=key, value=value)

    def get_state(self, key):
```

4.7. BEST PRACTICES FOR DAPR STATE MANAGEMENT

```
        with DaprClient() as client:
            response = client.get_state(store_name=self.store_name, key=key)
            return response.data

    def delete_state(self, key):
        with DaprClient() as client:
            client.delete_state(store_name=self.store_name, key=key)
```

This encapsulation allows developers to handle state interactions transparently, simplifying state logic management and aiding in applying systematic enhancements.

- **Cache Strategically:** Use caching layers to reduce load on state stores, especially for frequently accessed or invariant data. This can reduce latency and improve overall throughput.

3. Ensuring Robustness and Fault Tolerance:

While microservices allow for high degrees of fault isolation and resilience, state management must be equally resilient:

- **Implement Retry Mechanisms:** Use retry logic for transient failures when accessing state stores to ensure seamless operation during temporary network issues.

- **Utilize Idempotency:** Design state write operations to be idempotent, ensuring that retrying an operation does not lead to inconsistent states. This is especially critical in distributed systems where duplicate network requests may occur.

- **Leverage ETags Effectively:** Use ETags for optimistic concurrency control, preventing conflicting updates from overwriting each other and ensuring consistent data modifications.

4. Security and Compliance:

Security is a critical aspect of state management that should not be neglected:

- **Secure State API Communication:** Always use HTTPS to secure communication between microservices and the Dapr sidecar. Implement additional security measures such as API gateways and throttling to restrict API access.

- **Protect Sensitive Data:** Use integrated secret management solutions to handle sensitive information like credentials and connection strings. Dapr supports secret stores like Azure Key Vault and Kubernetes secrets.

- **Ensure Compliance:** Adhere to data protection laws and standards, ensuring that state management practices comply with relevant regulations such as GDPR or HIPAA.

```
apiVersion: dapr.io/v1alpha1
kind: Component
metadata:
  name: vault
spec:
  type: secretstores.azure.keyvault
  version: v1
  metadata:
  - name: vaultName
    value: "<your-key-vault-name>"
  - name: clientId
    value: "<your-client-id>"
  - name: clientSecret
    value: "<your-client-secret>"
```

This configuration facilitates the management of sensitive information securely, leveraging Dapr's ability to interface with Azure Key Vault for secret management.

5. Monitoring and Observability:

Robust monitoring and observability frameworks ensure early detection of anomalies and contribute to system reliability:

- **Instrument with Metrics:** Utilize monitoring tools to track state API latencies, error rates, and throughput. Additionally, log access patterns and state changes to provide comprehensive insights into system performance.

- **Trace State Transactions:** Implement distributed tracing to follow state transactions across services. Dapr integrates with tools like OpenTelemetry to enable detailed tracing data collection.

- **Alerting Strategies:** Develop real-time alerting systems connected to metrics for timely escalation of potential issues, ensuring rapid response and mitigation.

4.7. BEST PRACTICES FOR DAPR STATE MANAGEMENT

6. Continuous Improvement and Testing:

Finally, fostering a culture of continuous improvement around state management contributes to enhanced application efficacy:

- **Regular Load Testing:** Perform routine stress testing to evaluate how the state management layer behaves under extreme conditions. These tests help identify bottlenecks and guide scaling decisions.

- **Periodic Audits:** Routinely audit security measures, data access logs, and operational configurations to maintain alignment with evolving best practices and compliance requirements.

- **Feedback Loops:** Establish feedback mechanisms, leveraging state monitoring insights to iteratively improve systems, refine efficiency, and optimize for new performance milestones.

Through disciplined implementation of these best practices, developers can craft state management frameworks within Dapr-enabled microservices that are resilient, performant, and aligned with business growth ambitions. This proactive approach cultivates an architecture that gracefully handles evolving demands and remains ready for future integrations and enhancements.

Chapter 5

Dapr Bindings and Pub/Sub

This chapter examines the use of Dapr bindings and the publish-subscribe (pub/sub) pattern to facilitate seamless integration and communication within microservices architectures. It explains how Dapr bindings allow interaction with external systems via simple configurations and how pub/sub enables decoupled, event-driven communication between services. By exploring configuration techniques and practical use cases, this chapter highlights how these features contribute to creating scalable and efficient microservices solutions.

5.1 Exploring Dapr Bindings

Dapr (*Distributed Application Runtime*) is a portable, event-driven runtime that enables developers to easily build resilient, stateless, and stateful microservices that run in the cloud and edge. An essential feature of Dapr is its support for bindings, which simplify integration with a variety of external systems and services. These bindings facilitate seamless event-driven architectures by enabling applications to interact with cloud services, databases, message brokers, and many other external systems through a consistent and standardized interface.

Bindings in Dapr are classified into two types: input bindings and output bindings. Each plays a crucial role in the ecosystem, allowing developers to both receive external events into their service and output events from their service to an external system.

A **binding component** in Dapr abstracts the complexity involved in communicating with different services and exposes a unified API for developers. This abstraction allows developers to focus on business logic rather than learning the specifics of each external system or service. For example, an input binding could be configured to trigger an application whenever a new object is uploaded to a cloud storage bucket, while an output binding might send a message to a notification service.

The Dapr Bindings architecture revolves around the concept of event sources and destinations. By defining the bindings in a configuration file, developers can specify which events their applications are interested in and where to send outgoing events. The configuration typically involves defining the type of binding, setting up necessary metadata, and specifying the endpoint of the service the application should interact with.

To elucidate the mechanics of input and output bindings in Dapr, consider the following YAML configuration for a hypothetical input binding:

```
apiVersion: dapr.io/v1alpha1
kind: Component
metadata:
  name: example-binding
  namespace: default
spec:
  type: bindings.aws.sqs
  version: v1
  metadata:
  - name: accessKey
    value: "<AWS_ACCESS_KEY>"
  - name: secretKey
    value: "<AWS_SECRET_KEY>"
  - name: queueName
    value: "example-queue"
```

In this configuration, the example-binding component is set to listen to messages from an AWS SQS queue. It leverages Dapr's bind-

5.1. EXPLORING DAPR BINDINGS

ings.aws.sqs component type, requiring the necessary credentials and configuration details of the queue. This setup abstracts away the complexity of connecting directly to AWS SQS, allowing the developer to receive message events effortlessly.

For output bindings, the process is similar, with configurations determined by the destination service. Here is an additional example of output binding configuration, this time for sending messages to an external SMTP server:

```
apiVersion: dapr.io/v1alpha1
kind: Component
metadata:
  name: email-output-binding
  namespace: default
spec:
  type: bindings.smtp
  version: v1
  metadata:
  - name: host
    value: "smtp.example.com"
  - name: port
    value: "587"
  - name: username
    value: "<SMTP_USERNAME>"
  - name: password
    value: "<SMTP_PASSWORD>"
  - name: from
    value: "no-reply@example.com"
```

The binding configuration for SMTP can facilitate sending emails from the application through any SMTP server. By handling configuration in this way, developers avoid directly interfacing with SMTP protocols, making the application more portable and maintainable.

Within the application code, handling a binding involves implementing HTTP endpoints that get invoked by Dapr when a bound event occurs. Consider a simple Go application that listens for new messages from the previously configured queue:

```
package main

import (
  "fmt"
  "log"
  "net/http"
  "encoding/json"
)

func eventHandler(w http.ResponseWriter, r *http.Request) {
  // Read and process event data
```

```
   var data map[string]interface{}
   err := json.NewDecoder(r.Body).Decode(&data)
   if err != nil {
      http.Error(w, "Cannot parse JSON", http.StatusBadRequest)
      return
   }
   fmt.Printf("Received event: %+v\n", data)

   // Respond back to Dapr
   w.WriteHeader(http.StatusOK)
}

func main() {
   const subscribeURL = "/example-binding" // URL matches the metadata name in
         YAML config
   http.HandleFunc(subscribeURL, eventHandler)
   fmt.Printf("Listening on %s\n", subscribeURL)
   log.Fatal(http.ListenAndServe(":8080", nil))
}
```

This simple application sets up an HTTP server where Dapr will send POST requests containing incoming event data whenever a message arrives in the AWS SQS queue bound in configuration. The endpoint /example-binding matches the name of the binding in the configuration.

To address the way Dapr manages and communicates via bindings, it is essential to understand the interplay between HTTP and GRPC communication protocols. When a Dapr sidecar container is deployed alongside a service, it intercepts bindings and communicates events to the application using HTTP or GRPC. This architecture is conducive to microservices communications, where services should remain agnostic of the underlying communication protocol of external systems.

The versatility of Dapr bindings is also evident in the wide range of supported components, which include cloud services like Azure Blob Storage and AWS S3, messaging systems such as Kafka and NATS, databases like MongoDB and SQL Server, and other services including Webhooks and Twilio.

Managing state and ensuring reliable delivery are critical considerations in a robust event-driven architecture. Dapr helps ensure reliable delivery by providing built-in mechanisms for retrying failed events upon initial delivery failure. This reliability is paramount when developing complex systems interacting with third-party services where occasional downtime or slowdowns can occur.

5.1. EXPLORING DAPR BINDINGS

When using output bindings, developers have access to consistent APIs to send data to external systems. Here's a practical example in Python illustrating how an application might send data using an output binding configured to target a RabbitMQ message queue:

```python
import requests

def send_message_to_queue(data):
    dapr_port = 3500
    binding_url = f"http://localhost:{dapr_port}/v1.0/bindings/rabbitmq-output"

    payload = {
        "data": {
            "message": data
        },
        "operation": "create"
    }

    response = requests.post(binding_url, json=payload)
    if response.status_code == 200:
        print('Message successfully sent to the queue')
    else:
        print('Failed to send message', response.text)

if __name__ == "__main__":
    send_message_to_queue("Test message.")
```

In this example, the binding named rabbitmq-output is used to post a message to a RabbitMQ queue. The Dapr sidecar abstracts communication with RabbitMQ, allowing the developer to focus solely on the business logic around when and how messages should be sent.

Handling edge cases, such as transient failures or network issues, can be incorporated into Dapr binding mechanisms through policy definitions that instruct the runtime on the behavior upon encountering errors. Developers can specify retry policies, deadline management, and error handling strategies in the configuration, contributing to increased reliability and fault tolerance of the system.

Dapr's binding component framework is highly extensible. If a developer needs to integrate with a service not currently supported by an existing Dapr component, they can create a custom binding component. This extensibility ensures that applications can remain future-proof as new technologies and services emerge. Additionally, community contributions mean that support for new services is always expanding.

The power of Dapr bindings lies in their simplicity and scope, making it feasible to focus efforts on business logic and less on proprietary integrations or middleware. As enterprises increasingly adopt microservices architectures, the integration capabilities provided by Dapr become invaluable.

Being declarative in configuring bindings, Dapr enables consistency and repeatability in deployments. This consistency is crucial, particularly in continuous integration/continuous deployment (CI/CD) pipelines where environments must be easily replicated. It also aligns well with infrastructure as code (IaC) principles, assisting teams in maintaining systematic control over infrastructure setups.

In the ever-evolving landscape of cloud-native applications, technologies like Dapr provide a crucial advantage, enabling developers to build systems that are not only scalable and reliable but also far simpler in terms of operational management. By subsuming the complexity inherent in managing multiple different service providers and protocols, Dapr streamlines and accelerates microservice development.

5.2 Configuring Input and Output Bindings

Configuring input and output bindings in Dapr is a foundational aspect of enabling event-driven microservices architectures. These bindings facilitate the seamless integration and interaction between your application and external services or systems. By leveraging Dapr's bindings, developers can decouple their application logic from the specific interfaces and protocols required by these external systems, achieving operational efficiency and simplifying application maintenance.

Input bindings are used to bring events into the application from external sources, triggering certain actions or workflows in response to those events. Conversely, output bindings send data from your application to an external system, effectively allowing the application to notify other services or trigger workflows elsewhere. Both types of bindings are configured using a declarative approach in Dapr, employing YAML component files that describe the desired behavior and required metadata.

The configuration of input and output bindings begins by declaring

5.2. CONFIGURING INPUT AND OUTPUT BINDINGS

component configurations in YAML, specifying the component type, version, necessary metadata, and any additional parameters required for the binding operation. This configuration method harmonizes with contemporary DevOps practices involving infrastructure as code (IaC), enabling reproducible and consistent setup across various environments.

- Input Bindings Configuration

- Handling Input Events

- Output Bindings Configuration

- Sending Data via Output Bindings

- Enhanced Configuration Features

- Secrets Management

- Telemetry and Metrics

Input bindings in Dapr connect your application to external event sources. Examples of event sources might include cloud queues, cloud storage systems, or third-party event streams. The configuration typically involves specifying the type of event source and any credentials or parameters needed for successful communication.

Consider a configuration for an input binding that listens to events from a cloud-based message queue, such as Azure Service Bus. The YAML configuration might appear as follows:

```
apiVersion: dapr.io/v1alpha1
kind: Component
metadata:
  name: servicebus-queue
  namespace: default
spec:
  type: bindings.azure.servicebusqueues
  version: v1
  metadata:
  - name: connectionString
    value: "<YOUR_CONNECTION_STRING>"
  - name: queueName
    value: "orders"
```

In this example, the binding named servicebus-queue defines a connection to an Azure Service Bus queue named orders. The binding uses the bindings.azure.servicebusqueues component type and requires a connection string for authentication and authorization. By defining this input binding, events within the Service Bus queue can trigger application logic as defined in the respective application code.

Once the input binding is configured, the Dapr sidecar listens for events from the specified source and relays them to the application. Developers need to implement HTTP or GRPC endpoints to process these incoming events. For instance, a Java Spring Boot application might handle a Service Bus queue event as follows:

```
@RestController
public class EventController {

    @PostMapping("/servicebus-queue")
    public ResponseEntity<?> handleEvent(@RequestBody Map<String, Object>
        event) {
        System.out.println("Received event: " + event);

        // Process event data
        processOrderEvent(event);

        // Acknowledge receipt
        return ResponseEntity.ok().build();
    }

    private void processOrderEvent(Map<String, Object> event) {
        // Logic to process order event
        System.out.println("Processing order: " + event.get("orderId"));
    }
}
```

In this example, the application's REST controller listens at the endpoint /servicebus-queue, which corresponds to the binding's name. Upon receiving an event, the application processes it by parsing the received data and acting accordingly. The endpoint acknowledges the event by returning an HTTP 200 response to Dapr.

Output bindings enable applications to send messages or data to external systems, facilitating an outgoing communication pattern synonymous with modern event-driven architectures. Configuration for output bindings follows a similar declarative process, identifying the target service and defining the necessary parameters.

An example of configuring an output binding for an SMS service such as Twilio is illustrated below:

5.2. CONFIGURING INPUT AND OUTPUT BINDINGS

```
apiVersion: dapr.io/v1alpha1
kind: Component
metadata:
  name: sms-output
  namespace: default
spec:
  type: bindings.twilio.sms
  version: v1
  metadata:
  - name: accountSID
    value: "<TWILIO_ACCOUNT_SID>"
  - name: authToken
    value: "<TWILIO_AUTH_TOKEN>"
  - name: from
    value: "+1234567890"
```

This configuration, named sms-output, specifies an output binding that communicates with Twilio's SMS service, requiring credentials such as the account SID and authentication token. The from field defines the originating phone number for sent messages.

In the application, developers use consistent APIs, typically HTTP requests to the Dapr sidecar, to send data through output bindings. Consider a Node.js application that needs to send SMS messages using the configured Twilio binding:

```
const axios = require('axios');

async function sendSMS(to, body) {
    const daprPort = 3500;
    const bindingUrl = `http://localhost:${daprPort}/v1.0/bindings/sms-output`;

    const payload = {
        data: {
            to: to,
            body: body
        },
        operation: "create"
    };

    try {
        const response = await axios.post(bindingUrl, payload);
        console.log('SMS sent:', response.status);
    } catch (error) {
        console.error('Failed to send SMS:', error.message);
    }
}

sendSMS('+9876543210', 'Your order has been shipped!');
```

In this script, the application constructs a payload with the recipient's phone number and the message body. The Dapr sidecar processes this payload, handling the complexities of interfacing with Twilio to dispatch the SMS message.

The configuration of input and output bindings in Dapr can be enriched with advanced features such as secrets management, telemetry, and metrics. These enhancements align with modern best practices in cloud-native development and are critical in complex enterprise deployments.

Managing sensitive information such as API keys and passwords is facilitated by Dapr through integration with secret management solutions. By referencing secret keys in binding metadata, developers can avoid hardcoding sensitive information in their configuration files. Here's an example using Kubernetes secrets:

```
apiVersion: dapr.io/v1alpha1
kind: Component
metadata:
  name: secure-binding
  namespace: default
spec:
  type: bindings.uservice
  version: v1
  metadata:
  - name: apiKey
    secretKeyRef:
      name: mysecret
      key: api-key
```

In this configuration, the apiKey is securely sourced from a Kubernetes secret named mysecret, effectively decoupling credentials from the configuration files.

Monitoring the performance and reliability of your bindings is crucial for diagnosing issues and maintaining system health. Leveraging Dapr's telemetry capabilities enables comprehensive observability. Dapr can export metrics to compatible systems such as Prometheus or Zipkin, capturing details about binding execution times, failure rates, and other relevant metrics.

Implementing effective telemetry involves configuring your system to capture Dapr-specific metrics and ensuring that these metrics are visualized and interpreted appropriately. Here is a hypothetical enhancement in your deployment architecture involving Prometheus:

```
apiVersion: dapr.io/v1alpha1
kind: Configuration
```

```
metadata:
  name: myapp-config
  namespace: default
spec:
  tracing:
    enabled: true
    samplingRate: "1"
    exporterType: "zipkin"
  metric:
    enabled: true
    exporter:
      componentType: "prometheus"
```

The configuration above enables tracing and metric capturing through Prometheus and Zipkin, creating a robust framework for tracking binding performance and diagnosing operational issues.

The practice of configuring input and output bindings in Dapr signifies a core approach to achieving a truly decoupled and scalable architecture in modern distributed systems. By abstracting the details of interfacing with various external services and providing a consistent interaction model, Dapr bindings allow developers to focus on crafting high-quality business logic without getting bogged down in the intricacies of service integration.

With powerful conveniences like secrets management and telemetry, Dapr not only simplifies the developer's workflow but also enhances security, observability, and reliability of the system. As Dapr continues to evolve, adopting these practices ensures that applications are prepared for the complex demands of cloud-native and edge deployments, maintaining flexibility and sustainability in an ever-changing technological landscape.

5.3 Working with Event-Driven Architecture through Bindings

Event-driven architecture (EDA) holds significant prominence in the design and development of modern microservices. This architectural paradigm focuses on the production, detection, consumption, and reaction to events. Within this context, Dapr's bindings offer robust mechanisms to facilitate event-driven interactions between applications and external systems, streamlining the development and deployment of scalable, responsive systems that react to incoming data streams and triggers.

In an event-driven system, events are first-class citizens; they represent significant states or state changes such as "an order has been placed," "a user has registered," or "temperature exceeds the threshold." These events are used to inform other parts of the system that something of interest has happened. Dapr's bindings help to abstract away the nuanced technicalities of these events propagating through distributed services, contributing to reduced complexity and increased reliability.

- **Understanding Event Sources and Event Sinks**

    In the context of Dapr, an event source is where an event originates. For example, this could be a message queue that receives order notifications from an e-commerce platform. An event sink, conversely, is where processed events are dispatched, such as a database where these orders are persisted or an analytics system that aggregates order data for reporting.

    Bindings facilitate event-driven paradigms by interconnecting these sources and sinks. Input bindings allow applications to subscribe to events from diverse sources, acting as event processors. Output bindings, on the other hand, enable applications to publish events to destination services, such as messaging systems or notification services.

- **Designing an Event-Driven System with Dapr Bindings**

    The design of an event-driven system using Dapr bindings involves considerations such as event flow, data transformation, fault handling, and eventual consistency. Events must be efficiently captured, processed, and dispatched, often involving intermediate steps like data validation and enrichment.

- **Event Flow and Data Transformation**

    Capturing and transforming event data as it flows through your system is a critical task. Suppose we're working with a retail application that needs to process incoming order events from a message queue and subsequently update a database and notify

5.3. WORKING WITH EVENT-DRIVEN ARCHITECTURE THROUGH BINDINGS

a warehouse system. Here's an example setup using Dapr bindings:

1. **Order Received Event**: Captured by an input binding pointing to a message queue.
2. **Event Enrichment**: Order details are enriched by retrieving additional data, such as customer information, from external services.
3. **Persistence and Alerting**: Through output bindings, the enriched event updates a database and sends notification to a warehouse management system.

```
apiVersion: dapr.io/v1alpha1
kind: Component
metadata:
  name: order-queue
  namespace: default
spec:
  type: bindings.kafka
  version: v1
  metadata:
  - name: brokers
    value: "kafka-broker:9092"
  - name: topics
    value: "orders"
  - name: consumerGroup
    value: "order-processing-group"
```

This binding configuration sets up an input binding to a Kafka topic named orders, allowing the application to consume order events as they are published.

Similarly, an output binding might be configured to update a database:

```
apiVersion: dapr.io/v1alpha1
kind: Component
metadata:
  name: db-update-binding
  namespace: default
spec:
  type: bindings.sql
  version: v1
  metadata:
  - name: connectionString
    value: "Server=myServerAddress;Database=myDatabase;User Id=
      myUsername;Password=myPassword;"
  - name: tableName
    value: "orders_table"
```

The application can leverage these bindings to implement its logic. A possible implementation, say in Python, might look like this:

```
import requests

def process_order_event(order_event):
    # Enrich event with additional data
    customer_info = fetch_customer_info(order_event['customer_id'])
    enriched_event = {**order_event, **customer_info}

    # Update database
    update_database(enriched_event)

    # Notify warehouse
    notify_warehouse(enriched_event)

def update_database(data):
    dapr_port = 3500
    url = f"http://localhost:{dapr_port}/v1.0/bindings/db-update-binding"
    payload = {
        'data': data,
        'operation': 'insert'
    }
    response = requests.post(url, json=payload)
    assert response.status_code == 200

def notify_warehouse(data):
    # Send notification logic
    print("Warehouse notified with data:", data)

def fetch_customer_info(customer_id):
    # Simulate fetching customer data
    return {'customer_name': 'John Doe'}

# Main event processing mechanism
process_order_event({
    'order_id': '12345',
    'customer_id': '98765',
    'items': ['item1', 'item2']
})
```

In this code, the order event is captured and processed to enrich it with additional data before being persisted to a database and propagated to a warehouse notification system.

- **Fault Tolerance and Eventual Consistency**

    Handling failures gracefully is paramount in an event-driven architecture. Event processing might fail due to network issues, service errors, or downtime of external systems. Dapr addresses these concerns by offering built-in support for retries and error policies.

Bindings can be configured with retry policies to manage transient errors. Consider an example configuration that details how retries might be governed:

```
apiVersion: dapr.io/v1alpha1
kind: Component
metadata:
  name: retry-binding
  namespace: default
spec:
  type: bindings.redis
  version: v1
  metadata:
  - name: endpoint
    value: "redis://myredis:6379"
  - name: retries
    value: "5"
  - name: backoff
    value: "exponential"
  - name: maxInterval
    value: "10s"
```

This example uses an exponential backoff strategy, which is beneficial in reducing strain on external systems and preventing further failures from cascading.

Eventual consistency is another critical consideration. In distributed systems, achieving strong consistency is challenging. Dapr facilitates eventual consistency by ensuring at-least-once delivery semantics for events. This implies that while events may be delivered more than once due to failures, the system should be designed to tolerate such occurrences without adverse effects.

- **Decoupling and Scalability**

  A significant advantage of event-driven architecture is its support for decoupled systems. Through Dapr bindings, different services can communicate using well-defined events without needing insight into each other's implementations. This promotes scalability, as individual services can scale independently based on load, improving resource utilization.

  Decoupled systems also foster team productivity as development teams can work on isolated components with minimal dependencies. Furthermore, a well-designed event-driven architecture aids in partitioning data, enhancing data locality, and reducing network latency—a vital consideration in the age of cloud and edge computing.

- **Long-Running Workflows and Stateful Processing**

  Some events require orchestration across long-running workflows, involving several services and actions. Dapr can work in collaboration with workflow systems like Apache Airflow or Temporal to coordinate complex processes.

  Consider a scenario requiring staged event processing. An initial event may trigger a sequence of actions—for example, order verification, payment processing, and shipment initiation. Here is a simplified illustration:

  1. **Order Verification**: Triggered by an order-received event, confirming validity and stock availability.

  2. **Payment Processing**: The system initiates payment, involving external payment gateways.

  3. **Shipment Initiation**: Once payment is confirmed, a shipment event begins logistics management.

  Dapr's state management allows you to maintain context across stages. Each event state is associated with tokens or keys that assist in keeping track of the workflow's progress.

Embracing Dapr bindings within an event-driven architecture provides developers with powerful tools to build scalable, resilient, and agile systems. By abstracting the intricacies behind diverse message protocols, systems can be designed and deployed rapidly while maintaining high standards of reliability and performance.

The modularity achieved through bindings contributes to better maintainability, flexibility, and the ability to extend or modify functionalities without widespread implications. As the field of distributed computing progresses, Dapr remains at the forefront, offering credible solutions that simplify the challenges inherent in event-driven systems. Through continued adoption and innovation, event-driven architectures, combined with the power of Dapr, stand to redefine the future landscape of distributed systems.

5.4 Overview of Dapr Pub/Sub Mechanism

The publish-subscribe (pub/sub) pattern is a fundamental communication model in distributed systems, enabling scalable and decoupled interaction between microservices. Dapr (Distributed Application Runtime) implements a powerful, flexible pub/sub mechanism that supports asynchronous communication among services operating across different environments and cloud platforms. This section provides a comprehensive examination of the Dapr pub/sub mechanism, elucidating how it simplifies complex communication scenarios while enhancing the resilience and scalability of microservices architectures.

- **Core Concepts of Pub/Sub**: The pub/sub pattern entails publishers sending messages to a central broker, which then routes these messages to one or more subscribers based on predefined criteria. This model promotes decoupling by ensuring that publishers are not concerned with how that information is consumed, and subscribers do not need to know how data is generated. The abstraction provided by the broker enables system components to evolve independently.

  In a Dapr context, the pub/sub mechanism is supported by a designated stateful component, known as the pubsub component. This component abstracts diverse message brokers and systems such as Redis, RabbitMQ, Kafka, and Azure Service Bus, providing developers with a uniform interface to configure, send, and receive messages.

- **Configuring Pub/Sub Components**: Dapr pub/sub is configured by defining pub/sub components within YAML files. These configurations specify the type of pub/sub component and provide necessary metadata for establishing connections to message brokers. Below is an example configuration for a pub/sub component using Redis as the message broker:

```
apiVersion: dapr.io/v1alpha1
kind: Component
metadata:
```

```
name: redis-pubsub
namespace: default
spec:
  type: pubsub.redis
  version: v1
  metadata:
  - name: redisHost
    value: "localhost:6379"
  - name: redisPassword
    value: ""
  - name: consumerID
    value: "my-consumer-group"
```

In this Redis-based configuration:

- redisHost denotes the address of the Redis server.
- redisPassword holds the password for Redis, if secured.
- consumerID designates a unique identifier for the subscriber's consumer group.

This approach abstracts Redis's underlying connection details, focusing on the pub/sub pattern's consistency.

- **Publishing Messages**: Publishing messages in Dapr involves invoking a specific endpoint offered by the Dapr HTTP or GRPC API through which the message, titled by its topic, is relayed to the appropriate pub/sub component. Here is a Python example demonstrating how a service publishes messages to a specific topic:

```
import requests
import json

def publish_message(topic, data):
    dapr_port = 3500
    url = f"http://localhost:{dapr_port}/v1.0/publish/redis-pubsub/{topic}"

    headers = {
        "Content-Type": "application/json"
    }

    response = requests.post(url, headers=headers, data=json.dumps(data))

    if response.status_code == 204:
        print("Message published successfully")
    else:
```

5.4. OVERVIEW OF DAPR PUB/SUB MECHANISM

```
    print("Failed to publish message:", response.status_code)
# Example usage
publish_message("order-confirmed", {"order_id": "1234", "status": "confirmed"})
```

Here, the publish_message function sends an HTTP POST request to the Dapr sidecar, targeting a topic via the redis-pubsub component. The message payload in JSON format conveys data such as an order identifier and status.

- **Subscribing to Topics**: To receive and process messages, a service subscribes to specific topics. This subscription is established by defining one or more routes within the service code where the Dapr sidecar should deliver applicable messages. An example in Go illustrates how a service subscribes to a topic:

```go
package main

import (
  "encoding/json"
  "fmt"
  "net/http"
)

type OrderEvent struct {
  OrderID string `json:"order_id"`
  Status  string `json:"status"`
}

func orderConfirmedHandler(w http.ResponseWriter, r *http.Request) {
  var event OrderEvent
  if err := json.NewDecoder(r.Body).Decode(&event); err != nil {
    http.Error(w, "Invalid request", http.StatusBadRequest)
    return
  }
  fmt.Printf("Order confirmed: ID=%s, Status=%s\n", event.OrderID, event.Status)
  w.WriteHeader(http.StatusOK)
}

func main() {
  http.HandleFunc("/orders/confirmed", orderConfirmedHandler)
  fmt.Println("Listening for order confirmations on /orders/confirmed")
  http.ListenAndServe(":8080", nil)
}
```

In this Go example, a handler is set up to manage requests to the "/orders/confirmed" endpoint, which corresponds to the subscribed topic order-confirmed. The Dapr sidecar invokes this handler each time a message matching the topic is received.

- **Enabling Scalability and Fault Tolerance**: Dapr's pub/sub mechanism enhances the scalability of services by allowing seamless message broadcast and reception among multiple instances. When scaling services horizontally, multiple service instances can concurrently subscribe to topics, leveraging Dapr's consumer groups to distribute the load evenly and ensure messages are delivered efficiently.

  Fault tolerance is managed through built-in support for retries and dead-letter queues. Transient failures, such as network partitioning or resource unavailability, trigger automatic retries, ensuring reliable message delivery. If messages continuously fail to be processed, Dapr's support for dead-letter queues ensures that these messages are isolated, allowing developers to perform remedial actions.

- **Integrating with Multiple Brokers**: Dapr's abstraction layer accommodates various message brokers, empowering teams with the flexibility to choose or switch between different brokers based on requirements like latency, throughput, and geographic distribution. Each broker may offer unique configuration details in Dapr's YAML, but the uniform interaction pattern remains unchanged. Here we illustrate configuring a pub/sub component with Kafka:

```
apiVersion: dapr.io/v1alpha1
kind: Component
metadata:
  name: kafka-pubsub
  namespace: default
spec:
  type: pubsub.kafka
  version: v1
  metadata:
  - name: brokers
    value: "broker:9092"
  - name: consumerGroup
    value: "kafka-consumer-group"
  - name: authRequired
    value: "true"
  - name: saslUsername
    value: "user"
  - name: saslPassword
    value: "password"
```

5.4. OVERVIEW OF DAPR PUB/SUB MECHANISM

In this Kafka configuration, authentication details ensure secure communication with the Kafka broker, while topics can be dynamically assigned at runtime.

- **Eventual Consistency and Data Integrity**: The asynchrony inherent in the pub/sub model introduces challenges around consistency and data integrity. Dapr facilitates eventual consistency by offering at-least-once message delivery semantics. Although messages may be delivered more than once under certain conditions, services can be designed idempotently to handle repeated messages gracefully, safeguarding data integrity.

  Implementing idempotent consumers necessitates strategies such as maintaining unique identifiers for processed messages, leveraging distributed locks, or employing consistent hashing techniques. Furthermore, monotonic counters or timestamps enrich message payloads, providing logical ordering that aids consumer logic in sequencing and processing messages accurately.

- **Logging and Monitoring**: Robust monitoring and diagnostics are indispensable for optimizing the pub/sub mechanism's performance and detecting anomalies. Dapr provides telemetry options that capture insights into message flow, processing latency, throughput, and failure rates. Instrumentation involves exporting metrics to systems like Prometheus and correlating them with distributed tracing tools like OpenTelemetry.

  Example Dapr metric configuration for Prometheus:

```
apiVersion: dapr.io/v1alpha1
kind: Configuration
metadata:
  name: pubsub-metrics-config
  namespace: default
spec:
  tracing:
    enabled: true
    samplingRate: "1"
    exporterType: "otelagent"
  metric:
    enabled: true
    exporter:
      componentType: "prometheus"
```

This configuration documents how to enable metrics and tracing for comprehensive visibility into pub/sub operations, facilitating proactive optimizations and troubleshooting efforts.

- **Advanced Use Cases**: The versatility of Dapr's pub/sub model is evident in complex, real-world use cases such as:

    - Event Sourcing: Utilizing the pub/sub model to track every state change as a sequence of events, reconstructing past states by replaying these events.

    - CQRS (Command Query Responsibility Segregation): Combining pub/sub with other Dapr patterns to separate command handling and query models, enhancing performance and scalability.

    - Inter-Domain Events: Coordinating events across multiple domains (e.g., orders, payments, shipping) within a microservices framework, requiring sophisticated message routing and topic management.

Dapr's pub/sub mechanism simplifies the delivery and consumption of events across distributed services, powering scalable, resilient, and decoupled systems. By abstracting the complexities of direct broker interactions, developers can pivot focus towards building feature-rich applications without being burdened by underlying infrastructure details.

Furthermore, the cross-broker compatibility ensures that enterprises can adapt to evolving technological landscapes, selecting the best-fit message broker according to context-specific demands. The emphasis on reliability and operability, combined with telemetry and observability, positions the pub/sub mechanism as a cornerstone in the toolset for crafting modern cloud-native architectures. As adoption continues to surge, Dapr's pub/sub mechanism will remain integral to advancing the state of art in distributed system design.

5.5 Configuring Publishers and Subscribers

Configuring publishers and subscribers is a pivotal task in setting up the publish-subscribe (pub/sub) model in Dapr, allowing developers to implement an agile, scalable, and decoupled microservices architecture. The pub/sub pattern enables microservices to communicate asynchronously, supporting complex event-driven systems without requiring tight coupling between message producers and consumers.

The Dapr sidecar abstracts away the underlying details of managing direct interactions with message brokers. This section delves into configuring publishers and subscribers within the Dapr ecosystem, illustrating how to achieve seamless communication between services. Focus will be given to YAML component configurations and application code examples for various programming languages.

- **Defining Pub/Sub Components**

The foundation of configuring publishers and subscribers in Dapr involves defining and setting up pub/sub components. These YAML component files configure an external message broker, specifying connection details, and manage identities for authenticating publisher and subscriber processes. Each component has consistent fields to define its type, version, and metadata, representing a broker's endpoint, authentication credentials, and additional custom settings.

- **Example: Configuring a Redis Pub/Sub Component**

Here, we illustrate a basic configuration for Redis as a pub/sub component:

```
apiVersion: dapr.io/v1alpha1
kind: Component
metadata:
  name: redis-pubsub
  namespace: default
spec:
  type: pubsub.redis
  version: v1
  metadata:
```

```
- name: redisHost
  value: "localhost:6379"
- name: redisPassword
  value: ""
- name: consumerID
  value: "customer-group"
- name: processingTimeout
  value: "10s"
- name: redeliverInterval
  value: "5s"
```

In this configuration:

- redisHost specifies the hostname and port of the Redis server.
- redisPassword holds the password for authentication, if configured for security.
- consumerID provides a unique identity for consumer groups, aiding in load balancing across multiple instances.
- processingTimeout and redeliverInterval manage message handling durations and retry intervals, maintaining durable delivery semantics.

- **Configuring Publishers**

Publishing messages in a Dapr environment requires the service to interact with the Dapr sidecar using HTTP or GRPC interfaces. A publisher in this sense is a microservice that crafts and sends messages on specific topics, leveraging the pub/sub mechanism configured in the Dapr environment.

- **Example: Python Code for Message Publishing**

Suppose an order processing service publishes order confirmation events to a topic. A Python script using the requests library can serve as the publisher:

```python
import requests
import json

def publish_event(topic, message):
    dapr_port = 3500
```

5.5. CONFIGURING PUBLISHERS AND SUBSCRIBERS

```
    publish_url = f"http://localhost:{dapr_port}/v1.0/publish/redis-pubsub/{topic}"

    headers = {
        "Content-Type": "application/json"
    }

    response = requests.post(publish_url, headers=headers, data=json.dumps(message)
    )

    if response.status_code == 204:
        print(f"Event published to topic {topic}")
    else:
        print("Failed to publish event:", response.status_code)

# Example usage
order_event = {"order_id": "12345", "status": "confirmed"}
publish_event("order-confirmed", order_event)
```

This example shows how the service exposes an HTTP POST request to the Dapr sidecar, sending a JSON-formatted message to the specified topic.

- **Configuring Subscribers**

Subscribers in pub/sub architectures register interest in specific topics, handling messages as they are received. Dapr subscribers can be any service capable of handling incoming HTTP requests, as the Dapr sidecar invokes these handlers with messages upon receiving them from the broker.

- **Example: Node.js Subscriber Script**

Let's configure a Node.js application that subscribes to the order-confirmed topic:

```
const express = require('express');
const bodyParser = require('body-parser');

const app = express();
app.use(bodyParser.json());

app.post('/order-confirmed', (req, res) => {
    const orderEvent = req.body;
    console.log(`Order confirmed: ${JSON.stringify(orderEvent)}`);

    // Process the order event
    handleOrderConfirmation(orderEvent);

    res.status(200).send();
```

```
});

function handleOrderConfirmation(order) {
    // Business logic for handling order confirmation
    console.log('Processing order ID: ${order.order_id}');
}

const port = 3000;
app.listen(port, () => console.log('Subscriber listening on port ${port}'));
```

In this example, the application listens for HTTP POST requests at the /order-confirmed endpoint—the topic to which it subscribes. The Dapr sidecar routes messages to this subscriber, which handles message processing and acknowledgment.

- **Coordinating Multiplexed Communication**

Deploying scalable pub/sub systems necessitates deliberate planning of message flow and concurrent processing. Dapr assists in managing high-volume message traffic across numerous microservices by employing consumer groups and concurrent connection handling.

- **Consumer Group Behavior and Scaling**

Utilizing consumer groups ensures messages are processed only once by competing subscriber instances, allowing services to scale independently. Each instance maintains its entry in the group, enabling effective load-sharing even under increased load conditions. This behavior adheres to the *exactly-once* processing paradigm.

- **Example: Configuring Consumer Groups**

Here's a revision of the previous component configuration, highlighting consumer group usage:

```
apiVersion: dapr.io/v1alpha1
kind: Component
metadata:
  name: kafka-pubsub
  namespace: default
spec:
  type: pubsub.kafka
  version: v1
  metadata:
```

5.5. CONFIGURING PUBLISHERS AND SUBSCRIBERS

```
- name: brokers
  value: "localhost:9092"
- name: consumerGroup
  value: "order-processors"
- name: authRequired
  value: "true"
- name: saslUsername
  value: "kafka-user"
- name: saslPassword
  value: "kafka-password"
```

This configuration employs a Kafka cluster, designating the order-processors consumer group for subscriber scaling and division of labor.

- **Advanced Considerations and Best Practices**

Enabling smooth, high-performance communication in pub/sub systems extends beyond straightforward configuration. Consider these advanced practices to ensure robust operation:

- **Conflict Resolution and Idempotency**

Ensure service logic can distinguish and manage duplicate message delivery. Employ idempotent operations where the multiple processing of an event yields the same state as a single processing occurrence. Implement message IDs or versioning schemas to avoid redundant processing.

- **Security and Authentication**

Apply uniform access controls across Dapr components to ward off harmful activity. Ensure that publishers and subscriber roles are distinctly authenticated and authorized to interact with message brokers through protocols like OAuth or mutual TLS.

- **Monitoring and Observability**

Leverage built-in Dapr telemetry to track message processing time, failure occurrences, and network latencies. Instrument detailed logging to capture event flows and state transitions for diagnostic clarity.

```yaml
apiVersion: dapr.io/v1alpha1
kind: Configuration
metadata:
  name: pubsub-tracing-config
  namespace: default
spec:
  tracing:
    enabled: true
    samplingRate: "1.0" # Full trace logging
    exporterType: "otlp"
  metric:
    enabled: true
    exporter:
      componentType: "prometheus"
      options:
        offload: true
```

This configuration emphasizes complete trace capture using OpenTelemetry and Prometheus integration, equipped with offloading for minimal service disruption.

- **Planning for Resilience and Adaptability**

The adaptable nature of Dapr's pub/sub mechanism empowers applications to remain resilient in the face of inevitable network failures or increasing consumer demand. As systems expand, reliance on asynchronous messaging and processing facilitates uninterrupted operations by freeing service dependencies.

- **Conclusion**

Configuration of publishers and subscribers in Dapr facilitates comprehensive deployment and maintenance of resilient distributed systems. By excellent design and strategic configuration, these systems exhibit superior performance handling, reduced error rates, and flexible scaling abilities.

Dapr provides developers with the essential tools for implementing a pub/sub model that accommodates current operational requirements while preparing for unforeseen challenges. By following best practices and optimizing inter-service communications, teams can drive greater consistency, precision, and efficiency within their architectures. As enterprises extend into complex distributed systems, embracing technologies like Dapr proves invaluable in navigating dynamic cloud and edge environments.

5.6 Idempotent Subscriber Example

```
import redis
import json
import requests

# Initialize Redis client
redis_client = redis.StrictRedis(host='localhost', port=6379, db=0)

def process_message(message):
    message_id = message['id']
    if redis_client.exists(message_id):
        print(f"Duplicate message {message_id} ignored.")
    else:
        # Mark this message as processed in Redis
        redis_client.set(message_id, 'processed', ex=86400) # 1-day expiration
        # Process the message
        print(f"Processing message: {message_id}")
        # Example business logic, such as updating database
        update_business_logic(message)

def update_business_logic(data):
    # Simulate update logic
    print(f"Business logic updated with data: {data}")

# Simulated incoming message
incoming_message = {"id": "order-123456", "content": "New order received"}
process_message(incoming_message)
```

In this example, the process_message function ensures that a message is processed only if it has not been encountered before, using Redis as a cache to track previously handled messages. The ex parameter specifies a time-to-live for the cache entry, ensuring that memory is not unnecessarily consumed long-term.

- Utilizing Dead-Letter Queues: Dead-letter queues (DLQs) serve as critical components in enhancing the reliability and fault tolerance of a pub/sub system. They capture messages that cannot be delivered or processed despite multiple retry attempts. By leveraging DLQs, developers can isolate problematic messages, analyze root causes, and execute compensatory actions, maintaining service health and data consistency.

    Below is a conceptual representation of how DLQs are integrated within message workflows:

This diagram showcases a typical messaging workflow wherein messages undergo a designated number of retry attempts before resorting

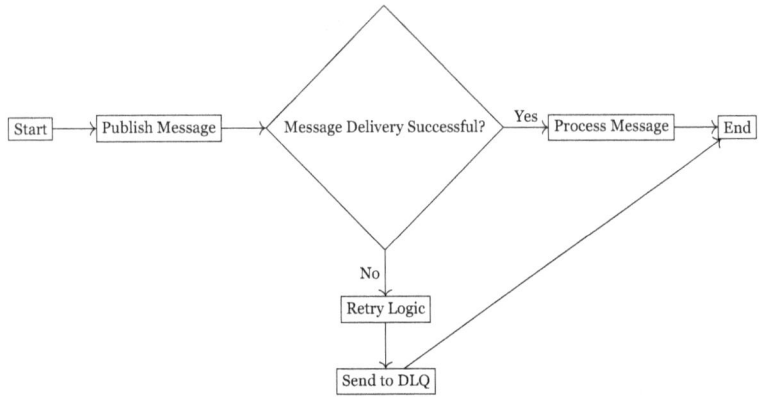

Figure 5.1: Message Workflow with DLQ Integration

to dead-letter queue submission due to persistent failures.

- Monitoring and Observability in Reliable Messaging: Ensuring observability is paramount in optimizing a reliable messaging setup. Dapr provides telemetry capabilities that can be integrated with standardized formats and platforms like OpenTelemetry and Prometheus to offer insight into message flows and error occurrences. Key metrics to monitor include:

- Message Throughput: Counts of successfully processed messages across topics.

- Retry Counts: Frequency and success rates of retry operations.

- DLQ Reports: Statistics on messages rerouted to DLQs, including failure reasons.

- Example: Visualization with Prometheus Configuration: A typical Prometheus monitoring setup visualizes message-related metrics to allow operators to take corrective actions preemptively:

```
apiVersion: dapr.io/v1alpha1
kind: Configuration
```

5.6. IDEMPOTENT SUBSCRIBER EXAMPLE

```
metadata:
  name: dapr-monitoring-config
  namespace: default
spec:
  metric:
    enabled: true
    exporter:
      componentType: "prometheus"
      options:
        scrapeInterval: "15s"
        labels:
          service: "order-service"
```

This example highlights a Prometheus exporter configured to scrape metrics data at a 15-second interval, providing a consistent view of messaging behavior.

- Best Practices for Achieving Reliable Messaging: Several best practices ensure that Dapr pub/sub implementations achieve high levels of reliability:

- Idempotent Processing: Consider deduplication strategies to safely handle repeated message deliveries.

- Dynamic Scalability: Implement autoscaling policies for your services based on message throughput and processing load.

- Circuit Breakers: Utilize circuit breaker patterns to prevent service overload during high retry attempts.

- Dependency Tracking: Monitor dependencies closely, ensuring that brokers and related components maintain high uptime and performance.

The power of reliable messaging in a Dapr-powered pub/sub system can scarcely be overstated. Its influence extends beyond immediate system stability and resilience, encompassing broader enterprise agility and responsiveness. By coupling the best practices of message processing with advanced Dapr configurations, developers can achieve confidence in delivering mission-critical data through intricate networks of microservices.

By continuously innovating upon existing robust frameworks, organizations can realize the potential of scalable, asynchronous communication patterns. This capability not only caters to current demands but also ensures preparedness for evolving future requirements in the distributed systems paradigm.

5.7 Advantages and Use Cases of Dapr Bindings and Pub/Sub

The adoption of Dapr bindings and the publish-subscribe (pub/sub) pattern brings transformative advantages to microservices architecture and event-driven systems. By abstracting complexity and fostering elasticity, these mechanisms enable developers to create responsive and scalable applications. In this section, we explore the distinct advantages Dapr provides and delve into real-world use cases that highlight the utility and flexibility of these components.

Advantages of Dapr Bindings and Pub/Sub

1. Decoupling of Services

One of the primary benefits of leveraging Dapr bindings and pub/sub is the decoupling of services. In a decoupled architecture, services interact through a common messaging infrastructure without direct dependencies on each other's implementation details. This separation allows individual services to evolve and scale independently, reducing interdependencies that can become bottlenecks in development and deployment processes.

In the Dapr framework, bindings abstract away the intricacies of connecting and interfacing with external systems, allowing developers to focus on core business logic instead. Similarly, the pub/sub model separates message producers from consumers via a broker, supporting seamless integration and communication.

2. Scalability

Dapr enhances scalability by efficiently distributing the load across multiple services. With pub/sub, publishers transmit messages to a broker, which disseminates them to subscribers—a mechanism that naturally supports load balancing. Subscriber services can scale horizontally, ensuring they handle incoming messages proportionately to the load.

5.7. ADVANTAGES AND USE CASES OF DAPR BINDINGS AND PUB/SUB

Bindings empower dynamic resource allocation by activating services only when necessary—like triggering functions based on external event sources—thereby optimizing utilization and cost effectiveness.

3. Flexibility and Portability

The platform-agnostic design of Dapr facilitates flexibility and portability. The same application code and configurations can run on any environment supported by Kubernetes or other container orchestrators, minimizing vendor lock-in risks. This flexibility allows applications to easily integrate with varied cloud-native technologies and services as they become available or mature.

Dapr's extensive support for different message brokers—such as Redis, Kafka, and Azure Service Bus—affords developers the choice of integrating with technologies that best align with their specific performance and operational preferences.

4. Fault Tolerance and Reliability

Dapr's built-in retry policies and support for dead-letter queues contribute to the fault tolerance and reliability of applications. This is crucial in distributed environments where intermittent failures, such as network glitches or temporary unavailability of services, are expected.

By implementing retry strategies and configuring DLQs, developers can ensure that transient failures do not derail the system, thus preserving data consistency and integrity over time.

Use Cases of Dapr Bindings and Pub/Sub

Use Case 1: E-Commerce Order Processing

In a competitive e-commerce landscape, efficiently handling transactions and order fulfilment is paramount. Using Dapr's pub/sub mechanism, an e-commerce platform can decompose into several focused microservices—such as order management, payment processing, and inventory management.

Workflow Outline:

- **Order Service**: When a user places an order, the Order Service publishes an order-created event. This service remains agnostic of the subsequent process flow details.

- **Payment Service**: Subscribed to the order-created topic, it manages payment authorization and dynamically publishes a payment-confirmed event.

- **Inventory Service**: It subscribes to the payment-confirmed topic, decrements stock levels, and generates a stock-allocated message.

- **Shipping Service**: Awaits the stock-allocated message to commence shipping operations.

Each service maintains its logic independent of the others. Scalability concerns can be addressed by increasing subscriber instances based on processing demand.

```
apiVersion: dapr.io/v1alpha1
kind: Component
metadata:
  name: e-commerce-pubsub
  namespace: default
spec:
  type: pubsub.redis
  version: v1
  metadata:
  - name: redisHost
    value: "localhost:6379"
  - name: redisPassword
    value: ""
  - name: consumerID
    value: "e-commerce-group"
```

```
package main

import (
  "bytes"
  "encoding/json"
  "fmt"
  "net/http"
)

func publishOrderCreated(orderID string) error {
    daprPort := "3500"
    topic := "order-created"
    url := fmt.Sprintf("http://localhost:%s/v1.0/publish/e-commerce-pubsub/%s",
        daprPort, topic)

    orderEvent := map[string]string{
      "order_id": orderID,
      "customer": "customer123",
      "items": "item1,item2",
    }
```

5.7. ADVANTAGES AND USE CASES OF DAPR BINDINGS AND PUB/SUB

```
   data, _ := json.Marshal(orderEvent)
   resp, err := http.Post(url, "application/json", bytes.NewBuffer(data))
   if err != nil {
      fmt.Println("Failed to publish order:", err)
      return err
   }
   defer resp.Body.Close()

   fmt.Println("Order creation event published:", orderID)
   return nil
}
func main() {
   publishOrderCreated("order12345")
}
```

Use Case 2: IoT Device Event Processing

Different applications, including IoT solutions, often require processing data from a multitude of devices, which generate events sporadically based on user interaction, sensor data, or environmental triggers.

Workflow Outline:

- **Sensor Devices**: Each device generates telemetry data, publishing it through a device-telemetry binding component.

- **Telemetry Processor**: This service, subscribing to the device-telemetry topic, stores data in a database and processes real-time analytics.

- **Alerting Service**: Subscribes to telemetry-anomalies to trigger alerts upon recognizing unusual patterns or threshold breaches.

Such architectures enable enhanced performance monitoring and timely intervention, thereby increasing the reliability and efficiency of IoT networks.

Use Case 3: Real-Time Notifications

Leveraging Dapr's pub/sub and bindings models, applications can deliver real-time notifications to users across various channels, such as SMS, email, or app alerts.

Workflow Outline:

- **Notification Hub**: Centralized to receive events from various triggers, including status changes, appointments, or offer initiations.

- **Communication Bridges**: Separate services handle messaging through diverse channels, potentially using output bindings for integration with systems like Twilio or SendGrid.

Here, Dapr facilitates seamless multi-channel communication without overburdening the core logic of primary microservices.

```
apiVersion: dapr.io/v1alpha1
kind: Component
metadata:
  name: sms-twilio
  namespace: default
spec:
  type: bindings.twilio.sms
  version: v1
  metadata:
  - name: accountSID
    value: "<TWILIO_ACCOUNT_SID>"
  - name: authToken
    value: "<TWILIO_AUTH_TOKEN>"
  - name: from
    value: "+1234567890"
```

In the rapidly evolving landscape of cloud-native technologies, Dapr stands at the forefront by abstracting complex service interactions and promoting cloud-agnostic practices. Its extensible component model supports diverse scenarios, ranging from hybrid on-premises/cloud strategies to multi-tenant application models, which demand consistent but versatile data processing pipelines.

For enterprises transitioning legacy systems to microservice-oriented designs, adopting Dapr simplifies the incremental modernization process. Its seamless integration with existing message brokers and support systems mitigates the operational challenges inherent in distributed ecosystems.

The strategic adoption of Dapr bindings and pub/sub brings a myriad of benefits, from streamlined communication across microservices to the promotion of modular, decoupled system design. Through real-world application in varied use cases—e-commerce, IoT, and communication systems—Dapr proves itself as a powerful enabler of event-driven architecture.

Its inherent flexibility reduces time-to-market, encourages innovation, and facilitates continuous integration and delivery practices. By anchoring system interactions within a framework designed for reliability and resiliency, organizations can approach their growth objectives with confidence and unwavering technical readiness, ensuring that the future of their architectural endeavors remains both agile and robust.

Chapter 6

Service Invocation and Resiliency

This chapter addresses the implementation of service invocation within Dapr and the built-in resiliency mechanisms that ensure robust microservices communication. It outlines the processes for configuring service discovery and enabling reliable interactions using HTTP and gRPC protocols. The discussion extends to implementing circuit breaker patterns, managing retries and timeouts, and enhancing observability, all aimed at developing fault-tolerant applications. These techniques are vital for maintaining service reliability and operational stability in distributed systems.

6.1 Service Invocation in Dapr

Service invocation is a fundamental aspect of microservices architecture, and Dapr provides a robust model to facilitate this communication. Dapr, or Distributed Application Runtime, abstracts the complexities involved in direct service-to-service communication by leveraging HTTP and gRPC protocols. This section explores how Dapr simplifies and enhances the process of service invocation, ensuring seamless interactions across distributed systems.

Dapr operates using a sidecar architecture, where each microservice instance is paired with a Dapr sidecar. This approach enables each service to communicate with other services through its associated sidecar. The sidecar handles service discovery, load balancing, and invoking desired services, thus offloading these responsibilities from the application logic.

```
dapr run --app-id serviceA --app-port 5001 -- dotnet run
```

The command above initiates a Dapr application with a specified app ID and port, demonstrating how Dapr integrates with microservices. Here, the dotnet service is started and managed by Dapr, listening on port 5001.

To invoke another service, the application does not communicate directly with the target service. Instead, it sends requests to its sidecar, specifying the target app ID. This interaction ensures that the service invocation is abstracted and managed efficiently by Dapr.

```
POST /v1.0/invoke/{targetAppId}/method/{method}
```

This endpoint illustrates the Dapr service invocation API call, where 'targetAppId' is the identifier of the target application, and 'method' represents the specific method to invoke. By utilizing such endpoints, applications can seamlessly interact with other services without being tightly coupled to them.

Dapr supports both HTTP and gRPC protocols for service invocation, allowing developers to opt for the most suitable protocol based on their specific requirements. HTTP is widely adopted for its simplicity, while gRPC offers advantages like higher performance and support for binary payloads, making it suitable for scenarios demanding efficient communication.

When using gRPC, Dapr provides autogenerated gRPC stubs for developers, which simplifies the integration process. For instance, if using protobufs, the service methods can be easily called through gRPC clients integrated into the application.

```
import grpc
import dapr_pb2_grpc
```

6.1. SERVICE INVOCATION IN DAPR

```
# Create a channel to Dapr sidecar
channel = grpc.insecure_channel('localhost:50001')
stub = dapr_pb2_grpc.AppCallbackStub(channel)

# Invoke the remote service method
response = stub.OnInvoke(dapr_pb2.InvokeRequest(method='methodName'))
```

This Python example demonstrates how to use gRPC for Dapr service invocation. It involves setting up a gRPC channel to the Dapr sidecar, using Dapr's autogenerated gRPC stubs to perform service calls efficiently.

Latency and reliability are critical for service invocations in microservices. Dapr incorporates retries and policies to handle transient failures and optimize communication. This built-in resilience ensures that temporary network issues do not lead to application failures, thereby improving overall reliability.

Beyond the simple invocation of services, Dapr offers extensibility through middleware, allowing for the customization of invocation paths. Middleware can handle cross-cutting concerns like security, logging, and data transformation in a centralized manner, before or after an invocation request.

```
apiVersion: dapr.io/v1alpha1
kind: Middleware
metadata:
  name: custom-middleware
spec:
  type: http.middleware.custom
  version: v1
  initTimeout: "50ms"
  properties:
    url: "http://localhost:3500/customMiddleware"
```

In this middleware configuration, a custom HTTP middleware is defined. This middleware could preprocess requests—such as authenticating or modifying request headers—before they are forwarded to the respective service endpoint.

Security in service invocation often involves mutual TLS (mTLS), which Dapr supports natively. Through mTLS, services can authenticate and encrypt messages, ensuring secure communication throughout the invocation process. The Dapr sidecar handles securing network traffic, reducing the need for in-depth protocol management in the application code.

The observability of service invocations is integral to understanding the behavior and performance of microservices. Dapr includes native support for tracing and logging, facilitating the monitoring of request flows across various services. It integrates with popular observability tools such as Zipkin, Jaeger, and Prometheus, providing comprehensive insights into service interaction patterns.

Dapr uses context propagation underpinned by the OpenTelemetry standard, passing trace contexts across services. Developers can analyze trace data to identify bottlenecks or failures in the invocation chain, enabling proactive system optimization.

```
{
  "traceparent": "00-4bf92f3577b34da6a3ce929d0e0e4736-00f067aa0ba902b7-01",
  "tracestate": "congo=t61rcWkgMzE"
}
```

This trace context example holds information required for tracing service invocation paths. With Dapr handling distributed tracing, pinpointing issues such as latency spikes or errors becomes more manageable.

Dapr's service invocation model is also compatible with polyglot environments, where services may be implemented in multiple programming languages. Through the use of standard protocols and autogenerated client libraries, interservice communication remains consistent and efficient, irrespective of the language used to develop the services.

Dapr's DNS-based service resolution provides a straightforward method for services to identify and locate each other. While Dapr's sidecar typically handles service discovery automatically, developers can use DNS for static configurations or conditions where explicit control is required.

```
http://serviceB.dapr:5002/method-name
```

This example demonstrates how a service can invoke another using Dapr's DNS resolution mechanism. It provides clarity and simplicity, removing the complexity often associated with service discovery in distributed systems.

Applications can scale dynamically in response to demand. With autoscaling capabilities integrated within Dapr, service invocation remains performant even under varying loads. Dapr's load balancing ensures that incoming invocation requests are distributed optimally across service instances, mitigating performance bottlenecks.

Dapr's service invocation model abstracts away intricate details, offering a simplified API that focuses on interaction, rather than connectivity and compatibility issues. This abstraction empowers developers to innovate and experiment with service communication patterns, focusing on application logic and end-user experiences.

Dapr's service invocation capabilities significantly streamline the development and operation of distributed applications. By providing a consistent and efficient communication layer, Dapr enhances microservice communication, ensuring that services can scale, evolve, and interoperate seamlessly.

6.2 Configuring Service Discovery

Service discovery is a vital component within microservices architecture, allowing services to dynamically find and communicate with each other. Dapr, a distributed application runtime, simplifies service discovery through its sidecar architecture, promoting decoupled interactions between services. This section delves into the intricacies of configuring service discovery using Dapr, elucidating its role in load balancing and the seamless integration of microservices.

Dapr's service discovery mechanism is tightly integrated with its sidecar pattern, where each microservice instance operates alongside a Dapr sidecar. This pairing ensures an isolated environment for each service to independently register and resolve its address with the Dapr runtime, irrespective of the underlying infrastructure. Unlike traditional service discovery methods, which often require configuring external registries, Dapr facilitates zero-configuration discovery where services leverage Dapr's internal capabilities.

To initiate service discovery, services need only communicate with their local Dapr sidecar using a common application protocol, such as HTTP or gRPC. The sidecar augments service requests with necessary metadata and efficiently routes them to the intended service instances. This ensures that services can dynamically discover each other without explicit querying or dependency on the external network settings.

CHAPTER 6. SERVICE INVOCATION AND RESILIENCY

```
dapr run --app-id service-discovery --app-port 6000 --protocol grpc -- python app.py
```

This command launches a Python application using Dapr, specifying gRPC as the communication protocol and setting the application ID to 'service-discovery'. It demonstrates Dapr's streamlined approach to register a service, abstracting the intricacies of service discovery from developers.

Dapr's built-in service registry automatically maintains the mapping of app IDs to their respective addresses. When a request is initiated, Dapr resorts to this registry to determine the appropriate service endpoint, eliminating manual intervention.

```python
import requests

def invoke_service(target_app_id, method_name, data):
    url = f'http://localhost:3500/v1.0/invoke/{target_app_id}/method/{
        method_name}'
    response = requests.post(url, json=data)
    return response.json()

response = invoke_service("inventory-service", "get-items", {"category": "electronics
    "})
print(response)
```

In the Python code snippet above, a request is made to inventory-service through Dapr's HTTP endpoint. Dapr handles service discovery by mapping the inventory-service app ID to its network address, before forwarding the request to the correct service instance.

For advanced configurations, Dapr supports name resolution components, which define how service names are resolved into endpoint addresses. The default component is mDNS (Multicast DNS) for local development, but in production environments, adopting a cloud-native component like Kubernetes service discovery is advisable to leverage robust DNS-level service discovery.

```yaml
apiVersion: dapr.io/v1alpha1
kind: Component
metadata:
  name: k8s-name-resolution
  namespace: default
spec:
  type: nameResolution.kubernetes
  version: v1
```

This YAML configuration attests to setting up a Kubernetes-based

6.2. CONFIGURING SERVICE DISCOVERY

name resolution component within Dapr. The Kubernetes name resolution component interconnects Dapr with the Kubernetes DNS, ensuring that service discovery adheres to established cloud-native patterns.

Apart from aligning with infrastructure-native solutions like Kubernetes, Dapr facilitates DNS resolution through a naming convention supporting lightweight configurations. The svc.cluster.local DNS suffix is appended to service names, guiding Dapr to resolve the service name according to the local DNS strategy within Kubernetes clusters.

To further enrich the flexibility of service discovery, Dapr supports integration with traditional service meshes like Istio. Integrating Dapr with Istio, for instance, confers additional benefits such as advanced traffic routing, A/B testing, and canary deployments. This dual-layer enhancement empowers complex deployments leveraging granular control of traffic policies, jointly bestowed by service meshes and Dapr.

Load balancing plays a crucial role in Dapr's service discovery mechanism, distributing incoming requests across service instances to ensure optimal utilization and high availability. Dapr employs sophisticated load balancing strategies, such as round-robin and least connections, to efficaciously manage traffic distribution.

```
apiVersion: dapr.io/v1alpha1
kind: Subscription
metadata:
  name: load-balancer-config
spec:
  topic: incoming-requests
  routes:
    - condition: "checkLoad"
      path: "least-connection"
```

In this YAML configuration example, Dapr's load balancing policy is tuned via a subscription model. It prescribes load-based routing policies, instructing Dapr to engage the least-connection strategy when routing incoming-requests.

Remarkably, Dapr's service discovery mechanism inherently fosters high resilience. The runtime environment autonomously handles failovers, re-attempting failed requests against healthy instances. Dapr comprehensively monitors and refreshes service registry entries, autonomically removing or reinstating service endpoints in response to health state changes.

Security considerations are paramount in service discovery. Dapr natively supports mutual TLS (mTLS) across service communications, ensuring encryption and secure identity assurance. The Dapr sidecars transparently manage mTLS handshakes, requiring minimal configuration from developers.

```
apiVersion: dapr.io/v1alpha1
kind: Component
metadata:
  name: mTLS-configuration
spec:
  type: security.tls
  version: v1
  metadata:
  - name: caSecret
    value: "ca-secret"
```

The aforementioned YAML configuration exemplifies setting mTLS within a Dapr environment. By configuring mTLS, service invocations become inherently secure against eavesdropping and spoofing attacks.

Tracing and observability are key to diagnosing service discovery behaviors in complex distributed systems. Dapr's support for OpenTelemetry facilitates tracing service discovery paths, capturing telemetry data indicative of service health and performance.

By enabling telemetry through integrations with platforms like Jaeger or Zipkin, developers can trace transaction flows between services. This visibility augments incident response, allowing practitioners to swiftly pinpoint anomalies and draw insights from invocation latency patterns.

Service discovery in Dapr is adeptly designed to cater to polyglot environments. Developers enjoy consistent service lookup experiences regardless of the programming language, promoting seamless microservice interactions without concern for language dependencies.

Dapr's service discovery mechanism revolutionizes how microservices identify and communicate across distributed environments. By encapsulating complex discovery logic within its sidecar pattern, Dapr offloads burdens from developers, empowering them to focus on refining application logic. Whether adopting a cloud-native architecture or experimenting with local development, Dapr bridges connectivity and provides a robust discovery layer pivotal to operational excellence in microservices ecosystems.

6.3 Implementing Circuit Breaker Patterns

The circuit breaker pattern is an essential design paradigm in microservices architectures, aimed at enhancing system resilience by preventing cascading failures. Dapr, with its intrinsic support for circuits, provides a robust framework for the application of circuit breaker patterns, shielding the system from inefficiencies and failures by regulating the flow of calls to a potentially failing service. In this section, we delve into the intricacies of implementing circuit breakers with Dapr, exploring the configuration and monitoring of circuit states to optimize service reliability.

A circuit breaker is a mechanism that monitors and governs the interaction between services, particularly in managing failures and maintaining operability during transient issues. It operates by allowing a specified number of failures before moving from a "closed" state (normal operation) to an "open" state (failing operation), ultimately halting requests to the struggling service to prevent further impact.

Implementing a circuit breaker pattern begins with defining what constitutes a failure and the thresholds for tripping the circuit breaker. Dapr's resiliency policy framework empowers developers to articulate these criteria in structured configurations.

```
{
    "apiVersion": "dapr.io/v1alpha1",
    "kind": "Configuration",
    "metadata": {
        "name": "service-circuit-breaker"
    },
    "spec": {
        "resiliency": {
            "policies": {
                "circuitBreaker": {
                    "trip": {
                        "consecutiveFailures": 5
                    },
                    "duration": "60s",
                    "interval": "10s"
                }
            }
        }
    }
}
```

This JSON configuration is for a basic circuit breaker policy within Dapr. It defines a policy that trips when five consecutive failures are detected, entering the "open" state for 60 seconds. The circuit breaker periodically attempts to reset, executing checks at 10-second intervals. Such policies mitigate the risk of cascading failures by withholding requests after repeated errors have been identified.

Upon tripping, the circuit breaker's open state can optionally feature a half-open stage, where a subset of requests is trialed to ascertain if the target service has recovered. This state transition is critical in re-establishing communication and dynamically recalibrating the circuit based on real-time outcomes.

Consider the following YAML configuration for a more nuanced circuit breaker policy:

```
apiVersion: dapr.io/v1alpha1
kind: Component
metadata:
  name: advanced-circuit-breaker
spec:
  type: middleware.http.circuitbreaker
  version: v1
  metadata:
  - name: policy
    value: "exceptionCount"
  - name: threshold
    value: "10"
  - name: recoveryTimeSpan
    value: "2m"
  - name: minServers
    value: "3"
```

The advanced configuration above demonstrates a setup where the circuit breaker trips based on a count of exceptions, setting the threshold at 10. Upon reaching this limit, the breaker enforces a recoverable timeout of 2 minutes after which it reassesses the service's health. The 'minServers' attribute secures a minimum number of healthy service instances before the system exponentially retries invoking the service.

Dapr's circuit breaker implementation leverages middleware, integrating seamlessly into service pipelines. This integration decouples the resiliency logic from application code, allowing developers to modify and enhance policies without altering business logic.

Beyond failure detection, circuit breakers require sophisticated monitoring to provide insights into system health and adjust parameters

6.3. IMPLEMENTING CIRCUIT BREAKER PATTERNS

dynamically. Dapr facilitates observability through metrics and integration with monitoring solutions like Prometheus. Observing circuit metrics helps understand the frequency of state changes, failure rates, and recovery times, enabling proactive tuning of circuit thresholds.

```
# HTTP Circuit Breaker Metrics example
circuit_breaker_open_total{policy="exceptionCount"} 3
circuit_breaker_half_open_total{policy="exceptionCount"} 5
circuit_breaker_closed_total{policy="exceptionCount"} 18
```

This output showcases an example of Prometheus metrics labelling for circuit breaker states, tracking the count of transitions between open, half-open, and closed states. These metrics facilitate real-time analysis of failures, empowering developers to iterate policies to minimize downtime effectively.

The application of circuit breaker patterns is evident in various domains such as network communications, database operations, and third-party integrations, each benefiting from enhanced reliability and fault tolerance. Dapr's extensible architecture allows for tailored circuit breakers specific to varying service dependencies, where heterogeneous requirements demand distinct configurations.

In scenarios where particular services are mission-critical, developers might choose to apply a dual-layer strategy comprising localized circuit breaker configuration alongside global policy management facilitated by Dapr. This ensures granular control while maintaining overarching resilience.

Resiliency testing forms a cornerstone of the development lifecycle, wherein simulated failure conditions validate the effectiveness of circuit breakers. Fault injection helps examine predictability when confronted with sudden spikes in latency or service unavailability, ensuring that circuit break configurations adapt to stress conditions.

Establishing circuit breaker patterns represents a paradigm shift towards fail-fast mechanisms in microservices. It proactively assesses system resilience, balances resource utilization, and orchestrates automated recovery—transformations instrumental to extending system lifecycles with minimal disruptions.

Dapr gives credence to circuit breaker patterns, harmonizing their implementation with contemporary development practices by abstracting intricate error processing. Investing in robust circuit breaker configurations begets overarching benefits for system availability, reliability, and scalability—the pillars of resilient application architecture in distributed environments.

6.4 Handling Retries and Timeouts

In distributed systems, handling retries and timeouts effectively is fundamental to achieving robust microservice interactions. These mechanisms enhance reliability by efficiently managing transient failures while preventing prolonged service unavailability. Dapr, through its runtime configuration capabilities, provides robust support for managing retries and timeouts to facilitate reliable service-to-service communication. This section elucidates on defining, configuring, and monitoring retries and timeouts using Dapr, complemented with substantial insights and technical details.

Retries involve the re-attempt of failed operations, introduced primarily to handle transient errors or momentary network blips. Configuring retries judiciously ensures that temporary faults do not cascade into persistent failures, enhancing the resilience of microservices interactions.

Timeouts delineate the period a system waits for an expected response before categorizing an operation as failed. Properly defined timeouts serve to quickly identify unresponsive services and relieve system resources that would otherwise be locked during prolonged waiting periods.

One of Dapr's key design tenets is abstracting complex retry and timeout logic away from application code, placing it within the configuration logic managed by the Dapr sidecar. This separation allows developers to fine-tune their systems' reliability settings without needing to alter application logic.

```
{
    "apiVersion": "dapr.io/v1alpha1",
    "kind": "Configuration",
    "metadata": {
        "name": "service-retry-timeout-config"
    },
    "spec": {
```

6.4. HANDLING RETRIES AND TIMEOUTS

```
"resiliency": {
    "policies": {
        "retry": {
            "policy": "fixed",
            "maxRetries": 5,
            "interval": "2s"
        },
        "timeout": "10s"
    }
  }
}
```

The above JSON configuration demonstrates how Dapr can be used to define retry and timeout policies. This configuration establishes a fixed retry strategy where failed requests are retried up to five times with a 2-second interval between each attempt. Furthermore, it ensures that each service call times out if no response is received within 10 seconds.

When configuring retries, it is crucial to determine the most suitable retry strategy for your application. Basic retry strategies available in Dapr include fixed retries, where every retry is executed after a constant delay, and exponential backoff, which introduces progressively longer wait periods between retries.

Exponential backoff is particularly relevant in avoiding network congestion and service overload, as it reduces the risk of immediately retrying failed requests en masse. Developers often implement exponential backoff with jitter—randomly adjusting backoff periods—further mitigating the potential for thundering herd problems.

```
apiVersion: dapr.io/v1alpha1
kind: Component
metadata:
  name: exponential-retry
spec:
  type: middleware.http.resiliency
  version: v1
  metadata:
  - name: policy
    value: "exponential"
  - name: maxRetries
    value: "3"
  - name: initialInterval
    value: "1s"
  - name: maxInterval
    value: "5s"
  - name: backoffMultiplier
    value: "2"
```

The YAML snippet illustrates configuring an exponential retry policy with a maximum of three retries, starting at a 1-second delay, and growing to a maximum of 5 seconds, doubling each time (backoff multiplier of 2).

Timeout configurations must strike a balance between system responsiveness and reliability. Too short a timeout may result in prematurely aborting valid responses, while an extended timeout can cause resource exhaustion, tying up threads that should be servicing other requests.

Dapr's timeout policy can comprehensively accommodate variable application demands by leveraging hierarchical timeouts at different architectural levels—from API client calls to low-level inter-service communications. Specifically, microservices interacting over networks with varying latencies may necessitate distinct timeout settings for optimal functionality.

In practice, developers should undertake empirical testing to identify suitable timeout durations based on real-world conditions and failover scenarios, hence optimizing service reliability through adaptive timeout policies.

Besides offering static configuration, Dapr supports dynamic adjustment of retries and timeouts based on external parameters or system load conditions. Such adaptability is crucial in environments experiencing fluctuating loads, enabling fine-tuning of resiliency settings aligned with workload characteristics.

```
import requests

def call_service_with_timeout(url, data, timeout):
    try:
        response = requests.post(url, json=data, timeout=timeout)
        response.raise_for_status()
        return response.json()
    except requests.exceptions.HTTPError as err:
        print(f"HTTP error occurred: {err}")
    except requests.exceptions.Timeout:
        print(f"Request timed out after {timeout} seconds.")
```

The Python example illustrates an HTTP request leveraging a timeout parameter, providing fundamental error handling logic to manage HTTP errors and timeouts effectively.

By employing retries and timeouts, Dapr solutions inherently improve fault tolerance. Coupled with circuit breakers, these mechanisms contribute to a fortified resilience strategy that safeguards against transient faults as well as more significant failures.

Observability into retry behaviors and timeouts is indispensable for understanding system reliability, where Dapr's integration with observability systems captures insightful metrics. With Prometheus or similar platforms, developers can oversee retry attempts, timeouts, and latencies, thereby garnering insights to optimize resiliency policies.

```
# Prometheus Metrics - Retry and Timeout Examples
dapr_retries_total{policy="fixed"} 14
dapr_request_timeout_total{policy="defaultTimeout"} 7
```

Prometheus metrics such as retries and timeouts offer quantified insights into ongoing operations, providing actionable data to finetune retry intensities or timeout durations.

Environments utilizing autoscaling mechanisms or experiencing sporadic traffic spikes particularly benefit from robust retry and timeout configurations. Adaptive policies ensure graceful degradation during overload conditions by dynamically moderating retry and timeout behaviors, maintaining availability and sustaining service quality.

When appropriately configured in Dapr, retries and timeouts embody a powerful abstraction that transforms error recovery from manual interventions or arbitrary error handling routines into disciplined, automated processes. Through configurable strategies, distributed systems can attain heightened resilience, maintaining operability even amidst unreliable network conditions or external service interruptions. Dapr's careful abstraction and facilitation of these patterns underpin ongoing advancements in the design and operation of scalable, distributed software architectures.

6.5 Observability in Service Invocations

Observability within distributed systems is imperative to manage, monitor, and diagnose applications effectively. In the context of microservices, observability in service invocations illuminates the pathways through which services interact, offering insights into their runtime behavior and performance characteristics. This section extensively explores how Dapr, a distributed application runtime, enhances observability for service invocations with integrated tools and practices, ensuring systems remain transparent, reliable, and resilient.

Observability constitutes three primary pillars: metrics, logs, and traces. Together, these elements provide comprehensive insights necessary for understanding the dynamic operational state of an application. Dapr natively supports each of these observability areas, furnishing developers with enriched perspectives regarding the performance and health of services.

Metrics are quantifiable data points that denote system performance, such as request rates, error rates, and latency measurements. Within Dapr, the collection of service invocation metrics involves capturing detailed information about request success and failure rates, response times, and overall throughput, among others.

To set up metrics observability using Dapr, developers can configure it to export metrics compatible with popular monitoring systems such as Prometheus. This enables efficient visualization and alerting on key metrics related to service interactions.

```
apiVersion: dapr.io/v1alpha1
kind: Component
metadata:
  name: prometheus
spec:
  type: exporters.prometheus
  version: v1
  metadata:
  - name: metricsEnabled
    value: "true"
  - name: scrapeInterval
    value: "15s"
  - name: scrapePath
    value: "/metrics"
```

The YAML configuration enables Prometheus in Dapr, facilitating automatic scraping of metrics at a 15-second interval from the specified path. Metrics encompass data like the average latency of successful service invocations and the percentage of failed requests, allowing operators to pinpoint performance bottlenecks and triage issues effectively.

Logs, the second pillar of observability, offer a historical account of

6.5. OBSERVABILITY IN SERVICE INVOCATIONS

service execution flows and interactions. Dapr enhances observability by consolidating logs from various microservices, integrating them into centralized logging systems, such as Elasticsearch, Fluentd, and Kibana (EFK) stack, or directly through popular cloud services.

```
kubectl logs dapr-operator-xxxxx -n dapr-system
```

Using the command above in Kubernetes environments, developers can directly access logs from Dapr components like the operator, sidecar, or placement service. Detailed logs provide crucial context around system errors and unexpected states, augmenting the debugging and troubleshooting processes.

Tracing, the third pillar, brings visibility to service invocation paths across distributed systems. Dapr inherently supports distributed tracing, allowing developers to trace end-to-end requests, capturing spans that represent operation durations as well as pertinent metadata, including error information and operational context.

Dapr enables seamless integration with open-source distributed tracing solutions such as Zipkin, Jaeger, and OpenTelemetry, which capture and visualize traces spanning multiple microservices.

```
apiVersion: dapr.io/v1alpha1
kind: Component
metadata:
  name: tracing
spec:
  type: exporters.zipkin
  version: v1
  metadata:
  - name: enabled
    value: "true"
  - name: exporterAddress
    value: "http://zipkin-collector.local:9411/api/v2/spans"
```

The configuration showcases how to enable Zipkin tracing within Dapr, where each service invocation is assigned a unique trace identifier propagated across microservice boundaries. These trace visualizations reveal critical path information, latency distributions, and dependency trees, offering a structured, temporal view of system operations.

Enabling observability within service invocations underpins a variety of use cases, including anomaly detection, capacity planning, and performance optimization. By acquiring holistic visibility of request and response cycles, developers can gain a nuanced understanding of workload behaviors, identifying latency peaks, traffic surges, or deviation from expected performance parameters.

In high-scale environments, observability data fuels AI-driven insights and automation strategies capable of preemptively scaling resources or rebalancing workloads to meet fluctuating demands, ensuring stable and responsive system behavior.

```
from opentelemetry import trace
from opentelemetry.exporter.jaeger import JaegerSpanExporter
from opentelemetry.sdk.trace import TracerProvider
from opentelemetry.sdk.trace.export import BatchSpanProcessor

trace.set_tracer_provider(TracerProvider())
tracer = trace.get_tracer(__name__)

# Configure Jaeger Exporter
jaeger_exporter = JaegerSpanExporter(
    service_name="inventory-service",
    agent_host_name="jaeger-agent.local",
    agent_port=6831,
)

# Adding the exporter to the tracing back-end
span_processor = BatchSpanProcessor(jaeger_exporter)
trace.get_tracer_provider().add_span_processor(span_processor)

with tracer.start_as_current_span("process-order"):
    # Simulated business logic execution
    time.sleep(1)
```

The Python code exemplifies implementing OpenTelemetry with a Jaeger exporter in a service, allowing finer-grained tracing of operations such as 'process-order'. The ability to inspect trace data provides critical insights into latency and execution behavior at both granular and aggregate levels.

Adopting observability practices via Dapr enhances the operational oversight of complex microservice architectures by creating a feedback loop between operational outcomes and system adjustments. Alerting frameworks, driven by observability data, notify operational teams of anomalies, enabling timely interventions that curtail emerging disruptions.

Through meticulous analysis of observability data, organizations can foster continuous improvement cycles—iteratively refining service invocations, optimizing resource deployments, and harmonizing the service interactions that support end-user experiences.

By implementing observability in Dapr, organizations achieve heightened transparency within microservice interactions, spotlighting operational inefficiencies while providing tangible pathways for optimization. Dapr's layered approach to observability—including distributed traces, expansive logging, and meticulous metric collection—cultivates comprehensive introspection into distributed application behavior, equipping organizations with the necessary insights to fortify, sustain, and advance their microservices ecosystems.

6.6 Developing Fault-Tolerant Applications

In the evolving landscape of cloud-native architectures, fault tolerance is an indispensable attribute of modern software systems. Fault-tolerant applications are designed to maintain functionality despite encountering problems such as network failures, service interruptions, or hardware malfunctions. Dapr (Distributed Application Runtime) provides a suite of abstractions and tools that empower developers to build robust, fault-tolerant microservices that minimize disruptions by managing failures gracefully. This section explores strategies for developing fault-tolerant applications using Dapr, illustrating mechanisms that enhance resilience and maintain operability when adversities occur.

Fault-tolerant systems embody redundancy, failover mechanisms, isolation, and graceful degradation, ensuring that a failure in one component does not cascade into systemic crashes. These systems typically employ patterns like retries, circuit breakers, bulkheads, and fail-safes to deliver reliability and resilience in the face of adversities.

One of the foundational features offered by Dapr for achieving fault tolerance is its sidecar pattern. The sidecar acts as an intermediary between services, providing standardized interfaces and managing aspects such as service discovery, communication protocols, and error handling. This pattern abstracts cross-cutting concerns from the application logic, enabling developers to focus on building core functionality while the sidecar manages resilience strategies.

At the heart of Dapr's strategy for fault-tolerant applications is its support for resilient communication patterns. By leveraging advanced retries, timeouts, and circuit breaker configurations, Dapr ensures that interactions between services remain robust against transient and persistent failures.

```
apiVersion: dapr.io/v1alpha1
kind: Configuration
metadata:
  name: fault-tolerant-settings
spec:
  resiliency:
    policies:
      retry:
        policy: backoff
        maxRetries: 5
        interval: "100ms"
      circuitBreaker:
        trip:
          failureThreshold: 0.1
          minimumNumberOfCalls: 10
        resetTimeout: "30s"
      timeout: "15s"
```

The YAML configuration above demonstrates how fault tolerance is configured within Dapr using a combination of resiliency policies. The retry policy adopts a backoff strategy with a specific interval, retrying failed requests up to five times. The circuit breaker trips if more than 10% of the calls fail, and a timeout ensures that calls are capped at a 15-second duration if unresponsive.

Resilience begins with the robust handling of communication failures. Dapr's sidecar manages both inbound and outbound service calls, seamlessly implementing retry logic and timeouts. The inclusion of circuit breakers addresses potential cascading failures by monitoring service responses and halting requests to malfunctioning services until they recover.

A critical aspect of developing fault-tolerant applications is embracing idempotency, where operations can be executed multiple times without producing undesirable side effects. Ensuring that services are idempotent allows Dapr to safely apply retries without concern for data corruption or operation duplication.

Isolation, achieved through patterns like bulkheads and service-level segmentation, prevents failures from propagating across service boundaries. Dapr facilitates isolation by providing dedicated sidecars for each service instance. This decoupling ensures that resource

6.6. DEVELOPING FAULT-TOLERANT APPLICATIONS

constraints or failures in one service do not degrade the performance or reliability of others.

State management and transactional integrity are essential in fault-tolerant architectures. Dapr's state management APIs offer transactional capabilities that facilitate atomic operations, allowing services to maintain consistency across distributed data stores.

```
import dapr.clients

with dapr.clients.DaprClient() as client:
    order_id = "order-123"
    order_data = {"productId": "298", "quantity": 1}

    # Save order state
    client.save_state(store_name="statestore", key=order_id, value=order_data)

    # Retrieve order state
    response = client.get_state(store_name="statestore", key=order_id)
    print(response.data)
```

The Python example illustrates using Dapr's state management API to save and retrieve application state data reliably. State persistence, facilitated by Dapr's pluggable state stores, allows services to recover from failures and maintain continuity without data loss.

Failover strategies in Dapr are inherently supported through load balancing and service mesh integrations. By dynamically redirecting requests from failing instances to healthy ones, Dapr ensures continuity in service availability, effectively handling node failures in cloud-native environments.

Monitoring is vital for fault tolerance, providing an observability layer that identifies potential issues before they escalate. Dapr incorporates profiling, logging, and tracing capabilities compatible with industry-standard observability tools like Grafana, Prometheus, and Zipkin. By analyzing trends and anomalies in metrics, logs, and traces, operators can uncover bottlenecks, balance loads, and refine resilience configurations proactively.

Automation and infrastructure as code (IaC) practices complement fault-tolerant application development by provisioning self-healing deployment environments. Resource scaling, container orchestration, and policy enforcement processes integrated within Kubernetes and Dapr establish adaptive infrastructure capable of responding to failures with minimal manual intervention.

Developing fault-tolerant applications calls for a multi-layered approach, combining redundancy with smart failure management strategies. The paradigms facilitated by Dapr, including robust error handling, stateful resilience, and automatic failover, form a synergy that drives forward reliable software practices. By amalgamating Dapr's capabilities, developers craft resilient architectures that excel in uptime, delivery, and performance—creating a technological foundation that aligns with the expectations and demands of modern cloud-native applications.

Chapter 7

Dapr's Role in Observability and Monitoring

This chapter explores how Dapr enhances observability and monitoring in microservices environments by providing comprehensive telemetry capabilities, including metrics, logs, and traces. It details configuring Dapr for effective monitoring, integrating with popular tools like Prometheus and Grafana, and implementing request tracing to identify performance issues. The chapter also covers creating custom metrics and following best practices to ensure efficient monitoring and debugging of Dapr-based applications, facilitating improved operational insights and system performance.

7.1 Overview of Observability in Microservices

Observability in the context of microservices is a pivotal topic, especially given the distributed and often complex architecture that microservices entail. Essentially, observability provides the ability to gain insights into system performance, health, and operation, which is vital for ensuring reliability, efficiency, and detectability of issues within microservices. As microservices are designed to perform discrete tasks and operate independently, yet also interact with one another to deliver complex functionalities, observability becomes crucial to trace, log, and monitor these interactions effectively.

A well-implemented observability strategy enables developers and operators to form a coherent understanding of system behavior, which is critical for troubleshooting and optimizing workflows. This involves the collection, storage, and analysis of telemetry data—comprising metrics, logs, and traces—across all components of a microservices-based application.

Metrics are quantitative measures that describe the performance and health of a system. They are typically numeric and aggregated over a fixed time interval, providing insight into various aspects such as system load, process utilization, memory usage, and network latency. Metrics are crucial in providing real-time insights and triggering alerts when anomalies or predefined thresholds are breached.

Logs are streams of timestamped records detailing a sequence of events. Logs serve as the forensic evidence for what happened in the system and are indispensable during fault analysis and debugging. Efficient logging requires structured data, including contextual information pertinent to the event being logged, aiding in effective querying and analysis.

Traces provide a more granular view by capturing the flow and timing of requests as they traverse through the different services. A trace follows a request across its journey in the system, offering visibility into latencies and identifying potential bottlenecks. Traces are instrumental in understanding request paths, ensuring compliance with service-level objectives (SLOs), and diagnosing inefficiencies.

7.1. OVERVIEW OF OBSERVABILITY IN MICROSERVICES

One key aspect of observability is that these telemetry attributes should not be viewed in isolation, but rather in conjunction with one another. Together, they create a comprehensive picture of the system. The practices of combining and analyzing metrics, logs, and traces can be instrumental in detecting patterns, predicting failures, and enhancing the robustness of microservices architectures.

Integration and Tools

To effectively gather and utilize telemetry data, integration with suitable tools and platforms is essential. Tools such as Prometheus, Grafana, and Elasticsearch provide sophisticated methods for collecting, querying, and visualizing telemetry data. They enable teams to set up dashboards, alerting mechanisms, and reporting systems that are vital for proactive monitoring.

Prometheus, for example, is an open-source system monitoring and alerting toolkit that excels at collecting and querying time-series data. Prometheus's ability to scrape metrics data from endpoints is highly beneficial. Consider the following code snippet demonstrating a basic configuration for Prometheus deployment:

```
global:
  scrape_interval: 15s # By default, scrape targets every 15 seconds.
  evaluation_interval: 15s # Evaluate rules every 15 seconds.

scrape_configs:
  - job_name: 'microservices_app'
    static_configs:
      - targets: ['localhost:9100', 'localhost:9200']
```

This configuration instructs Prometheus to scrape metrics from endpoints running at localhost ports 9100 and 9200 every 15 seconds, specifically tailored to a microservices deployment. These metrics can then be visualized using Grafana, which seamlessly connects with Prometheus to provide rich visual insights.

Grafana enables the creation of dashboards built from a variety of data sources, offering comprehensive visuals for metrics analysis.

Designing for Observability

Designing systems with observability in mind from the onset ensures that each microservice is equipped to produce the necessary telemetry data. Critical to this design is the instrumentation of applications. Instrumentation facilitates the collection of telemetry data by embedding sensors in code. These sensors are strategically placed to capture meaningful data at crucial points during execution, such as request arrival, processing stages, database queries, and external service calls.

Instrumentation can be achieved through libraries and frameworks that are integrated into services during development. OpenTelemetry, for example, offers a standardized set of APIs, libraries, and agents to enable observability in distributed systems. This open-source project is instrumental in generating, capturing, and exporting telemetry data through an API consistent across multiple platforms and environments.

Consider the following Python example demonstrating basic instrumentation using OpenTelemetry for tracing:

```
from opentelemetry import trace
from opentelemetry.sdk.trace import TracerProvider
from opentelemetry.sdk.trace.export import BatchSpanProcessor
from opentelemetry.exporter.otlp.trace_exporter import OTLPSpanExporter

# Setting up a trace provider
trace.set_tracer_provider(TracerProvider())
tracer = trace.get_tracer(__name__)

# Exporter for OTLP format
span_exporter = OTLPSpanExporter(endpoint="http://localhost:4317", insecure=
    True)
span_processor = BatchSpanProcessor(span_exporter)
trace.get_tracer_provider().add_span_processor(span_processor)

# Creating a trace
with tracer.start_as_current_span("operation"):
    # Simulate a process or operational task
    print("Tracing an operation")
```

This example sets up an OTLP exporter to transmit trace data from the application to an external collector service. Properly leveraging such frameworks simplifies the process of building observability into applications and enhances capabilities in tracing distributed transactions.

Challenges and Considerations

While observability provides substantial benefits, it is vital to handle it with certain considerations to prevent complexities, overhead, or misuse:

- *Data Overhead*: The constant recording or transmission of metrics, logs, and traces can generate significant data volumes. Careful design around what data is collected and how it is managed is crucial. Aggregation, sampling, and rate limiting can help control data growth.

- *Security and Compliance*: With increased observability, the potential exposure to sensitive information also increases. Proper access controls, data anonymization techniques, and adherence to compliance standards such as GDPR are necessary to protect both data and privacy.

- *Performance Impact*: Instrumentation and telemetry collection, if not optimized, can add latency to microservices. It is critical to ensure that observability mechanisms do not adversely impact the system's response times or throughput.

- *Integration Complexity*: Integrating observability tools with a microservices architecture can become complex due to the ever-changing nature of services and infrastructure. Leveraging standardized interfaces and reusable components can help mitigate these complexities.

Future Trends

As microservices architectures continue to evolve, observability will increasingly leverage advances in artificial intelligence and machine learning to predict anomalies and suggest corrective actions. This evolution aims at not merely observing the present state but also intelligently forecasting future states by analyzing telemetry data patterns over time.

Precision in observability ensures that microservices operators can maintain the required level of confidence in their systems under diverse and dynamic conditions, fostering an environment for innovation and agility.

The overview provided context and clarification around the role of observability in microservices, underscoring the importance of metrics, logs, and traces in creating resilient systems. As technology and methodologies continue to advance, the continuous improvement and implementation of effective observability will maintain their critical status in fostering highly available and dependable microservice architectures.

7.2 Telemetry with Dapr

Telemetry in the realm of microservices involves the systematic collection, processing, and analysis of data that reflects the collective behavior, performance, and health of individual services and the system as a whole. Dapr (Distributed Application Runtime), a portable, event-driven runtime, plays a significant role in the telemetry landscape by providing built-in observability capabilities. This section aims to delve deeply into how Dapr facilitates telemetry, offering extensive insights into its operational intricacies and methods of implementation.

Dapr is engineered to simplify the building of modern distributed applications by abstracting away complex infrastructure needs such as state management, service invocation, and observability. It adopts sidecar architecture, where each microservice runs alongside a Dapr sidecar. This architectural choice allows Dapr to intercept requests, manage state, and perform telemetry duties independently from the application code.

- **Telemetry Components:** Dapr collects telemetry data through three primary components: metrics, logs, and traces. These elements are vital for producing a comprehensive observability framework.

Metrics with Dapr:

Dapr automatically exports several metrics that offer insights into various facets of system performance. Metrics are exposed via a Prometheus-compatible endpoint, allowing seamless integration with monitoring systems that support Prometheus. Metrics in Dapr include data points such as latency distributions, request counts, error rates, and sidecar resource usage.

Here is how a typical Dapr metrics endpoint is configured:

```
apiVersion: dapr.io/v1alpha1
kind: Configuration
```

7.2. TELEMETRY WITH DAPR

```
metadata:
  name: myappconfig
spec:
  metrics:
    enabled: true
    rules:
      - name: "myapp_successful_request_count"
        query: "sum(increase(dapr_http_client_request_count{app_id=\"myapp\",
          code=\"200\"}[5m]))"
```

In this configuration, the metrics are configured to collect data on HTTP request counts that return a 200 status code, allowing teams to monitor successful interactions with the service.

Logs with Dapr:

Logging with Dapr is streamlined by its abstraction capabilities, enabling developers to focus on core logic rather than logging intricacies. Dapr assigns specific log categories and levels (e.g., Info, Debug, Error) facilitating precise logging across the service landscape. Each instance (or pod in Kubernetes environments) of a Daprized application generates logs for the service and Dapr sidecar.

Logs are formatted to include rich contextual metadata information, aiding teams in tracking service interactions and server messages through Dapr's sidecar container. It also supports structured logging, often required to parse logs efficiently.

Tracing with Dapr:

Request tracing provides unparalleled insight into the flow of data through a service ecosystem. Dapr leverages distributed tracing to enable visibility into call chains, pinpointing latencies, bottlenecks, and service dependencies. Utilizing standards such as W3C trace context, Dapr ensures trace continuity across service boundaries.

OpenTelemetry integration in Dapr helps emit trace data in a standardized manner. The traces can be exported to various backend systems like Zipkin, Jaeger, or any OpenTelemetry-compatible tracing system.

Consider the following configuration for enabling distributed tracing with Dapr:

```
apiVersion: dapr.io/v1alpha1
kind: Configuration
metadata:
  name: mytracingconfig
spec:
```

```
tracing:
    samplingRate: "1"  # 1 = 100\% trace sampling
zipkin:
    endpointAddress: "http://localhost:9411/api/v2/spans"
```

This setup provides guidance on collecting span data and creates a comprehensive trace through the system. The samplingRate parameter determines the percentage of requests to be traced, which is crucial for balancing detail against performance and storage considerations.

- **Implementing Telemetry with Dapr:** Integrating telemetry with Dapr is remarkably straightforward compared to conventional practices. The sidecar model automates the instrumentation process, allowing teams to access rich telemetry data with minimal code changes.

Here is a concise example of a simple microservice leveraging Dapr's telemetry:

```
import flask

app = flask.Flask(__name__)

@app.route('/process', methods=['GET', 'POST'])
def process():
    # Processing logic here —Dapr sidecar handles telemetry
    return "Processing request successfully"

if __name__ == '__main__':
    app.run(port=8080)  # Run service on port 8080
```

In this example, the Dapr sidecar automatically captures telemetry data for requests to the '/process' endpoint, including traces and metrics detailing execution time, request counts, and associated metadata.

- **Insights and Use Cases:** Implementing telemetry through Dapr can unlock significant operational efficiencies and reveal valuable insights into both system and component levels. It empowers organizations to respond proactively to changes, enhancing both reliability and performance.

  1. Performance Optimization: Telemetry aids in pinpointing inefficient services or methods that use excessive system resources or

introduce unnecessary latencies, enabling developers and operators to make informed optimizations.

2. Fault Diagnosis: Debugging distributed systems is challenging due to the asynchronous and stateless nature of microservices. Dapr telemetry provides necessary observations to trace issues and correlate system behaviors with underlying problems.

3. Scaling Decisions: Metrics on average load and failure distribution help determine which services require additional resources, assisting dynamic scaling.

4. Compliance and Security Monitoring: Detailed logging and trace analytics can ascertain compliance with security policies, while facilitating audits and incident investigations.

5. End-to-end Visibility: Tracing and comprehensive logging provide visibility across all services, supporting effective management of service-level objectives (SLOs) and agreements (SLAs).

- **Challenges and Considerations:** Despite its advantages, implementing telemetry with Dapr requires attentiveness to specific challenges:

- Data Volume and Management: Telemetry data grows rapidly, necessitating strategic decisions around storage solutions and data retention policies to keep costs manageable.

- Overhead Management: Although the sidecar model simplifies deployment, it introduces additional network hops and can impact resource utilization. Efficient resource planning and performance benchmarking are essential.

- Security and Compliance: Telemetry inherently stores sensitive data which may include user information or system operation details. Ensuring robust encryption and access control is mandatory to prevent data breaches.

- Integration Complexity: Understanding and configuring diverse backends for telemetry data storage, visualization, or alerting can require considerable expertise, particularly in a multi-cloud or hybrid environment.

Implementing Dapr's telemetry capabilities leads to improved responsiveness to faults, better performance management, and comprehensive understanding from system-level operations to specific service interactions. Despite potential challenges in data management and performance overhead, these can be appropriately managed through considered design and strategy.

Through its versatile support for integration with popular observability platforms, Dapr stands out as a powerful enabler of reliable and scalable microservices architectures. Its ability to encompass both horizontal scalability and vertical integration with CI/CD pipelines, automated deployments, and modern DevOps practices escalates the telemetry landscape to new heights, ultimately culminating in superior system health and operational excellence.

7.3 Configuring Dapr for Monitoring

Effective monitoring is a cornerstone of managing modern applications built on microservices architectures. Dapr, an open-source runtime that simplifies the development of distributed applications, provides comprehensive tools for monitoring through its observability features. This section delves into the procedures and considerations involved in configuring Dapr to support robust monitoring capabilities, explicating on steps and best practices to harness Dapr's potential in this realm.

The primary goal of configuring Dapr for monitoring is to ensure seamless collection, processing, and visualization of telemetry data — metrics, logs, and traces — from various microservices and their sidecar components. By standardizing this process, Dapr enables developers and operators to maintain an operational overview, quickly diagnose issues, and optimize performance.

- **Step 1: Installing Dapr**
  Before configuring monitoring features, Dapr must be correctly installed and initialized in your environment, whether it's a local development machine or a cluster system like Kubernetes. Installation typically involves downloading the Dapr CLI and running

the initialization command, which sets up the necessary dependencies.

```
# Install Dapr CLI
wget -q https://raw.githubusercontent.com/dapr/cli/master/install/install.
    sh -O - | /bin/bash

# Initialize Dapr runtime (local environment)
dapr init
```

This setup pulls and runs the Dapr runtime's containers on a loopback network alongside your services, deploying components like Redis and Zipkin for state management and tracing, respectively.

- **Step 2: Configuring the Dapr Sidecar**
  In Kubernetes environments, Dapr runs as a sidecar alongside each application pod. This configuration is managed by annotating the pod template within the deployment manifests, thus linking a service to its corresponding Dapr sidecar.

```
apiVersion: apps/v1
kind: Deployment
metadata:
  name: front-end
spec:
  replicas: 3
  template:
    metadata:
      annotations:
        dapr.io/enabled: "true"
        dapr.io/app-id: "front-end"
    spec:
      containers:
      - name: server
        image: myapp/server:latest
        ports:
        - containerPort: 8080
```

These annotations automatically bind telemetry features like tracing and metrics to the application without modifying the entire codebase. Furthermore, dapr.io/app-id is crucial as it serves as the primary identifier across Dapr resources.

- **Step 3: Configuring Metrics Collection**
  Dapr exports a comprehensive set of metrics in a Prometheus format. By default, these metrics come enabled and can be queried using Prometheus-compatible tools. When integrating

with Prometheus, the primary task is to configure the system to scrape the Dapr sidecar's metrics endpoint.

```
scrape_configs:
  - job_name: 'dapr_sidecar'
    metrics_path: '/v1.0/metrics'
    kubernetes_sd_configs:
    - role: pod
    relabel_configs:
    - source_labels: [
        __meta_kubernetes_pod_annotation_dapr_io_enabled]
      action: keep
      regex: true
```

In Kubernetes, this example instructs Prometheus to target pods with the annotation dapr.io/enabled: "true" and to scrape metrics from the path /v1.0/metrics. This configuration ensures that any pod running a Dapr sidecar will have its telemetry data automatically captured.

- **Step 4: Logging Setup and Configuration**
  Logging in Dapr involves streams from both the main application and its sidecar. It is prudent to adopt a centralized logging approach to aggregate logs from different services into a single platform for easy analysis.

  Here is an example of integrating Dapr logs with a central logging solution like Elastic Stack:

```
apiVersion: apps/v1
kind: DaemonSet
metadata:
  name: fluentd
spec:
  template:
    spec:
      containers:
      - name: fluentd
        image: fluent/fluentd-kubernetes-daemonset
        env:
          - name: FLUENT_ELASTICSEARCH_HOST
            value: "elasticsearch-logging"
          - name: FLUENT_ELASTICSEARCH_PORT
            value: "9200"
```

The configuration uses Fluentd to aggregate and forward logs from all nodes in a Kubernetes cluster to Elasticsearch. Integrating such setups can be accomplished by ASP.NET, Java, or any language-specific logging backends that push logs to stdout or a custom interface.

- **Step 5: Tracing Configuration**
  Enabling distributed tracing in Dapr involves setting the tracing configuration to determine how much trace data is collected and where it is sent. Dapr supports exporting trace data to platforms supporting Zipkin or OpenTelemetry.

  ```
  apiVersion: dapr.io/v1alpha1
  kind: Configuration
  metadata:
    name: mytracing
  spec:
    tracing:
      samplingRate: "0.5" # 50% requests are sampled
      openTelemetryCollector:
        endpoint: "http://otel-collector:4317"
  ```

  This configuration specifies the sampling rate and the OpenTelemetry collector's endpoint for trace data export. By controlling the sampling rate, teams can balance between granularity and system performance burdens.

- **Advanced Considerations**
  When configuring Dapr for monitoring, several advanced considerations can optimize both the quality and efficiency of telemetry data handling:

    - **Security and Privacy Concerns**: Clarity around what data is logged or traced is important to avoid unintentionally exposing sensitive information. It's crucial to implement permission controls, use TLS for data in transit, and consider tokenization or anonymization for stored data.

    - **Performance Implications**: While Dapr's autonomous mechanisms in collecting telemetry alleviate some workloads, they can still impose network and CPU overhead. Benchmarking pre- and post-deployment helps in understanding the true resource footprint. Additionally, load testing validates that the monitoring setup persistently operates at production scale without introducing bottlenecks.

    - **Resource Limitations and Quotas**: Implementing quotas for Sidecar resources ensures that observability doesn't impede the core functionalities of services, particularly in resource-constrained environments. This means setting appropriate memory and CPU limits based on expected sidecar workloads.

- **Configuration Versioning and Management**: Telemetry configurations should be maintained as part of a version-controlled system. Continuous integration pipelines should handle deploying updated configurations seamlessly across environments, preventing drift and maintaining consistency.

- **Alerting and Visualization**: The telemetry data collected through Prometheus, Elasticsearch, and tracing systems is not inherently useful until it is interpreted. Integrating data visualization tools like Grafana, Kibana, or Jaeger can transform raw data into comprehensible insights. Setting up alerting rules within these tools ensures teams receive timely notifications of potential issues.

- **Conclusion**
Configuring Dapr for monitoring is an essential endeavor to harness the full benefits of microservices-based applications. The standardized procedures laid out ensure that systems are equipped with precise, real-time insights via metrics, logs, and traces. While conducting these configurations, attention to detail is crucial, particularly concerning data privacy, security considerations, and system performance impacts.

This foundational setup for monitoring creates a resilient and scalable platform, allowing developers and system administrators to focus on enhancing the core functionalities of services, addressing issues proactively, and optimizing system behavior for overall reliability and efficiency. With Dapr's extensive support for integration and flexibility in configuration, it stands poised as a powerful ally in ensuring application-wide observability within fast-evolving, distributed systems.

7.4 Integrating with Monitoring Tools

Integrating Dapr with a variety of monitoring tools is essential to leverage the full power of its observability features within distributed microservices environments. Monitoring tools provide the necessary infrastructure and interfaces for collecting, aggregating, visualizing, and alerting based on telemetry data, which includes metrics, logs, and traces. This section delves deeper into the practical steps and strategies for effectively integrating Dapr with prominent monitoring solutions such as Prometheus, Grafana, and Elasticsearch, among others.

The integration with these tools enables teams to interpret and respond to the telemetry data generated by the Dapr runtime, ultimately enhancing system reliability, performance, and operability.

Integrating Dapr with Prometheus

Prometheus is an open-source systems monitoring and alerting toolkit widely used for capturing and storing time-series data. Dapr's metrics are inherently compatible with Prometheus, thanks to their export in a Prometheus-friendly format.

Step-by-Step Integration Guide:

- **Set Up Prometheus:**

    Begin by installing Prometheus in your infrastructure. For Kubernetes, Prometheus can be deployed using Helm charts or Kubernetes manifests tailored for your environment.

    ```
    helm repo add prometheus-community https://prometheus-community.github.io/helm-charts
    helm repo update
    helm install prometheus prometheus-community/prometheus
    ```

    This installation ensures a fully functioning Prometheus instance ready to scrape metrics from Dapr sidecars.

- **Configure Prometheus to Scrape Dapr Metrics:**

    Adjust Prometheus's configuration file to include a new scrape target for Dapr sidecars. The metrics endpoint '/v1.0/metrics' should be incorporated into the Prometheus scrape configurations.

```
scrape_configs:
  - job_name: 'dapr'
    kubernetes_sd_configs:
      - role: endpoints
    relabel_configs:
      - source_labels: [__meta_kubernetes_endpoint_port_name]
        action: keep
        regex: dapr-metrics
```

These adjustments ensure that Prometheus aggregates data offered by all services annotated for Dapr monitoring.

- **Visualize Data in Prometheus UI:**

  Once configuration is complete, you can navigate to the Prometheus web UI to query and explore Dapr-generated metrics. Queries can be defined using PromQL, Prometheus's query language, to extract meaningful insights.

Visualizing with Grafana

Grafana is a leading open-source analytics and monitoring tool that specializes in visualizing time-series data. Its compatibility with Prometheus makes it an ideal choice for rendering visuals for Dapr telemetry.

Integration Steps:

- **Install Grafana:**

  Grafana can also be installed similarly to Prometheus. Below commands demonstrate using Helm charts to deploy Grafana within a Kubernetes cluster:

  ```
  helm repo add grafana https://grafana.github.io/helm-charts
  helm repo update
  helm install grafana grafana/grafana
  ```

- **Add Prometheus as a Data Source:**

  Navigate to the Grafana UI, and under configuration settings, select data sources to add Prometheus. Enter the appropriate URL endpoint where Prometheus is serving data (e.g., 'http://<PROMETHEUS-SERVICE>:9090').

7.4. INTEGRATING WITH MONITORING TOOLS

- **Create and Import Dashboards:**

  Grafana supports pre-built dashboard templates for Dapr if available or permits constructing custom dashboards by configuring metrics directly via Grafana's interface using PromQL. Dapr offers sample dashboards that can be adjusted based on telemetry requirements.

  ```
  {
    "dashboard": {
      "title": "Dapr Metrics",
      "panels": [
        {
          "type": "graph",
          "title": "Request Count",
          "targets": [
            {
              "expr": "sum(rate(dapr_grpc_client_method_counts{}[5m])) by (instance)"
            }
          ]
        }
      ]
    }
  }
  ```

  This JSON defines a simple panel in Grafana that tracks request counts across instances, providing visuals for performance evaluations.

Integrating with Elasticsearch

Elasticsearch is an open-source distributed search and analytics engine that can be used to aggregate logs and traces from Dapr and other microservices.

Setup and Integration Process:

- **Deploy Elasticsearch:**

  Kubernetes users can opt for deploying Elasticsearch using the official Helm charts or standard deployment manifests. Consider the following Helm chart deployment:

  ```
  helm repo add elastic https://helm.elastic.co
  helm repo update
  helm install elasticsearch elastic/elasticsearch
  ```

- **Configuring Log Shipping:**

Utilize Fluentd or another log-forwarding solution within your environment to capture logs from Dapr-enabled applications and send them to Elasticsearch.

```
<source>
  @type tail
  path /var/log/dapr/*.log
  pos_file /var/log/dapr/log.pos
  tag dapr.*
</source>
<match dapr.**>
  @type elasticsearch
  host elasticsearch-master
  port 9200
  logstash_format true
</match>
```

This configuration file captures and forwards logs from the standard Dapr log directory to a specified Elasticsearch index.

- **Leverage Kibana for Visualization:**

    Elasticsearch is typically paired with Kibana to create dashboards and perform analytics on log data. Once logs are ingested, Kibana can provide an interactive way to query and visualize this data, enhancing your ability to monitor Dapr and application interactions through comprehensive dashboards.

Enabling Distributed Tracing with Zipkin and Jaeger

Distributed tracing solutions such as Zipkin and Jaeger can both be integrated with Dapr for full visibility across service calls.

Zipkin Integration:

- **Deploy Zipkin:**

    For local testing, Zipkin can be started quickly via Docker:

    ```
    docker run -d -p 9411:9411 openzipkin/zipkin
    ```

- **Configure Dapr for Zipkin Export:**

    Adjust the tracing configuration on the Dapr configuration file, setting the endpoint to point to the Zipkin collector.

    ```
    tracing:
      samplingRate: "0.1"
      zipkin:
        endpointAddress: "http://localhost:9411/api/v2/spans"
    ```

7.4. INTEGRATING WITH MONITORING TOOLS

This configuration tracks a portion of requests for performance analysis.

Jaeger Integration:

- **Deploy Jaeger:**

Equivalent to Zipkin, Jaeger can be up and running using Docker or Helm in Kubernetes environments.

```
docker run -d --name jaeger \
  -e COLLECTOR_ZIPKIN_HTTP_PORT=9411 \
  -p 5775:5775/udp \
  -p 6831:6831/udp \
  -p 6832:6832/udp \
  -p 5778:5778 \
  -p 16686:16686 \
  -p 14268:14268 \
  -p 14250:14250 \
  -p 9411:9411 \
  jaegertracing/all-in-one:1.23
```

- **Adjust Dapr Settings for Tracing:**

Ensure Dapr's OpenTelemetry tracing configuration setup, directing spans to Jaeger.

```
tracing:
  samplingRate: "0.2"
  openTelemetryCollector:
    endpoint: "http://localhost:55680"
```

With Dapr and Jaeger integrated, you can visualize complex service relationships and diagnose latency issues through the Jaeger UI.

Automated Alerts and Management

Implementing automated alerts is an instrumental feature of these integrated monitoring systems. Configuring alerts via Prometheus server rule files, such as:

```
groups:
  - name: DaprAlerts
    rules:
    - alert: HighRequestLatency
      expr: histogram_quantile(0.99, sum(rate(dapr_grpc_client_duration_bucket{le
          ="+Inf"}[5m])) by (le)) > 0.5
      for: 5m
```

```
labels:
    severity: "high"
annotations:
    summary: "High Request Latency Detected"
    description: "Request latency over threshold (>0.5s) for longer than 5 minutes."
```

These rules notify teams in real-time when anomalies or breaches in performance thresholds occur.

Integrating Dapr with monitoring tools is a core capability that enables data-driven decisions and system stability across microservices ecosystems. The synergy between Dapr's telemetry engine and external dashboards, storage, and alert frameworks effortlessly creates a cohesive, insightful observability infrastructure.

Achieving seamless integration requires not only proper tool setup but an understanding of each tool's capabilities, an effort that translates telemetry data into actionable insights concerning system performance, health, and user experience. This comprehensive monitoring solution is what ultimately allows developers and IT operators to sustain, scale, and enhance the performance of Dapr-based distributed applications effectively.

7.5 Tracing Requests with Dapr

Tracing requests is a crucial aspect of observability in microservices architectures, providing visibility into the path a request takes as it traverses through various services. Dapr offers powerful distributed tracing capabilities that facilitate the tracking of requests, helping developers and operators diagnose performance issues, identify bottlenecks, and optimize system interactions. This section aims to elucidate the underlying mechanisms, configurations, and applications of tracing within a Dapr-enabled environment.

Distributed tracing is designed to capture and record trace data for each request processed by the system. This data includes timing information, service interactions, and critical metadata, enabling the reconstruction of request paths and dependencies between services. Tracing provides insights into latency distributions, failure points, and flow inconsistencies, which are vital for maintaining and enhancing the reliability of microservices deployments.

Understanding Distributed Tracing

Distributed tracing in microservices allows tracking of requests across multiple services and their interconnected paths. By capturing detailed trace data, it becomes possible to visualize how an application performs, why certain operations failed, and how each service component interacts.

A trace consists of a series of spans, each representing a unit of work done by the service or application component. Spans comprise various data points such as operation names, timestamps, metadata, and links to parent spans, which together form a directed acyclic graph (DAG) depicting the request flow.

Key Concepts:

- **Trace:** A collection of spans that model the workflow of a request through different components.
- **Span:** The fundamental unit of work in tracing, capturing metadata for a single operation.
- **Context Propagation:** Involves carrying trace information across service boundaries, ensuring continuity and coherence of traces.

Implementing Tracing in Dapr

Dapr natively supports distributed tracing via sidecars using standardized trace context formats, effectively abstracting the complexity involved in instrumenting applications for tracing. The OpenTelemetry standard allows Dapr to integrate seamlessly with various tracing backends.

Step-by-Step Configuration:

1. Enable Tracing in Dapr Configuration:

The first step to implement request tracing is to configure the tracing settings within the Dapr configuration file, defining sampling rates and specifying endpoint addresses for trace exports.

```
apiVersion: dapr.io/v1alpha1
```

```
kind: Configuration
metadata:
  name: tracingconfig
spec:
  tracing:
    samplingRate: "0.5" # 50% sampling rate for tracing.
    zipkin:
      endpointAddress: "http://zipkin:9411/api/v2/spans"
```

This configuration specifies a 50% sampling rate, meaning half of all requests will be traced. The traces are sent to a Zipkin-compatible backend for storage and analysis.

2. **Deploy a Tracing Backend:**

To store and analyze trace data, deploy a tracing backend like Zipkin or Jaeger. For example, deploying Zipkin using Docker can be achieved as follows:

```
docker run -d -p 9411:9411 openzipkin/zipkin
```

This step ensures that the Zipkin server is ready to receive and manage trace data from Dapr sidecars.

3. **Optimize Service Annotations:**

For Kubernetes deployments, ensure Dapr annotations are present within your deployment manifests for each microservice as follows:

```
apiVersion: apps/v1
kind: Deployment
metadata:
  name: service-a
spec:
  replicas: 2
  template:
    metadata:
      annotations:
        dapr.io/enabled: "true"
        dapr.io/app-id: "service-a"
    spec:
      containers:
      - name: app
        image: myorg/service-a:latest
        ports:
        - containerPort: 8080
```

These annotations enable the automatic inclusion of tracing capabilities provided by Dapr's sidecar architecture.

4. **Review Instrumentation:**

7.5. TRACING REQUESTS WITH DAPR

While Dapr abstracts much of the complexity of manual instrumentation, consider reviewing application code for potential enhancements, such as adding custom span metadata.

```
from opentelemetry import trace

tracer = trace.get_tracer(__name__)

with tracer.start_as_current_span("service_operation") as span:
    span.set_attribute("custom.metadata", "value")
    # Operational logic
```

Custom attributes provide context-specific information that aids in detailed analysis and troubleshooting of transactions.

Deep Analysis of Trace Data

Once tracing is established, analysis and visualization tools like Zipkin or Jaeger's web interface can be leveraged to gain insights from trace data:

- **Latency Analysis:** Assessing latency for requests helps identify patterns and intermittencies, guiding targeted optimizations or refactoring efforts.

- **Error Analysis:** Identifying errors and correlating logs with traces establishes a clearer picture of failure sources, crucial for diagnosis and bug fixes.

- **Bottleneck Identification:** Tracing highlights services contributing most to overall latency or operations frequently failing, assisting prioritization for resource allocation or further investigation.

Sample Use Cases

Tracing requests within Dapr-empowered architectures unveils opportunities to improve application resiliency and operational efficiencies. Some notable applications and use cases include:

1. Performance Tuning:

By monitoring trace latencies, operators can pinpoint bottlenecks in service decision chains, recognize inefficient query execution paths, or adjust microservice distributions dynamically to scale inductively with demand.

2. **Debugging and Fault Isolation:**

Trace paths reveal the precise sequence of service calls leading to an error state, showing where in the call tree a failure might have originated, allowing engineers to isolate and resolve issues swiftly through contextual and forensic debugging.

3. **Dependency Mapping:**

Traces effectively map service dependencies, providing a bird's-eye view of how components interact. This real-time dynamic mapping assists in evaluating the impact of architectural changes on dependent systems or live experiments under chaos engineering protocols.

4. **Impact Analysis:**

Introducing new features, configuration alterations, or code deployments can be scrutinized by analyzing their impact on service response times and error rates, negating regressions or unplanned drift in service quality.

Challenges and Considerations

While tracing reduces complexity in understanding service interactions, it also introduces several challenges:

- **Sampling Limitations:** While high sampling rates capture more in-depth insights, they can incur increased processing loads and storage costs. Balancing granularity and resource efficiency is imperative.

- **Data Security:** Distributed traces may inadvertently capture sensitive user information. Ensuring trace data is sufficiently redacted, encrypted, or anonymized mitigates exposure risks.

- **Scalability of Trace Backends:** Trace data grows exponentially. Adequate scaling and efficient indexing strategies for backends like Zipkin or Jaeger are vital to ensure performance isn't compromised.

Dapr's approach to tracing requests provides developers and operators with an extensive, robust view of microservice interactions and performance. By integrating distributed tracing efficiently, it becomes possible to maintain high levels of service quality and reliability, essential in today's always-on, distributed environments.

With comprehensive trace management, Dapr enables proactive optimization, precise fault detection, and robust dependency monitoring, fostering a proactive culture of continuous improvement. The integration simplicity combined with the powerful observability framework epitomizes Dapr's role in modern cloud-native infrastructure—balancing efficiency, scalability, and transparency.

7.6 Custom Metrics and Logging

In the domain of microservices, custom metrics and logging are vital for capturing non-standardized metrics and detailed log information that reflect specific business and operational requirements. Dapr—the Distributed Application Runtime—facilitates the creation and management of custom metrics and logs, empowering developers and administrators to fine-tune observability to match application-specific needs.

Understanding Custom Metrics

Custom metrics are user-defined quantitative measures that extend beyond default telemetry. They provide insights tailored to the particular operational goals or business logic of an application. Custom metrics might include specific API request counts, data pipeline processing speeds, cache hit ratios, and more.

Key Characteristics of Custom Metrics:

- **Granularity:** Define metrics with a resolution that suits the operational requirements, whether high frequency for real-time monitoring, or aggregated spans for trend analysis.

- **Contextual Insight:** Embed metrics with metadata relevant to the operational context, aiding in more precise interpretation and actionability.

- **Emphasis on Application Performance:** Custom metrics focus heavily on aspects like request throughput, latency profiles, error distributions, or specific business transactions, which are not captured by default instrumentation.

Implementing Custom Metrics with Dapr

Dapr's extensible architecture allows for seamless integration and updating of custom metrics within its telemetry ecosystem.

Creating Custom Metrics:

1. **Define the Metric:** Identify the metric type—counter, gauge, histogram, or summary—based on what you aim to measure. Counters are ideal for monotonically increasing values such as requests served, while gauges represent fluctuating values like current memory usage.

2. **Code Implementation:** Utilize a language-specific client library that adheres to standardized interfaces (e.g., OpenTelemetry) to instrument the application code. Below is an example using Python to implement a custom metric using OpenTelemetry's metrics API.

```
from opentelemetry import metrics
from opentelemetry.sdk.metrics import MeterProvider
from opentelemetry.sdk.metrics.export import ConsoleMetricsExporter,
    PeriodicExportingMetricReader

# Initialize metrics provider
metrics.set_meter_provider(MeterProvider())
meter = metrics.get_meter(__name__)

# Define a counter metric
request_counter = meter.create_counter(
    "myapp_requests_handled",
    description="Counts the number of handled requests",
)

# Increments the counter
def handle_request():
    # Logic to handle a request
    request_counter.add(1)
```

This example defines a simple counter myapp_requests_handled that increments each time a request is processed.

3. **Exporting Metrics:** Configure the appropriate backend for metrics storage and visualization. The use of export mechanisms, such as the OpenTelemetry Collector, enables data funneling to monitoring platforms like Prometheus for long-term storage, querying, and visualization.

7.6. CUSTOM METRICS AND LOGGING

```
exporter = ConsoleMetricsExporter()
reader = PeriodicExportingMetricReader(exporter)
```

This configuration prints metrics to the console, although in production, you would define an exporter appropriate to the environment, such as a Prometheus exporter.

4. **Integration with Dapr Sidecar:** For metrics to be consumed, ensure that your application correctly interacts with the Dapr sidecar. This might involve exposing custom metrics endpoints or interposing Dapr APIs during instrumentation process.

Advanced Logging in Dapr

Logs document application execution and are pivotal for understanding events, errors, and operational flows that occur within an application. Dapr augments traditional logging capabilities by collating detailed log data in a structured format via the sidecar architecture.

Creating Custom Logs:

1. **Setup the Logging Framework:** Utilize structured logging practices that align with the application's environment. Language-specific logging libraries are employed to capture, format, and output logs. Here's an example using Python's built-in 'logging' module with adjustments for structured logging.

```python
import logging

# Configure logger settings
logger = logging.getLogger(__name__)
logging.basicConfig(level=logging.INFO, format="%(asctime)s | %(
    levelname)s | %(message)s")

# Log messages with context
def process_transaction(tx_id, amount):
    logger.info("Processing transaction", extra={"transaction_id": tx_id, "
        amount": amount})
    # Transaction processing logic
```

This logging setup ensures messages are timestamped and include metadata like transaction specifics, supporting detailed traceability and contextual analysis.

2. **Centralize Log Aggregation:** Dapr logs can be collected using

log aggregators like Fluentd or Logstash. These agents collect, filter, and centralize logs from multiple services, which can be sent to an Elasticsearch backend for testing and long-term storage.

```
<source>
  @type tail
  path /var/log/dapr/*.log
  pos_file /var/log/dapr/pos.file
  tag dapr.services
</source>

<match dapr.services>
  @type stdout
  @log_level info
  @type elasticsearch
  host elasticsearch
  port 9200
  index_name dapr-logs
</match>
```

By tailoring such configurations, the Dapr environment dynamically adjusts the scope of logging to balance storage limitations and informational yield.

3. **Analyzing Logs with Kibana:** Using Kibana, a visualization layer for elastic search data clusters, enables advanced dashboards and querying capabilities. Logs can illuminate application workflow patterns, isolate errors, and provide metrics on operations that intersect with application logic.

```
{
  "title": "Dapr Application Logs",
  "panels": [
    {
      "type": "visualization",
      "title": "Log Severity Count",
      "metrics": [
        {
          "type": "count",
          "schema": "metric",
          "field": "_index"
        }
      ],
      "aggs": [
        {
          "type": "terms",
          "field": "log.level",
          "order": "desc"
        }
      ]
    }
  ]
}
```

7.6. CUSTOM METRICS AND LOGGING

This simple panel configuration aggregates logs based on severity, aiding in rapid identification of fault spikes or warning trends across Dapr service log records.

Benefits and Use Cases

Harnessing custom metrics and structured logs provides an array of benefits and wide applications in cloud-native environments:

- **Performance Monitoring:** Detailed metrics offer precise assessments of individual service performance, assisting in real-time adjustments and capacity planning.

- **Security and Compliance:** Logs generate auditable trails, facilitating traceability and adherence to security policies, vital for compliance requirements.

- **Operational Insights:** Custom metrics grant visibility into application-level operations, tracking application behavior, cohort analysis, and feature usage.

- **Fault Detection:** Structured logs enable rapid pinpointing of errors through keyword-based searches, filters, and correlations, fast-tracking the debugging cycle.

Challenges and Considerations

- **Log Volume Management:** Excessive custom logging can introduce significant data overhead. Implementing a comprehensive retention policy and log levels (DEBUG, INFO, WARN) mitigates unnecessary storage use.

- **Metric Overhead:** While collecting extensive metrics can be beneficial, understanding the trade-off between detail and system load remains essential.

- **Standard Consistency:** Ensuring custom metrics and logs adhere to consistent formatting standards ensures seamless integration and usability across different tools or teams.

- **Telemetry Security:** Custom metrics and logs may capture sensitive operational or business information. It is crucial to enforce data encryption, authentication measures, and access controls safeguarding this telemetry data.

Conclusion

Dapr's capacity for supporting custom metrics and logging showcases its flexibility and robustness as a distributed application runtime. The ability to tailor observability to meet unique application challenges and capture custom logic data points empowers organizations to drive superior performance and reliable operations.

As microservice complexities escalate, the thoughtful design and implementation of a comprehensive telemetry strategy are pivotal in sustaining high-quality service delivery. Dapr's seamless blend of powerful telemetry components supports all facets of metrics and logging infrastructure, fostering operational excellence within modern technological landscapes.

7.7 Best Practices for Observability

Observability is an evolving discipline that plays a crucial role in the management of modern microservices systems. It refers to the capability of a system to expose its internal states by producing structured telemetry data, including metrics, logs, and traces. This section delves into best practices for observability, emphasizing strategies that enable comprehensive insights into system behavior and facilitate effective management of microservice architectures.

While designing and implementing observability practices, it is important to achieve a balance—ensuring the depth of information without overwhelming system resources or cloud data storage. Proper observability not only aids in fault detection and performance monitoring but also in understanding application behaviors, thereby allowing teams to drive continuous improvement in service reliability and user satisfaction.

Design for Observability and Instrumentation

7.7. BEST PRACTICES FOR OBSERVABILITY

Integrate Observability Early:

Observability should be an integral aspect of system design and codebase development from the onset rather than an afterthought. Embedding observability into the development lifecycle ensures that services are equipped to produce consistent and useful telemetry data right from the initial deployment.

- **Instrumentation Strategy:** Plan where, how, and what to instrument. Consider key points in code that interact with external services, user requests, database access, or contain critical business logic.

- **Uniform Instrumentation Libraries:** Employ common libraries for instrumentation, such as OpenTelemetry, across all services to ensure uniformity and ease of integration.

Example of Instrumenting Once in a Shared Library:

```
public class MetricsLibrary {
    private static final Meter meter = GlobalMeterProvider.get().get("myappMeter");

    public static final LongCounter requestCounter = meter.counterBuilder("requests")
        .setDescription("Counts total number of requests")
        .build();

    public static void incrementRequestCounter() {
        requestCounter.add(1);
    }
}
```

Using a shared library for instrumentation like the above Java example ensures consistency across multiple microservices.

Metrics Collection and Analysis

Define Key Metrics:

Identify and track key performance indicators (KPIs) and system health metrics that correlate directly with business goals and customer experiences such as latency, error rates, request counts, and resource usage (CPU, memory).

- **Hierarchical Metrics Structure:** Categorize metrics by service, function, or business transaction to provide targeted insights and improve navigability.

Automate Collection and Aggregation:

Automating the collection process reduces manual overhead and allows aggregation of metrics for trend analysis and capacity planning.

- **Custom Dashboards and Alerts:** Create comprehensive dashboards and set up intelligent alerts for detection of anomalies or KPIs breaches, integrating with tools like Prometheus and Grafana.

```
{
  "dashboard": {
    "title": "Performance Metrics",
    "panels": [
      {
        "type": "graph",
        "title": "Request Latency",
        "targets": [
          {
            "expr": "histogram_quantile(0.95, sum(rate(
                http_request_duration_seconds_bucket{app='myapp'}[5m])) by (job,
                le))",
            "legendFormat": "{{job}}"
          }
        ]
      }
    ]
  }
}
```

Effective Logging Practices

Structure Logs for Contextual Clarity:

Logs must include vital context such as timestamps, levels (INFO, WARN, ERROR), and contextual metadata (user IDs, transaction IDs) to foster easy traceability.

- **Avoid Log Overhead:** Implement dynamic log levels to adjust verbosity during different operational states, ensuring essential information is captured without overwhelming storage.

- **Centralized Log Management:** Direct logs to centralized solutions like Elasticsearch to enable real-time querying and retrospective analysis.

7.7. BEST PRACTICES FOR OBSERVABILITY

```
<match **>
  @type elasticsearch
  host elasticsearch.cluster.service
  port 9200
  logstash_format true
  flush_interval 5s
</match>
```

This configuration forwards application logs to an Elasticsearch backend, facilitating further analysis through Kibana.

Enhancing Tracing Processes

Comprehensive Distributed Tracing:

Distribute tracing uniformly across all service interactions to construct a coherent view of user journeys and operational patterns. Utilizing OpenTelemetry, Dapr propagates trace context seamlessly through entire service meshes.

- **Optimize Sampling Rates:** Set trace sampling policies that balance insight depth against performance and storage costs.

```
apiVersion: dapr.io/v1alpha1
kind: Configuration
metadata:
  name: tracingconfig
spec:
  tracing:
    samplingRate: "0.25"  # Tracing 25% of requests
    openTelemetryCollector:
      endpoint: "http://otel-collector:4317"
```

Use OpenTelemetry collectors for aggregating and exporting trace data to backends like Jaeger or Zipkin for visualization.

Security and Compliance

Ensure Data Security:

Implement encryption for telemetry data both in transit and at rest to safeguard against breaches. Control access to telemetry dashboards and data, ensuring compliance with regulatory requirements such as GDPR.

Continuous Feedback and Improvement

Iterative Monitoring and Adjustments:

Set up feedback loops based on telemetry data to iteratively improve the observability framework. Review KPIs regularly and adjust metrics, dashboards, or alert thresholds in alignment with evolving business objectives or operational shifts.

- **Anomaly Detection and Insights:** Leverage machine learning models integrated within monitoring solutions to detect deviations or anomalies earlier, minimizing downtime and optimizing performance dynamically.

```
groups:
- name: AvailabilityAlerts
  rules:
  - alert: HighErrorRate
    expr: sum(rate(http_requests_total{status=~"5.."}[5m])) by (job) > 0.01
    for: 2m
    labels:
      severity: "critical"
    annotations:
      summary: "High Error Rate Detected"
      description: "Error rate exceeds 1\% for {{ $labels.job }}"
```

Alerts function as primary signals for recognizing potential disruptions and commencing problem-solving mechanisms.

Observability encompasses an expansive framework that equips an organization with the insight to drive resolutions, improvements, and proactive decisions. Establishing best practices in implementing metrics, structured logging, and seamless tracing is crucial in achieving a coherent and actionable observability framework. As microservices evolve, observability strategies must adapt dynamically, leveraging automation, adaptive policies, and intelligent insights to confidently support and advance service objectives.

The practices outlined ensure that telemetry data illuminates the internal states of distributed systems. When entwined with a feedback-oriented framework, they pave the way for enduring operational excellence and a keen competitive advantage, ensuring steadfast compliance with user expectations and market demands.

Chapter 8

Security and Dapr

This chapter delves into the security features and considerations essential for protecting microservices built with Dapr. It covers Dapr's security model, focusing on transport layer security (TLS) to protect service-to-service communication, and strategies for managing secrets and access control. Additionally, it discusses implementing authentication measures and securing API interactions. By following best practices, developers can ensure robust security, safeguarding data integrity and confidentiality in Dapr-integrated applications.

8.1 Security Challenges in Microservices

Microservices architecture is a methodology where an application is structured as a collection of loosely coupled services. Each service is fine-grained and runs a unique process. This architectural style enables the continuous delivery/deployment of large, complex applications. However, it also introduces unique security challenges that must be addressed to protect the integrity of the system.

In microservices, the independent and distributed nature of services elevates the attack surface, exposing more potential vulnerabilities compared to monolithic systems. One primary security challenge is the secure communication between microservices. Unlike monolithic applications that rely on a single deployment environment with in-process communication, microservices require networking protocols for service-to-service communication, such as HTTP, gRPC, or messaging queues. This opens possibilities for various attack vectors, such as man-in-the-middle attacks, where data could be intercepted during transmission.

To mitigate these risks, Transport Layer Security (TLS) is often employed to encrypt the communication between services, ensuring data confidentiality and integrity. Implementing TLS in a microservices architecture involves managing certificates and keys across a distributed network, which introduces its own set of challenges. The certificates must be properly issued, renewed, and securely stored, requiring robust secret management strategies.

```
# Example of enabling TLS for a microservice running on a Kubernetes cluster
kubectl create secret tls my-microservice-tls \
  --cert=path/to/tls.crt \
  --key=path/to/tls.key
```

Another challenge is securing the service-to-service authorization. When a request is made from one microservice to another, the receiving service must authenticate and authorize the requestor. Microservices often handle a wide variety of roles and permissions, necessitating a dynamic access control system. This is often addressed using OAuth2 or JSON Web Tokens (JWT), where each service verifies the identity and permissions of the calling service before processing any request.

```
{
  "iss": "auth.my-company.com",
  "sub": "user@example.com",
  "aud": "microservice-2",
  "roles": ["read", "write"],
  "exp": 1717947123,
  "iat": 1617943123
}
```

Additionally, microservices must be resilient to denial-of-service (DoS) attacks, where malicious actors aim to overwhelm services with excessive requests, causing degradation or a total denial of service. Rate limiting and circuit breaker patterns can be applied to prevent such

8.1. SECURITY CHALLENGES IN MICROSERVICES

attacks. Rate limiting ensures that no service receives more requests than it can handle effectively, while circuit breakers help avoid repeatedly invoking a failing service, allowing it time to recover.

```
{
  "name": "service-rate-limiter",
  "type": "rate-limiter",
  "config": {
    "maxRequestsPerSecond": 100
  }
}
```

The distribution of microservices across multiple environments — ranging from on-premises servers to cloud deployments — further complicates security efforts. Each environment might employ different levels of inherent security, and the interaction between services across these environments necessitates consistent security policies, robust identity management, and secure communication channels to protect sensitive data.

Moreover, logging and monitoring play critical roles in ensuring microservices' security. Adequate logging provides necessary insights into the operational state of microservices, helping promptly detect and respond to security incidents. Monitoring tools and services, often deployed as part of a larger DevOps strategy, are essential to identify anomalous behaviors that might indicate attempts at breaching security.

Microservices inherently leverage third-party libraries and frameworks, offering pre-built functionalities that accelerate development. However, they also introduce additional security risks, as vulnerabilities within these dependencies could be exploited. It is essential to regularly update dependencies and promptly patch known vulnerabilities as they are discovered.

The dynamic and ephemeral nature of microservices, which are often spun up and down based on demand, poses additional challenges for traditional security measures. Microservices can appear and disappear frequently, making it difficult to maintain a list of active services and apply consistent security controls. Solutions such as service meshes have emerged to handle the complex communication and security requirements in microservices. Service meshes provide a dedicated infrastructure layer for managing service-to-service communications, enabling features like load balancing, retries, and secure communication with minimal application code modifications.

```
import jwt

token = "eyJhbGciOiJIUzI1NiIsInR5cCI6IkpXVCJ9..."

try:
    # Decode the token using the JWT library and verify signature
    decoded = jwt.decode(token, "secret-key", algorithms=["HS256"])
    # Check expiration and audience claims
    if decoded["exp"] > current_time and decoded["aud"] == "microservice-2":
        print("Token is valid")
except jwt.ExpiredSignatureError:
    print("Token has expired")
except jwt.InvalidTokenError as e:
    print(f"Invalid token: {e}")
```

Error handling in microservices also presents unique security challenges. Error messages may inadvertently reveal implementation details that could be exploited by attackers. This makes it critical to design error handling mechanisms that provide useful feedback for debugging without exposing sensitive details. Logging systems must be configured to ensure error messages do not leak critical information.

As the number of microservices increases, so does the complexity of managing and securing them. Automation becomes key in handling these complexities without sacrificing security. Continuous integration/continuous deployment (CI/CD) pipelines must include automated security testing to verify that each microservice is deployed with the necessary security configurations.

```
# Using OWASP ZAP for automated security testing
docker run --rm -v $(pwd):/zap/wrk:rw \
    -t owasp/zap2docker-stable zap-baseline.py \
    -t http://my-microservice:8080 \
    -r test_report.html
```

Securing a microservices architecture requires addressing unique challenges that do not typically appear in monolithic systems. Organizations must employ comprehensive strategies encompassing encryption, access control, threat detection, and environmental consistency to protect their systems from potential security threats. Choosing and implementing the right tools, adhering to best practices, and fostering a security-driven culture are all necessary for effectively safeguarding microservices-based systems.

8.2 Dapr Security Model

Dapr (Distributed Application Runtime) is designed to simplify the building of microservices by providing a set of distributed system building blocks. With the adoption of Dapr, understanding its security model is vital to ensuring that microservices interact safely and securely within distributed environments. The Dapr security model encompasses several layers, including service-to-service communication, component interaction, and identity and access management, each contributing to the overall security posture of Dapr-based applications.

Central to Dapr's security approach is its reliance on Transport Layer Security (TLS) to protect data in transit. TLS encryption ensures that all communication between Dapr runtime instances and the applications they facilitate is secure from eavesdropping and tampering. By default, mutual TLS (mTLS) is enabled in Dapr, requiring both client and server to authenticate their identities to each other, significantly reducing the risk of man-in-the-middle and spoofing attacks.

```
# Enabling mTLS for Dapr by deploying the Dapr control plane with mTLS enabled
kubectl create namespace dapr-system
kubectl apply -f https://raw.githubusercontent.com/dapr/dapr/master/charts/dapr/
    crds.yaml
# Initialize dapr with mTLS
dapr init --kubernetes --install-mtls
```

In addition to securing service communication, Dapr offers a robust model for securing components, including middleware, state stores, and secret stores. Each component in Dapr is defined through a configuration YAML file where security policies can be specified. Secure handling of sensitive information, such as credentials and API keys, is crucial. Dapr encourages the use of secret stores, which provide encrypted storage and retrieval of secrets, ensuring that sensitive data is never exposed in plain text.

```
apiVersion: dapr.io/v1alpha1
kind: Component
metadata:
  name: my-secrets
  namespace: default
spec:
  type: secretstores.local.env
```

```
metadata:
- name: secretKey
  value: supersecretvalue
```

Component-level security also involves managing access based on roles and permissions. With Dapr's policy model, administrators can define who can access specific services or components using access policies. This can be further enhanced by leveraging identity providers such as OAuth2 or OpenID Connect, where Dapr can be configured to validate tokens presented by clients to ascertain their identities and permissions.

Dapr's security model also addresses the challenge of securing its powerful sidecar architecture. Every Dapr-enabled application operates alongside a Dapr sidecar instance, which manages communication and provides access to Dapr's building blocks. In this context, securing the API surface of sidecars is essential. Dapr provides mechanisms for authenticating calls made to the sidecars by requiring API tokens or mutual TLS, ensuring that only authorized clients can invoke Dapr APIs.

To illustrate these security features in action, consider a scenario where a microservice needs to securely store and retrieve a user's preferences using a state store managed by Dapr. The state store component can be configured to use an encrypted backend, and access to this store can be tightly controlled using Dapr's component security policies.

```
apiVersion: dapr.io/v1alpha1
kind: Component
metadata:
  name: statestore
  namespace: default
spec:
  type: state.azure.blobstorage
  metadata:
  - name: accountName
    secretKeyRef:
      name: azure-storage-secret
      key: account-name
  - name: accountKey
    secretKeyRef:
      name: azure-storage-secret
      key: account-key
```

In this configuration, 'secretKeyRef' provides an additional layer of security by referencing secrets stored securely within a Kubernetes secret store. This ensures that sensitive credentials are accessed securely by

8.2. DAPR SECURITY MODEL

the state store component when necessary.

Beyond component-level security, Dapr also implements security features across network boundaries. When Dapr applications are deployed in clustered environments, such as Kubernetes, security policies must extend to inter-cluster communication. Dapr supports automated certificate management to ease the burden of managing TLS certificates and keys over extensive deployments. Using open protocols for certificate issuance and renewal, such as through Cert Manager or HashiCorp Vault, Dapr can dynamically handle certificates for each service instance, reducing the complexity and risk of certificate mismanagement.

A critical aspect of the Dapr security model is its governance and compliance capabilities, allowing organizations to adhere to security regulations and standards. Dapr facilitates audit logging, providing traceability for actions performed within the Dapr system. Audit logs are profound for security incident response planning, allowing detection and analysis of potentially malicious activities.

```
{
  "method": "POST",
  "url": "http://localhost:3500/v1.0/state/statestore",
  "headers": {
    "Authorization": "Bearer eyJhbGciOiJIUzI1NiIsInR5cCI6IkpXVCJ9..."
  },
  "data": {
    "key": "userPreferences",
    "value": {
      "theme": "dark",
      "notifications": true
    }
  }
}
```

Understanding the Dapr security model extends beyond basic encryption and authentication mechanisms to include practices that protect the broader ecosystem. With security threats constantly evolving, the Dapr community emphasizes the importance of keeping up-to-date with the latest security patches and vulnerabilities. Regularly updating the Dapr runtime and its components ensures that applications benefit from continued improvements and mitigations against newly discovered threats.

Additionally, secret management in Dapr emphasizes lifecycle management to ensure secure creation, distribution, usage, and eventual expiration or rotation of secrets. This aids in reducing the risk of credential exposure due to espionage, accident, or expiration.

While Dapr simplifies the complexities of microservices architectures, it doesn't exempt developers and DevOps teams from understanding underlying security principles. Integrating Dapr's security features effectively demands a cohesive strategy that aligns with the application's security requirements. Dapr's extensibility allows for customization of security policies and integrations with existing security frameworks, providing flexibility to meet diverse application needs.

Incorporating Dapr into a microservices architecture involves comprehensively understanding and applying its security model. From TLS across services to managing access and secrets, Dapr enables robust secure-by-design measures. Organizations adopting Dapr can leverage these capabilities to reduce security vulnerabilities in their distributed applications and focus on delivering resilient and high-performing services. As microservices landscapes grow increasingly complex, the ability to seamlessly implement consistent and effective security policies remains critical, with Dapr offering strong foundations upon which to build.

8.3 Transport Layer Security (TLS) in Dapr

Transport Layer Security (TLS) is a cornerstone of secure communications in network applications, providing encryption, authentication, and integrity for data exchanged between clients and services. In the context of Dapr, TLS plays an essential role in securing communication between microservices, thereby ensuring the confidentiality and integrity of messages exchanged in a distributed system. Dapr's implementation of TLS, particularly mutual TLS (mTLS), offers enhancements specifically tailored to the microservices architecture it supports.

TLS operates based on cryptographic protocols that establish a secure channel between parties, protecting data from unauthorized interception or tampering. In a typical Dapr deployment, where multiple microservices might operate in diverse environments, TLS ensures that data passing over potentially insecure networks such as public clouds is encrypted, rendering it intercept-resistant.

The default configuration in Dapr employs mutual TLS (mTLS), a variant of TLS where both parties, the client and server, authenticate each other during the TLS handshake process. This bi-directional authentication is crucial for microservices, as it ensures that both service endpoints are verified, effectively mitigating man-in-the-middle and spoofing attacks.

```
# Initialize Dapr on Kubernetes with mTLS enabled
dapr init --kubernetes --install-mtls=true
```

Dapr automates several elements of TLS management which would otherwise require significant manual configuration. This includes automating the issuance and renewal of certificates, thereby reducing operational overhead and minimizing vulnerabilities related to expired or improperly managed certificates.

TLS Certificate Management in Dapr

Certificate management is a critical aspect of maintaining secure communications. Dapr leverages the Kubernetes Certificate Authority (in Kubernetes environments) to issue and rotate certificates used for mTLS. Certificates are used to establish trust between Dapr sidecars and must be carefully managed to minimize risks such as unauthorized access or data leaks due to expired or illicitly acquired certificates.

Automating the certificate lifecycle involves generating, distributing, and renewing certificates as needed without human intervention. Dapr's certificate authority automatically rotates certificates to maintain security, reducing the risk associated with expired certificates and ensuring continued secure communication.

```
apiVersion: dapr.io/v1alpha1
kind: Configuration
metadata:
  name: dapr-ca-config
  namespace: dapr-system
spec:
  mtls:
    enabled: true
    workloadCertTTL: "24h"
    allowedClockSkew: "15m"
```

The Dapr configuration above demonstrates typical settings for the certificate authority, specifying the workload certificate's time-to-live (TTL) and allowed clock skew, ensuring that security policies align with organizational needs for resiliency and trust.

Security Enhancements Through mTLS

Mutual TLS enhances security beyond traditional TLS by enforcing identity verification on both ends of the connection, ensuring that clients and servers mutually confirm each other before data exchange. This setup deters malicious attempts to impersonate services or clients, a concern prevalent in distributed architectures where numerous services interact across varied networks.

In a microservices environment utilizing Dapr, mTLS ensures that microservices initiated by unauthorized entities are unable to illicitly access or interact with valid service instances. This security guarantee is fundamental for applications operating with sensitive data or under stringent compliance requirements.

```
import ssl
import socket

hostname = 'example.microservice'
context = ssl.create_default_context(ssl.Purpose.CLIENT_AUTH)
context.load_verify_locations(cafile="/path/to/ca-bundle.crt")
context.load_cert_chain(certfile="/path/to/cert.pem", keyfile="/path/to/key.pem")

with socket.create_connection((hostname, 443)) as sock:
    with context.wrap_socket(sock, server_hostname=hostname) as ssock:
        print(ssock.version())
```

The Python code provided demonstrates how TLS verification can be programmed, including certificate loading and context management to ensure that both the client certificate (loaded using load_cert_chain) and the server's presented certificate are verified.

TLS Configuration and Debugging in Dapr

To effectively leverage TLS in Dapr, understanding how to configure and debug TLS settings is crucial. TLS issues can arise from certificate misconfigurations, expired certificates, untrusted certificate authorities, or network misconfigurations. Dapr provides logs and diagnostic tools that aid developers in understanding and resolving such issues efficiently.

When configuring TLS, it is important to test configurations in a development environment before rolling out changes into production. This includes verifying certificate validity, mTLS handshake compliance, and ensuring that all service interactions require authentication. Tools such as OpenSSL can be utilized to test TLS connectivity and validate certificate legitimacy across services.

```
# Testing TLS connection using OpenSSL
openssl s_client -connect example.microservice:443 -servername example.microservice
```

Executing the above command will allow verification of a service's certificate and chain, providing insights into the certificate's Common Name (CN), expiry dates, and signing authority.

TLS Best Practices in Dapr Deployments

- **Certificate Management**: Regularly renew and rotate certificates with automated tools to prevent expired certificates from becoming a security liability. Use short-lived certificates where possible to minimize the impact of a leaked certificate.

- **Configuration Stability**: Ensure consistent TLS configurations across environments. Use infrastructure-as-code (IaC) to deploy configurations to prevent human error.

- **Testing and Monitoring**: Implement comprehensive monitoring to catch TLS handshake failures and certificate errors. Utilize logs to trace anomalies that might indicate faulty certificates or misconfigurations.

- **Security Policies**: Define strict access controls that ensure only authorized identities are granted certificates. Monitor certificate issuance and renewal logs for unusual patterns.

By applying these practices, organizations can leverage Dapr's TLS capabilities effectively, ensuring that microservices communicate securely, thereby reducing the attack surface and protecting sensitive data.

Dapr's TLS integration simplifies securing microservices, automating the complex tasks of certificate management and mutual authentication. TLS and mTLS support in Dapr not only protect communication channels but also facilitate compliance through strong authentication mechanisms. Understanding these functionalities and incorporating best practices ensures robust security implementation within distributed systems leveraging Dapr.

8.4 Component Security and Secret Management

Within microservices architectures, components such as middleware, databases, and state stores play pivotal roles in enabling functionality and handling data. In Dapr, components are essential building blocks that allow developers to interface with external services like message brokers, configuration providers, and more. Securing these components and properly managing secrets—such as credentials and API keys—are crucial to ensure that applications remain resilient against threats and unauthorized access.

Understanding the security around components involves examining the multiple layers of protection that can be applied to shield data, restrict access, and manage sensitive information. Dapr's approach to component security and secret management provides a structured methodology to safeguard components, ensuring that applications are both secure and compliant with industry standards.

Component security in Dapr focuses on facilitating the secure integration and operation of external services necessary for microservice functionality. Each component in Dapr is defined through configuration YAML files that specify the type of component and metadata necessary for its proper functioning. Integrating security at this level ensures that data processed by these components is protected from unauthorized parties.

Securing Dapr components begins with configuring permissions and access control. By default, Dapr provides minimal access, emphasizing a least-privilege approach. This approach reduces the risk of components inadvertently exposing data or becoming entry points for attackers to exploit.

```
apiVersion: dapr.io/v1alpha1
kind: Component
```

8.4. COMPONENT SECURITY AND SECRET MANAGEMENT

```
metadata:
  name: secure-messaging
  namespace: default
spec:
  type: pubsub.redis
  metadata:
  - name: redisHost
    value: myredis:6379
  - name: redisPassword
    secretKeyRef:
      name: redis-secrets
      key: password
```

In the above configuration, the redis component uses secret management to keep the sensitive 'redisPassword' information private. By referencing Kubernetes secrets, Dapr prevents exposure of plaintext credentials in component definitions.

Secret management is a practice that involves the handling of sensitive information such as passwords, API keys, and configuration settings that applications use in a secure manner. Dapr provides a native secret management facility that allows integration with cloud-native secret stores like Kubernetes Secrets, Azure Key Vault, and HashiCorp Vault, among others. These integrations offer secure storage, access control, and auditing capabilities, ensuring that secrets are handled with organizational security policies.

The typical workflow for secret management in Dapr includes secret creation, secure transmission to applications at runtime, and use within applications without exposing them in transit.

```
apiVersion: dapr.io/v1alpha1
kind: Component
metadata:
  name: mysecretstore
  namespace: default
spec:
  type: secretstores.kubernetes
  metadata:
  - name: namespace
    value: default

apiVersion: dapr.io/v1alpha1
kind: Configuration
metadata:
  name: appconfig
  namespace: default
spec:
  secrets:
    scopes:
    - storeName: mysecretstore
```

```
defaultAccess: deny
allowedSecrets:
- secret1
- secret2
```

The scope-based configuration in the example restricts access to specific secrets ('secret1' and 'secret2'), aligning with the principle of least privilege. Only secrets explicitly listed are accessible, mitigating exposure risk even if the application is compromised.

For effective secret management, certain principles and practices must be adhered to, ensuring robust security posture:

- Limit Exposure: Secrets should be confined to the minimal number of services; services should not access secrets they do not need. Use access scopes diligently to enforce this principle.

- Rotate Secrets Regularly: To minimize the risk associated with leaked secrets, employ automated processes or secret management tools to rotate them at defined intervals.

- Monitor and Audit Access: Maintain comprehensive logs of all access and use events related to secrets. This aids in detecting unauthorized access attempts or anomalies indicative of a breach.

```
# Command to decode a Kubernetes secret for review
kubectl get secret redis-secrets -o jsonpath="{.data.password}" | base64 --decode
```

Decoding and reviewing secrets should be performed only by authorized personnel to understand usage audits and access patterns.

- Use Strong Encryption: Secrets stored in Dapr's secret store integrations must be irreversibly encrypted. Select backed encryption standards that align with industry best practices (e.g., AES-256).

- Implement Principle of Least Privilege: Configure access policies that restrict secret usage to only necessary components or services within the architecture.

Dapr's ability to integrate with established secret management solutions translates to enhanced security without radically altering existing

8.4. COMPONENT SECURITY AND SECRET MANAGEMENT

workflows. For cloud-native applications, this means seamless incorporation with Azure Key Vault, AWS Secrets Manager, or Google Cloud Secret Manager, allowing enterprises to leverage advanced security features such as centralized management, automated secret rotation, and compliance features.

A significant advantage of using a centralized secret manager alongside Dapr is its capability to standardize how secrets are handled throughout an organization. This ensures consistent compliance with security policies and protocols across all development and operational teams, reducing the risk of security oversights.

```
apiVersion: dapr.io/v1alpha1
kind: Component
metadata:
  name: azurekeyvault
  namespace: default
spec:
  type: secretstores.azure.keyvault
  metadata:
  - name: vaultName
    value: myvault
  - name: spnClientId
    secretKeyRef:
      name: azure-sp-secrets
      key: client-id
  - name: spnClientSecret
    secretKeyRef:
      name: azure-sp-secrets
      key: client-secret
```

The Azure Key Vault example demonstrates how to define the integration within Dapr using 'secretKeyRef' to securely manage the client id and secret needed for authentication with the vault.

Securing components and managing secrets is a multifaceted process that requires a strategic approach to mitigate risks associated with exposing sensitive data. Dapr's capabilities streamline this process through automated integration, industry-standard practices, and operational transparency. These functionalities enable application developers to focus on building distributed systems without compromising on security.

Understanding and implementing comprehensive component security and secret management measures are quintessential for protecting modern applications utilizing Dapr. By following best practices and leveraging secure integration with established secret management services, organizations can enhance the security of their microservices architectures, reinforcing their ability to deliver reliable, secure software solutions.

8.5 Access Control and Authentication

Access control and authentication are fundamental security principles in safeguarding microservices architectures. Within Dapr, a robust framework for defining and enforcing access policies and verifying client identities supports these principles, ensuring secure and efficient communication across services. Understanding and implementing effective access control mechanisms and authentication processes is critical to protect against unauthorized access and potential data breaches.

Access control is the selective restriction of access to resources, ensuring only authenticated and authorized users or services can perform actions or access data. In Dapr, this is achieved through a combination of authentication and authorization mechanisms to manage the identities of clients and enforce permissions across services and components.

Dapr leverages role-based access control (RBAC) to assign permissions to different roles within an application. This method allows administrators to control access rights based on the roles that users or services assume, without having to define permissions individually for each entity.

A typical implementation of RBAC in Dapr might involve defining policies that specify which roles have access to particular components or actions. This way, Dapr distinguishes between different entities within its architecture and grants or denies access accordingly.

```
apiVersion: dapr.io/v1alpha1
kind: Policy
metadata:
  name: access-policy
  namespace: default
spec:
  roles:
  - name: admin
    actions:
    - read
    - write
```

8.5. ACCESS CONTROL AND AUTHENTICATION

```
- name: viewer
  actions:
  - read
```

The configuration snippet defines an access policy, providing an example of how roles such as 'admin' and 'viewer' are granted different levels of access — a fundamental concept in implementing RBAC.

Authentication verifies the identity of a user or service, serving as the first line of defense against unauthorized access. Dapr supports various authentication protocols and mechanisms to ensure that only authenticated entities can interact with the system.

One common protocol for authentication in microservices is OAuth2, which allows users to authenticate securely across services via tokens. OpenID Connect (OIDC) extends OAuth2 to provide identity verification alongside authentication, enabling Dapr to assert user identities efficiently.

In Dapr, authentication can be configured to authenticate users through external identity providers such as Auth0, Azure Active Directory, or Google Identity Platform. These integrations streamline the management of user identities, leveraging established providers' secure frameworks worldwide.

```
apiVersion: dapr.io/v1alpha1
kind: Configuration
metadata:
  name: oauth-config
  namespace: default
spec:
  auth:
    identityProviders:
    - type: oauth2
      metadata:
      - name: clientId
        value: your-client-id
      - name: clientSecret
        value: your-client-secret
      - name: authorizationUri
        value: https://auth.example.com/oauth2/authorize
      - name: tokenUri
        value: https://auth.example.com/oauth2/token
```

By configuring an identity provider in Dapr, applications can authenticate users by exchanging an authorization code for an access token, securely verifying identities before access is granted.

JSON Web Tokens (JWT) are a compact and self-contained way of securely transmitting information between parties as a JSON object. They are used extensively in microservices for authentication and information exchange, owing to their simplicity and security.

JWTs contain encoded information about the user's identity and claims, allowing services to authenticate requests by verifying JWT signatures. Dapr can be configured to validate incoming JWT tokens before processing requests, adding a security layer that ensures services trust only valid and authenticated requests.

```
import jwt

encoded_jwt = "eyJhbGciOiJIUzI1NiIsInR5cCI6IkpXVCJ9.eyJzdWIiOiIxMjM0NT..."
secret_key = "secret"

def verify_jwt(token, key):
    try:
        decoded = jwt.decode(token, key, algorithms=["HS256"])
        if "scope" in decoded and "access_service" in decoded["scope"]:
            return "Access granted"
    except jwt.ExpiredSignatureError:
        return "Token expired"
    except jwt.InvalidTokenError:
        return "Invalid token"

    return "Access denied"

print(verify_jwt(encoded_jwt, secret_key))
```

This Python example illustrates how services can use JWTs to authenticate incoming requests, verifying the token's validity and any associated claims before permitting access.

Secure configurations often consist of controls that protect applications from both internal and external threats. In Dapr, these controls include defining secure default policies that deny access unless explicitly granted. This zero-trust approach encourages a security-first mindset, ensuring that any deviation from allowable actions is explicitly defined and monitored.

It is recommended to start with deny-all policies and progressively define roles and rules that explicitly allow necessary actions or access, reducing the likelihood of open access points that could be exploited by malicious actors.

```
apiVersion: dapr.io/v1alpha1
kind: Policy
```

8.5. ACCESS CONTROL AND AUTHENTICATION

```
metadata:
  name: zero-trust-policy
  namespace: default
spec:
  default:
    rule: deny-all
  roles:
  - name: analyst
    actions:
    - query
```

In this configuration, the default action is to deny all operations unless the 'analyst' role is assigned, effectively minimizing potential security gaps.

As Dapr exposes APIs that enable microservices to communicate and access Dapr features, securing these APIs is imperative to maintaining a strong security posture. Securing Dapr APIs involves implementing authentication and authorization at the API level, ensuring that only legitimate requests from verified sources are processed.

API tokens can be used alongside TLS to authenticate and encrypt communications between services, ensuring sessions are protected both in-flight and at rest.

```
# Example Header with API Token Authentication
curl -X GET "https://api.dapr.com/resource" -H "Authorization: Bearer eyJhb..."
```

By using such headers in requests, Dapr can authenticate API calls, controlling access based on provided tokens.

Access control and authentication are critical to enforcing secure and reliable service operations in Dapr-enabled environments. By implementing robust authentication mechanisms like OAuth2 and JWT, defining clear access control policies, and securing Dapr APIs, organizations can ensure their systems resist unauthorized access, support appropriate permissions, and protect sensitive data.

Dapr's built-in support for established security protocols allows for scalable and consistent access management across microservices frameworks, enabling developer teams to integrate seamless and secure identity verification systems tailored to their organizational needs. These comprehensive measures facilitate the creation of secure microservice applications while supporting agility and innovation in development processes.

8.6 Secure Communication with Dapr API

Communication between microservices involves exchanging sensitive data over potentially insecure networks, making security a critical consideration in system design. The Dapr API, a core component of the Dapr runtime, provides a standardized interface for microservices to interact with each other and with Dapr's building blocks. Ensuring secure communication with the Dapr API is paramount for maintaining data integrity, confidentiality, and system reliability.

The Dapr API consists of several subsystems, including the HTTP/-gRPC API for service invocation, state management, pub/sub messaging, and more. Each subsystem requires secure communication protocols to protect data from interception, tampering, and unauthorized access.

```
# Establishing secure communication with mTLS enabled for Dapr
dapr init --kubernetes --install-mtls=true \
  --enable-daprd-api-authentication
```

The command above initializes Dapr on a Kubernetes cluster with mTLS enabled, ensuring secure communications between services.

- **Role of mTLS in Dapr API Security**

    Mutual TLS (mTLS) in Dapr ensures that both parties involved in a communication session — the client and the server — are authenticated, preventing communication with unauthorized entities. This bi-directional trust model prevents compromised services or external actors from impersonating valid services, which could otherwise lead to data breaches or unauthorized operations.

    mTLS requires the following components to function:

    - **Certificates**: Both client and server certificates are issued by a trusted Certificate Authority (CA). The certificates must be validated as part of the TLS handshake.
    - **Private Keys**: Each party holds a private key corresponding to their certificate, ensuring that only the genuine holder

8.6. SECURE COMMUNICATION WITH DAPR API

can initiate or accept secure communications.

- **Trust Stores**: Each party maintains a list of trusted CAs, ensuring that only recognized certificates are accepted for creating secure connections.

```
apiVersion: dapr.io/v1alpha1
kind: Configuration
metadata:
  name: secure-setup
  namespace: default
spec:
  features:
  - name: dapr-mtls
    enabled: true
  - name: api-token-auth
    enabled: true
```

The Dapr configuration illustrated above specifies enabling 'dapr-mtls' and API token authentication, providing an additional layer of security for service communications.

- **Leveraging API Tokens for Resource Access Control**

    API tokens facilitate granular access control by verifying that only authenticated requests are honored by the Dapr API. When a service or client sends a request to a Dapr API endpoint, the token included in the request headers is verified. Access is granted based on the token's validity and the permissions associated with it.

    Tokens serve as a method to securely convey claims about the sender and the requested permissions. These claims are evaluated against the access policies defined within the Dapr deployment, allowing or denying access to resources or operations.

```
# Example HTTP GET request using an API token
curl -X GET "https://api.dapr.com/v1.0/state/store" \
  -H "Authorization: Bearer eyJhbGciOiJIUzI1NiIsInR..."
```

The request includes a bearer token in the Authorization header, which the Dapr API verifies before processing the request.

- **Securing gRPC Communications**

    Besides HTTP, Dapr supports gRPC for communication, leveraging the advantages of a binary protocol that is more efficient for data serialization, particularly in high-performance microservices deployments. Just like HTTP, gRPC communications must be secured to maintain confidentiality and integrity.

To secure gRPC with TLS in Dapr, a similar strategy as with HTTP is adopted; certificates and private keys are used to establish secure channels, preventing unauthorized interceptions or modifications of the transmitted data.

```go
package main

import (
    "log"
    "google.golang.org/grpc"
    "google.golang.org/grpc/credentials"
)

func main() {
    creds, err := credentials.NewClientTLSFromFile("path/to/cert.pem", "")
    if err != nil {
        log.Fatalf("failed to load credentials: %v", err)
    }
    conn, err := grpc.Dial("service-host:50051", grpc.WithTransportCredentials(creds))
    if err != nil {
        log.Fatalf("did not connect: %v", err)
    }
    defer conn.Close()

    log.Println("Connected with gRPC using TLS")
}
```

The Go code demonstrates establishing a secure TLS-enabled gRPC connection, where client certificate credentials are loaded to authenticate during the connection setup.

- **Log and Monitor API Interactions**

    Monitoring and logging API interactions are essential for identifying potential security incidents such as unauthorized access attempts, anomalies in usage patterns, or suspicious transfers of large data volumes. Logging can also help audit access to sensitive endpoints, ensuring compliance with security policies and regulations.

    Implement logging on API endpoints to capture details such as request origins, payload sizes, authentication tokens, and access outcomes. This information can be aggregated in centralized logging systems for real-time analysis and response to security threats.

```
# Example of enabling logging for a Dapr sidecar
dapr run --app-id myapp --components-path ./components/ \
  --log-level debug
```

By setting a higher log level, such as 'debug', detailed information about API requests and responses is captured, aiding in diagnostic and monitoring tasks.

- **Implementing Best Practices for Dapr API Security**
    - **Enable TLS Everywhere**: Enforce TLS for all communications, whether inter-component, external, or internal, ensuring that sensitive data is encrypted during transit.
    - **Regularly Rotate Keys and Certificates**: Implement a robust policy for regular rotation of cryptographic keys and certificates to mitigate risks associated with compromised credentials.
    - **Validate API Tokens**: Use short-lived tokens or implement token revocation mechanisms to reduce exposure risks linked to invalid or misused tokens.
    - **Leverage the Principle of Least Privilege**: Configure API access policies to grant the minimum required permissions needed by services to function, reducing the impact of any potential security breach.
    - **Stay Informed on Security Best Practices**: Keep abreast of evolving security threats and best practices, applying updates or patches to mitigate new vulnerabilities or exploits.

Secure communication with the Dapr API is integral to any trustworthy microservice architecture. By leveraging TLS, mTLS, API tokens, secure gRPC communications, and comprehensive logging, developers ensure that microservices interact safely, protecting sensitive information and maintaining system integrity. Applying best security practices aligns with these efforts, facilitating the deployment of resilient and secure applications that can withstand a dynamic threat landscape.

8.7 Best Practices for Dapr Security

As microservices architectures expand in complexity and scale, ensuring robust security becomes a fundamental concern. Dapr, with its distributed application runtime, provides developers with tools to efficiently build these architectures. However, leveraging Dapr effectively necessitates implementing best security practices tailored to mitigate specific risks associated with distributed systems.

Security best practices for Dapr cover a holistic approach encompassing secure deployment configurations, data protection, authentication and authorization, component and secret management, regular audits, and incident response preparedness. By incorporating these strategies, organizations can significantly enhance security and ensure their microservices architectures are resilient against evolving threats.

A secure deployment is foundational to operating secure services. When configuring Dapr in production environments, the following practices should be considered:

- **Enforce TLS for All Communications**: TLS should be enabled by default for all service-to-service and client-to-service communications, encrypting data-in-transit and protecting against eavesdropping and man-in-the-middle attacks.

  ```
  # Initialize Dapr with TLS enabled
  dapr init --kubernetes --install-mtls=true
  ```

- **Apply Network Policies**: Use network policies to restrict inter-service communications within your Kubernetes cluster, allowing only the necessary services to communicate, thus minimizing exposure to potential lateral movement by attackers.

  ```
  apiVersion: networking.k8s.io/v1
  kind: NetworkPolicy
  metadata:
    name: allow-app-communications
    namespace: dapr-system
  spec:
    podSelector:
      matchLabels:
        app: myapp
    policyTypes:
    - Ingress
    - Egress
  ```

8.7. BEST PRACTICES FOR DAPR SECURITY

```
ingress:
- from:
  - podSelector:
      matchLabels:
        app: otherapp
egress:
- to:
  - podSelector:
      matchLabels:
        app: dapr-sidecar
```

- **Limit External Exposure**: Where possible, deploy Dapr components internally within your network, limiting external facing endpoints to only those necessary for public interactions. Employ firewalls and access control lists (ACLs) to enforce these limits.

- **Role-Based Access Controls (RBAC)**: Define and enforce RBAC policies to control access to Dapr's administrative functions and component configurations, ensuring only authorized individuals can manage or modify critical resources.

Data protection comprises strategies to secure data both at rest and in transit. Fundamental practices in this area include:

- **Encrypt Data at Rest**: Leverage Dapr's integration with cloud providers' secret stores to encrypt sensitive data and avoid storing plaintext secrets within the service configuration.

```
apiVersion: dapr.io/v1alpha1
kind: Component
metadata:
  name: azure-secrets
  namespace: default
spec:
  type: secretstores.azure.keyvault
  metadata:
  - name: vaultName
    value: my-vault
  - name: spnClientId
    secretKeyRef:
      name: azure-sp-secrets
      key: client-id
  - name: spnClientSecret
    secretKeyRef:
      name: azure-sp-secrets
      key: client-secret
```

- **Rotate Secrets Regularly**: Implement secret rotation policies to refresh credentials periodically, mitigating risks associated with credential leaks or unauthorized access.

- **Utilize Secrets Engines**: If using HashiCorp Vault or similar platforms for secrets management, configure Dapr to query secrets at runtime instead of embedding them in static files, reducing the attack surface.

A key element of securing any distributed system is ensuring robust authentication and authorization for all service components. Recommended practices are:

- **Use Strong Authentication Mechanisms**: Configure Dapr to integrate with OAuth2 or OpenID Connect providers, enhancing the authentication of services and clients via well-established protocols.

- **Deploy JWT for Access Management**: Implement JSON Web Tokens (JWT) to manage access scopes and permissions across services, reducing the potential for unauthorized operations.

```
import jwt

def verify_jwt(token, secret_key):
    try:
        payload = jwt.decode(token, secret_key, algorithms=["HS256"])
        permissions = payload.get("permissions", [])
        if "read:service" in permissions:
            return True
    except jwt.ExpiredSignatureError:
        return False
    except jwt.InvalidTokenError:
        return False

    return False
```

The example function checks a JWT's validity and its claimed permissions, ensuring only legitimate requests proceed.

Continuous monitoring provides insights into system behavior, deterring potential malicious activities and ensuring adherence to security practices:

- **Implement Continuous Monitoring**: Use tools to monitor API calls and log access events, helping detect anomalies or suspicious attempts to access resources.

- **Conduct Security Audits**: Regular audits—conducted internally or via third parties—should verify compliance with security policies and identify areas for improvement.

- **Incident Response Planning**: Establish a clear incident response strategy to rapidly address and mitigate any detected security incidents, ensuring system resilience and continuity.

- **Patch and Update Management**: Establish processes for ensuring all Dapr components and dependencies are kept up to date with the latest security patches and updates.

To further enhance the security posture of microservices architectures employing Dapr, focusing on secure design principles and patterns is essential:

- **Zero Trust Architecture**: Employ a zero-trust approach where each request, irrespective of its origin, is authenticated and authorized based on defined security policies, reducing implicit trust exposure.

- **Service Mesh Integration**: Integrate with service meshes such as Istio or Linkerd for consistent policy deployment and management of service-to-service security, facilitating centralized configuration.

- **Layered Security Approach**: Implement security controls at multiple layers within the architecture, ensuring that even if one control fails, others provide continued protection.

Best practices for Dapr security encompass comprehensive methodologies that cater to the layered nature of microservices environments. Through secure deployment configurations, effective data protection, stringent authentication and authorization processes, continuous monitoring, and resilient design patterns, Dapr users can construct fortified application ecosystems. These practices not only protect against current threats but also anticipate future attack vectors, ensuring the ongoing security of applications built with Dapr.

Chapter 9

Advanced Dapr Features and Integrations

This chapter explores the advanced features of Dapr and how they integrate seamlessly with existing systems to enhance microservices applications. It addresses the development of custom components, explores deployment strategies in multi-cloud and hybrid environments, and discusses implementing advanced actor patterns. Moreover, it details optimizing performance and presents real-world case studies, highlighting practical integrations and innovative applications of Dapr in complex distributed environments.

9.1 Integrating with External Systems

Integrating with external systems is a fundamental capability of Dapr, designed to enable seamless communication and data exchange between microservices and third-party services or applications. This section delves into the methodologies and practices that facilitate such integrations, paying particular attention to both synchronous and asynchronous interactions. Through a combination of theoretical discussions and practical examples, we aim to provide a comprehensive understanding of how Dapr can be effectively employed to achieve robust system integration.

At the core of Dapr's integration capabilities are its building blocks, which abstract and simplify interaction with external systems. These include service invocation, pub/sub messaging, input/output bindings, and state management. By leveraging these building blocks, developers can focus on application logic rather than the intricacies of system communication protocols.

- **Service Invocation**

Service invocation in Dapr enables direct communication between services, akin to remote procedure calls (RPC). It abstracts the complexity of service discovery and network communication, providing a straightforward interface for invoking methods on external systems. The communication can be either HTTP or gRPC, offering flexibility based on specific use cases.

To initiate a service invocation, Dapr uses a request similar to the following example to call a method on a remote service:

```
POST /v1.0/invoke/<app-id>/method/<method-name>
Content-Type: application/json

{
    "data": {
        "key1": "value1",
        "key2": "value2"
    }
}
```

The key components of the request are the application ID of the target service and the method to be invoked. The payload and headers can be configured as per the requirements of the specific external service.

Service invocation can be further illustrated with a Dapr Python SDK example, showcasing how to call a remote service method:

```
from dapr.clients import DaprClient

with DaprClient() as client:
    response = client.invoke_method(
```

9.1. INTEGRATING WITH EXTERNAL SYSTEMS

```
        app_id='external-service',
        method_name='remoteMethod',
        data=b'{"key1": "value1"}',
        http_verb='POST'
)
print(response.text())
```

This snippet demonstrates how Dapr abstracts the complexity of service invocation, enabling developers to interact with external systems using high-level commands without needing to manage the underlying communication details.

- **Asynchronous Communication with Pub/Sub**

Publish/Subscribe, commonly known as pub/sub, is a messaging pattern that facilitates asynchronous communication between services. In Dapr, this enables microservices to subscribe to specific topics to receive messages published by others, providing a decoupled integration approach. This pattern is particularly beneficial when systems require high scalability and low latency.

To leverage Dapr's pub/sub capabilities, developers configure different components, such as message brokers, capable of handling messages. Consider the following YAML configuration for a Redis pub/sub component in a Dapr application:

```
apiVersion: dapr.io/v1alpha1
kind: Component
metadata:
  name: redis-pubsub
  namespace: default
spec:
  type: pubsub.redis
  version: v1
  metadata:
  - name: redisHost
    value: localhost:6379
  - name: redisPassword
    value: ""
```

Once configured, microservices can publish to and subscribe from topics using straightforward commands. Below is an example of how to publish a message to a topic from a Node.js application using the Dapr JavaScript SDK:

```
const dapr = require('dapr-client');
const daprClient = new dapr.DaprClient();
```

```
const msg = { message: 'Hello World' };

daprClient.pubsub.publish('redis-pubsub', 'greeting-topic', msg)
    .then(() => console.log('Message published successfully'))
    .catch(err => console.error('Error publishing message: ', err));
```

Subscribing to this topic requires setting up a listener within the same or a different microservice:

```
const express = require('express');
const app = express();

app.use(express.json());

app.post('/topics/greeting-topic', (req, res) => {
    console.log('Received message:', req.body);
    res.status(200).end();
});

app.listen(3000, () => console.log('Subscriber listening on port 3000'));
```

This code captures a message published to the 'greeting-topic', demonstrating how Dapr enables microservices to communicate asynchronously with minimal setup.

- **Input/Output Bindings**

Through input/output bindings, Dapr connects microservices with external services in a highly abstracted manner, facilitating the ingestion and dispatch of data from various external sources. Input bindings allow an application to subscribe to events or data streams, triggering operations when data arrives, while output bindings enable sending data from an application to an external system.

As an example, consider integrating with a cloud storage service to trigger actions when new files are uploaded. The following YAML configuration sets up an input binding for Azure Blob Storage:

```
apiVersion: dapr.io/v1alpha1
kind: Component
metadata:
  name: azureblob-input
  namespace: default
spec:
  type: bindings.azure.blobstorage
  version: v1
  metadata:
  - name: accountName
```

9.1. INTEGRATING WITH EXTERNAL SYSTEMS

```
  value: yourStorageAccountName
- name: accountKey
  value: yourStorageAccountKey
- name: container
  value: yourContainerName
```

The application receives data as it is uploaded to the specified blob storage, enabling it to process each new file systematically. An output binding could similarly be set up to write processed data back to another service or topic.

- **State Management for External Systems**

While often used internally within microservices for maintaining state, Dapr's state management building block also facilitates integration with persistent storage systems. Through this, external systems' data can be retained and manipulated efficiently. By modeling data interactions using Dapr's state API, applications can achieve consistency and reliability without coupling tightly to any specific storage technology.

Here is an example illustrating how to store and retrieve state using the Dapr HTTP API:

```
# Save state
POST /v1.0/state/store
Content-Type: application/json

[
    {
        "key": "order-123",
        "value": {"product": "book", "amount": 1}
    }
]
```

```
# Retrieve state
GET /v1.0/state/store/order-123
```

The abstracted interface allows developers to utilize various backends like Redis, Azure Cosmos DB, or Amazon DynamoDB through the same state API, thus simplifying the data handling process across different storage systems.

By harnessing these building blocks, Dapr offers a flexible and powerful means to integrate microservices with external systems across different communication patterns and data requirements. This not only simplifies the development process but also enhances the overall architecture's scalability, reliability, and maintainability. As modern applications increasingly rely on a multitude of services and environments, Dapr ensures that integration remains seamless and robust.

9.2 Custom Components Development

Custom components development in Dapr is an advanced topic that empowers developers to extend the functionality of Dapr beyond the built-in components provided. This capability is crucial for applications with unique requirements that cannot be fulfilled by existing components. Understanding how to develop custom components allows developers to implement new integrations, which can address specific business needs or technical constraints. This section provides a detailed exploration of the concepts, considerations, and processes involved in developing custom components for Dapr.

- **Understanding the Role of Custom Components**

    In Dapr, components are modular pieces that define the behavior of Dapr building blocks, such as state stores, pub/sub message brokers, and input/output bindings. While Dapr provides a wide array of default components supporting various technologies, there are use cases where these components do not suffice, including proprietary systems or specialized infrastructure.

    Developing custom components involves creating an implementation that adheres to the component interfaces defined by Dapr. This implementation is then deployed alongside application code, allowing the application to leverage Dapr's building blocks with custom capabilities.

- **Component Model and Specification**

    Each custom component must conform to a specific model, which includes defining metadata, establishing communication protocols, and implementing the required CRUD (Create, Read, Update, Delete) operations for stateful components. Understanding this model is critical to crafting components that integrate seamlessly with Dapr.

9.2. CUSTOM COMPONENTS DEVELOPMENT

The specification of a Dapr component often resides in a YAML file, which describes essential metadata, such as component type, version, and detailed settings. Consider the following example of a component specification for a hypothetical custom database:

```
apiVersion: dapr.io/v1alpha1
kind: Component
metadata:
  name: customdb
  namespace: default
spec:
  type: state.mycustom.db
  version: v1
  metadata:
  - name: dbEndpoint
    value: "http://localhost:5000"
  - name: dbUser
    value: "user"
  - name: dbPassword
    value: "password"
```

The component's specification ensures Dapr can load and configure the custom component appropriately during runtime.

- **Implementing a Custom State Store Component**

  Implementing a custom state store involves defining a server that adheres to Dapr's state management API. A minimal state store must implement operations including retrieving state, saving state, and deleting state.

  Here's a simplified example illustrating the implementation of a custom state store component in Go. This component interfaces with a REST API to perform state operations:

```
package main

import (
    "encoding/json"
    "log"
    "net/http"
    "io/ioutil"
    "github.com/gorilla/mux"
)

type inMemoryStateStore struct {
    store map[string][]byte
}

func (s *inMemoryStateStore) saveState(w http.ResponseWriter, r *http.
    Request) {
    var items []stateItem
    body, _ := ioutil.ReadAll(r.Body)
```

255

```go
    json.Unmarshal(body, &items)

    for _, item := range items {
        s.store[item.Key] = item.Value
    }

    w.WriteHeader(http.StatusOK)
}

func (s *inMemoryStateStore) getState(w http.ResponseWriter, r *http.Request) {
    key := mux.Vars(r)["key"]
    value, found := s.store[key]

    if !found {
        w.WriteHeader(http.StatusNotFound)
        return
    }

    w.Write(value)
}

func (s *inMemoryStateStore) deleteState(w http.ResponseWriter, r *http.Request) {
    key := mux.Vars(r)["key"]
    delete(s.store, key)

    w.WriteHeader(http.StatusOK)
}

func main() {
    store := &inMemoryStateStore{
        store: make(map[string][]byte),
    }

    router := mux.NewRouter()
    router.HandleFunc("/state", store.saveState).Methods("POST")
    router.HandleFunc("/state/{key}", store.getState).Methods("GET")
    router.HandleFunc("/state/{key}", store.deleteState).Methods("DELETE")

    log.Fatal(http.ListenAndServe(":5000", router))
}

type stateItem struct {
    Key string `json:"key"`
    Value []byte `json:"value"`
}
```

In this example, the custom state store component uses an in-memory map to save, retrieve, and delete state items. The API routes expose the necessary operations so that Dapr can interact with the state management interface.

- **Security and Configuration Considerations**

  Security is a critical aspect of custom components, particularly when component interactions involve sensitive data or operations. Developers must ensure secure transport via HTTPS and validate input data rigorously to protect against common vulnerabilities such as injection attacks.

Additionally, the configuration of custom components should be managed carefully. Sensitivity to changes in configuration can be managed dynamically, ensuring the component adapts without needing downtime or manual intervention. Configuration settings might include endpoints, credentials, and specific performance tuning parameters.

For example, environment variables can be used to manage sensitive data such as passwords or API tokens:

```
export CUSTOM_DB_PASSWORD="securepassword"
```

In your application, access these variables securely:

```
import (
    "os"
    "fmt"
)

func main() {
    password := os.Getenv("CUSTOM_DB_PASSWORD")
    fmt.Println("Using database password from environment:", password)
}
```

- **Testing and Validation**

    Rigorous testing and validation are essential before deploying custom components in a production environment. This includes unit testing individual functions, integration testing with Dapr, and end-to-end testing with the entire application ecosystem.

    For instance, testing the functionality of a custom state store component can be done using a combination of mock data and testing frameworks. In Go, 'httptest' is commonly used for testing HTTP-based components:

```
package main

import (
    "net/http"
    "net/http/httptest"
    "testing"
    "strings"
    "io/ioutil"
```

```
)
func TestSaveState(t *testing.T) {
    store := &inMemoryStateStore{}
    store.initialize()

    req, _ := http.NewRequest("POST", "/state", strings.NewReader('[{"key":
        "test", "value": "42"}]'))
    rr := httptest.NewRecorder()
    handler := http.HandlerFunc(store.saveState)
    handler.ServeHTTP(rr, req)

    if status := rr.Code; status != http.StatusOK {
        t.Errorf("handler returned wrong status code: got %v want %v", status,
            http.StatusOK)
    }
}
```

This test ensures that the 'saveState' function responds correctly to a valid request. Further tests would likely cover edge cases and invalid inputs to ensure robustness.

- **Deployment and Monitoring**

    Once developed and tested, custom components should be deployed as part of a broader Dapr application, ensuring they are registered correctly and available to the microservices requiring them. Monitoring the performance and availability of custom components can be achieved by integrating logging and observability tools, such as Prometheus and Grafana.

    Including meaningful logs and metrics within your component code enables easier debugging and optimization. Here's a simple illustration of logging requests in the state store component:

```
func (s *inMemoryStateStore) saveState(w http.ResponseWriter, r *http.
    Request) {
    log.Println("Saving state from request")
    // Rest of the save logic...
}
```

With efficient logging in place, developers can diagnose issues and monitor system health proactively.

Developing custom components in Dapr represents a sophisticated strategy to tailor microservice environments precisely to application demands. Through thoughtful implementation and testing, these components help bridge the gaps between existing capabilities and unique application requirements, enhancing flexibility and extensibility in distributed systems.

9.3 Multi-Cloud and Hybrid Deployments

The deployment of applications across multiple cloud providers and hybrid environments, known as multi-cloud and hybrid deployments, is an increasingly important strategy in today's enterprise architectures. Dapr is strategically positioned to facilitate these deployments by providing an abstraction layer that manages the complexity of connecting services across diverse infrastructures. This section examines the principles, methodologies, and advantages of using Dapr for multi-cloud and hybrid cloud deployments, along with practical implementations and considerations.

Understanding Multi-Cloud and Hybrid Environments

Multi-cloud environments involve utilizing services from multiple cloud providers, such as AWS, Microsoft Azure, and Google Cloud Platform, to host various parts of an application. Hybrid environments integrate on-premises infrastructure with cloud services, offering a blend of private and public cloud resources. These strategies are employed to increase resilience, optimize performance, and meet regulatory compliance.

The inherent challenges in these environments include interoperability between different platforms, consistent performance, latency issues, and managing disparate services collectively. Dapr addresses many of these challenges by providing uniform interfaces and a consistent architecture that abstracts provider-specific implementations.

Deploying Dapr in Multi-Cloud Settings

Dapr's sidecar architecture makes it a fitting choice for multi-cloud deployments, as it decouples the application logic from cloud-specific services by hosting functionalities such as state management, service invocation, and pub/sub as external components. Each component can be deployed near the cloud service it interfaces with, optimizing for network latency and data transfer costs.

Consider a multi-cloud deployment where an e-commerce platform utilizes AWS for payment processing and Google Cloud for product catalog services. Using Dapr's state management and service invocation, the application components can be deployed in proximity to their respective cloud services, facilitating efficient communication.

An environment setup might include the following steps:

- Deploy Dapr on Kubernetes clusters across different cloud providers. Utilize services such as EKS (Elastic Kubernetes Service) on AWS and GKE (Google Kubernetes Engine) on Google Cloud.

- Configure Dapr components for each cloud service. Create YAML configurations for Dapr components such as state stores and pub-/sub for each cloud platform. An example configuration for an AWS DynamoDB state store:

```
apiVersion: dapr.io/v1alpha1
kind: Component
metadata:
  name: dynamodb-state
  namespace: default
spec:
  type: state.aws.dynamodb
  version: v1
  metadata:
  - name: region
    value: us-west-2
  - name: tableName
    value: OrderStateTable
  - name: accessKey
    value: YOUR_ACCESS_KEY
  - name: secretKey
    value: YOUR_SECRET_KEY
```

- Establish service invocation between components. Dapr enables interoperability between services residing on different cloud platforms through its service discovery mechanism, supporting hybrid URL schemas and gRPC for cross-cloud calls.

Implementing Hybrid Cloud Deployments with Dapr

Hybrid cloud deployments demand seamless integration between on-premises systems and cloud-hosted services. Dapr provides the nec-

9.3. MULTI-CLOUD AND HYBRID DEPLOYMENTS

essary abstraction to manage these interactions without exposing the complexity to the application layer.

For instance, a hybrid scenario may involve maintaining sensitive financial records in an on-premises Oracle database while utilizing cloud services for computational tasks and user interfaces. Dapr components can be configured to access the Oracle database locally and invoke computational services hosted on the cloud.

Sample component configuration for connecting to a local Oracle database:

```
apiVersion: dapr.io/v1alpha1
kind: Component
metadata:
  name: oraclestorage
  namespace: default
spec:
  type: state.sql.database
  version: v1
  metadata:
  - name: connectionString
    value: "oracle://localdbHost:1521/service"
  - name: user
    value: "admin"
  - name: password
    value: "securepassword"
```

The application's cloud services can be configured to interact with this component through Dapr's state API, abstracting the database vendor specifics.

Security and Compliance in Multi-Cloud and Hybrid Deployments

Security is a non-negotiable aspect of deploying applications in multi-cloud and hybrid architectures. Dapr facilitates secure communications through mutual TLS between services, ensuring encrypted data transfer both within and across cloud environments. Additionally, deploying Dapr with proper namespace and identity definitions helps in maintaining isolated and secure service interactions.

Regulatory compliance can be a significant driving factor for hybrid cloud deployments, where data residency requirements may dictate on-premises data storage. Dapr aids compliance efforts by enforcing consistent data handling practices through its state management components while ensuring extensibility for audit logging and monitoring.

Observability Across Distributed Infrastructure

Comprehensive observability is crucial for maintaining performance and reliability across multi-cloud and hybrid deployments. Dapr integrates with tools such as Prometheus and Grafana for metrics collection and visualization, providing actionable insights into service health and interaction.

Implementing a monitoring solution involves:

- Configure Dapr sidecar diagnostics. Enable tracing and logging features by setting environment variables in the component configurations or deploying Dapr with tracing extensions compatible with OpenTelemetry.

- Leverage distributed tracing for performance analysis. Dapr's integration with Zipkin or Jaeger can help track end-to-end execution paths across hybrid deployments, identifying bottlenecks and failure points. This involves setting up tracing components, as shown:

```
apiVersion: dapr.io/v1alpha1
kind: Component
metadata:
  name: tracing
  namespace: default
spec:
  type: tracing.zipkin
  version: v1
  metadata:
  - name: enabled
    value: "true"
  - name: exporterAddress
    value: "http://zipkin:9411/api/v2/spans"
```

- Utilize aggregated logs for diagnostics. By redirecting and centralizing logs from multiple cloud platforms into a single dashboard, operations teams can perform cohesive analytics and adopt automation for incident responses.

Case Study: A Financial Enterprise

Consider a financial institution employing a hybrid cloud strategy to run analytical tasks on raw data stored securely on-premises. The institution leverages Dapr to stitch together disparate systems, optimizing for computational efficiency and regulatory compliance.

- Data processing services deployed on Azure access customer data stored locally by invoking Dapr's service invocation and state management components.
- Publication of risk analysis results to Algo-trading algorithms hosted on AWS using Dapr's pub/sub building block, ensuring timely insights without leaking sensitive data.
- Strict data movement policies, enforced through Dapr's security practices, ensure that only sanctioned data interactions occur between the systems.
- Visibility and control are maintained using Grafana dashboards and alerting mechanisms monitoring Dapr's telemetry, ensuring smooth operations across dynamic infrastructure.

Through Dapr's adaptable framework, the institution harmonizes hybrid and multi-cloud operations, facilitating innovation while adhering to stringent regulatory mandates.

Deploying applications across multi-cloud and hybrid environments with Dapr empowers organizations to leverage diverse technological strengths, optimize resource allocations, and fulfill comprehensive business and regulatory demands. As these deployment strategies continue to evolve, Dapr's abstraction and extensibility ensure it remains a valuable tool for developers navigating the complexities of modern infrastructure.

9.4 Advanced Actor Patterns

In distributed computing, actor patterns serve as a powerful conceptual model for constructing scalable and resilient applications. Dapr incorporates actor patterns seamlessly, providing a robust framework for building stateful objects that can manage their own state and behavior independently. This section delves into the advanced patterns employed with Dapr actors, highlighting their ability to coordinate complex workflows, optimize system resource management, and ensure data integrity across distributed services.

- **Understanding the Actor Model**: The actor model abstracts system components as actors, each possessing a distinct identity, encapsulated state, and behavior. Actors communicate with one another through asynchronous message passing, thereby promoting concurrency and isolation. Dapr's actor implementation is built on this model, facilitating the construction of scalable microservices that handle individual tasks or pieces of business logic.

  Dapr actors differ from traditional microservices by their intrinsic capacity to manage state inherently within the actor instance, eliminating reliance on external databases for transient operations. This attribute makes Dapr actors particularly suitable for fine-grained state management and event-driven applications.

- **Actor Lifecycles and Their Management**: One of the core considerations when working with actors is managing their lifecycle. An actor's lifecycle dictates how the actor is activated, maintained, and deactivated within the system. Dapr automates lifecycle management, creating actors upon demand and deactivating them after periods of inactivity to optimize resource usage.

  Dapr employs configurable settings to dictate lifecycle behaviors, including:

    - Actor Idle Timeout: Defines how long an actor remains in memory without receiving requests. If this timeout elapses, the actor is deactivated. This can be configured in the actor configuration settings, typically expressed in a YAML format:

      ```
      idleTimeout: "5m"
      ```

    - Actor Scan Interval: Specifies the interval for scanning inactive actors. Shorter intervals may lead to more frequent deactivation, affecting performance, while longer intervals preserve resources but may delay memory reclamation.
    - Drain Rebalanced Actors: Ensures a smooth transition when actors are relocated within a cluster by completing

9.4. ADVANCED ACTOR PATTERNS

ongoing operations before deactivation. This ensures that workloads are distributed evenly without causing performance bottlenecks.

- **Implementing Actor Patterns for Distributed Workflows**: Advanced actor patterns commonly involve workflow orchestration, whereby multiple actors work together to complete cohesive operations. Consider the Saga pattern, an important pattern for managing complex, long-running transactions across distributed systems. By orchestrating tasks through distinct actors, developers can coordinate actions while maintaining consistency and facilitating compensation when failures occur.

An example scenario could involve processing an e-commerce order through multiple steps, each managed by separate actors: inventory allocation, payment processing, and order shipment. The following pseudocode illustrates this interaction:

```
class OrderProcessor(ActorType):
    def processOrder(self, orderDetails):
        transactionId = generateTransactionId()
        self.startSaga(transactionId, orderDetails)

    def startSaga(self, transactionId, orderDetails):
        # Begin by reserving inventory
        inventoryActor = self.getActor('InventoryService')
        inventoryActor.reserveInventory(
            transactionId,
            orderDetails.items
        )

    def inventorySuccess(self, transactionId, details):
        # Proceed to charge payment
        paymentActor = self.getActor('PaymentService')
        paymentActor.processPayment(transactionId, details.paymentInfo)

    def paymentFailure(self, transactionId, reason):
        # Compensate the inventory reservation
        inventoryActor = self.getActor('InventoryService')
        inventoryActor.releaseInventory(transactionId)

    def paymentSuccess(self, transactionId, details):
        # Finalize by arranging shipment
        shippingActor = self.getActor('ShippingService')
        shippingActor.shipOrder(transactionId, details.shippingInfo)

    def orderCompleted(self, transactionId):
        # Complete the saga successfully
        log.info(f"Order {transactionId} completed.")
```

```
def orderFailed(self, transactionId, reason):
    # Handle failed saga
    log.error(f"Order {transactionId} failed due to {reason}.")
```

This example illustrates the orchestration between inventory, payment, and shipping actors, enabling a distributed transaction mechanism where compensatory actions play a critical role in handling failures.

- **State Consistency and Persistence**: Actors are distinguished by their ability to manage state seamlessly. Managing state consistency is crucial, particularly when actors are responsible for sequential operations that depend on prior states. In Dapr, actor state management is facilitated through state persistence, which saves actor states in configurable state stores.

For example, persisting actor state to a Redis store involves setting up a state configuration:

```
apiVersion: dapr.io/v1alpha1
kind: Component
metadata:
  name: redis-state
  namespace: default
spec:
  type: state.redis
  version: v1
  metadata:
  - name: redisHost
    value: redis-master.default.svc.cluster.local:6379
  - name: actorStateStore
    value: "true"
```

Actors interact with this state store transparently, allowing automatic state retrieval and updates, thus ensuring consistency across operations.

- **Concurrency Management and Thread Safety**: Actors facilitate orchestration of concurrent operations, capitalizing on the actor model's message-passing capabilities to manage complex logic without extensive locking mechanisms. This is achieved through serializable message processing, where actors handle one operation at a time, thereby preventing race conditions.

9.4. ADVANCED ACTOR PATTERNS

Nonetheless, actors managing or interacting closely with shared resources must be engineered with thread safety. This is especially relevant in scenarios where actors interact with external databases, file systems, or network-based APIs.

Careful sequence coordination and state validation checks are imperative for maintaining application integrity and performance. The use of sophisticated locking structures or transactional operations might be necessary, depending on the complexity and demands of the operations involved.

- **Distributed Event-Driven Patterns with Actors**: Dapr actors integrate seamlessly with event-driven systems, allowing applications to respond dynamically to changes and events. By subscribing to events or changes in other services' states, actors can initiate workflows or adapt behaviors proactively.

  Consider an event-driven pattern where actors subscribe to a pub/sub system to receive task notifications, allowing distributed processing within the collective actor system. The following example demonstrates actor subscription to an event topic:

  ```
  def orderNotificationReceived(self, message: dict):
      orderId = message.get("orderId")
      self.handleOrderNotification(orderId)
  ```

  Simultaneously, actors can publish results or statuses back to the event stream, enhancing dynamic responsiveness between diverse system components.

- **Monitoring Actors in Production Environments**: Advanced actor systems necessitate comprehensive monitoring and diagnostics to sustain performance and identity bottlenecks. Dapr provides tracing and logging capabilities, enabling developers to monitor actor interaction paths and system efficiency.

  Implementing actor monitoring involves setting instrumented observability components directly into the actor codebase. Leveraging logging libraries and integrated telemetry can provide a detailed view of actor lifecycles, transaction paths, and network flows:

```python
import logging

class InventoryService(ActorType):
    def init(self):
        logging.basicConfig(level=logging.INFO)

    def reserveInventory(self, transactionId, items):
        logging.info(f"Reserving inventory for transaction {transactionId}: {items}")
        # Perform reservation logic
```

Additionally, visualizing captured metrics using tools like Grafana can help track system load and resource allocation, facilitating proactive scaling and optimization strategies.

Advanced Dapr actor patterns provide a flexible, scalable framework for managing stateful, concurrent interactions across distributed systems. By mastering these patterns, developers can exploit actor model benefits to construct robust, resilient applications capable of meeting complex and dynamic business requirements. As systems scale and evolve, Dapr's actor framework establishes a foundation for innovation and continuity within the distributed computing landscape.

9.5 Leveraging Dapr with Event-Driven Architectures

Integrating Dapr with event-driven architectures can significantly enhance the adaptability, scalability, and maintainability of modern applications. Event-driven architectures (EDAs) serve as a blueprint for designing systems that react to changes and process events asynchronously, decoupling event producers from consumers. Dapr provides a robust foundation to implement these architectures, offering features that streamline the management of event flows between distributed services. This section explores how Dapr can be efficiently harnessed in building event-driven systems, emphasizing the role of pub/sub components, bindings, and observability tools.

At the core of event-driven architectures is the principle of decoupling: event producers (or sources) generate events independent of event consumers (or sinks). This pattern enables scalability and flexibility, as components can evolve independently. An EDA primarily consists of three components:

- Event Emitters: Components or services generating events.

- Event Routers: Mechanisms that distribute events between producers and consumers, often leveraging message brokers or pub-/sub systems.

- Event Listeners: Components that consume events to trigger specific operations.

In such architectures, artificial extensions like event sourcing or CQRS (Command Query Responsibility Segregation) may be employed to enhance system design.

Dapr's pub/sub building block abstracts the complexities involved with implementing pub/sub patterns, providing seamless integration with several message brokers such as Redis, Azure Service Bus, Kafka, and more. This abstraction allows developers to focus on business logic without delving into the intricacies of integrating with these platforms directly.

Consider a system where user actions within an application need to be logged for analytics. The user service publishes events such as "userLoggedIn" or "userClickedButton," while the analytics service subscribes to these events. The following are steps and configurations necessary to establish this communication with a Kafka message broker:

- Set Up a Kafka Pub/Sub Component: First, configure the Kafka component using Dapr's component specification language.

```
apiVersion: dapr.io/v1alpha1
kind: Component
metadata:
  name: myKafkaPubSub
  namespace: default
spec:
  type: pubsub.kafka
  version: v1
  metadata:
  - name: brokers
    value: kafka-broker.kafka:9092
  - name: consumerGroup
    value: myGroup
```

CHAPTER 9. ADVANCED DAPR FEATURES AND INTEGRATIONS

```
- name: authRequired
  value: "false"
- name: topics
  value: user-actions
```

- **Publish an Event**: In the user service, publish events using Dapr's pub/sub API. Here's an example in Python that publishes an event when a user logs in:

```python
from dapr.clients import DaprClient

with DaprClient() as client:
    order_event = {"userId": "12345", "event": "userLoggedIn"}
    client.publish_event(
        pubsub_name="myKafkaPubSub",
        topic_name="user-actions",
        data=order_event,
        data_content_type='application/json'
    )
    print("Published user login event.")
```

- **Subscribe to Events**: The analytics service subscribes to events via HTTP or gRPC endpoints registered with Dapr. Coupled with a consumer group, this ensures idempotency and fault tolerance across distributed instances.

```javascript
const express = require('express');
const app = express();

app.use(express.json());

app.post('/user-actions', (req, res) => {
    const event = req.body;
    console.log('Processing user actions: ', event);
    // Perform analytics operations
    res.sendStatus(200);
});

const port = 3000;
app.listen(port, () => console.log(`Analytics service listening on port ${port}`));
```

Another pivotal feature Dapr provides is input/output bindings, enabling microservices to interact with external systems as triggers for events. Input bindings listen for events occurring in these systems, while output bindings allow the emission of data to them. Dapr's bindings support multiple systems, including cloud event queues, databases, and file storage services.

9.5. LEVERAGING DAPR WITH EVENT-DRIVEN ARCHITECTURES

For instance, consider an application that processes incoming support tickets from a cloud queue. When incoming tickets appear, input bindings can invoke a service method, automating the workflows:

- Configure the Binding: Set up an input binding for a queue, such as Azure Queue Storage, which triggers the application:

```
apiVersion: dapr.io/v1alpha1
kind: Component
metadata:
  name: azurequeue-binding
  namespace: default
spec:
  type: bindings.azure.storagequeues
  version: v1
  metadata:
  - name: storageAccount
    value: mystorageaccount
  - name: storageAccessKey
    value: your-access-key
  - name: queue
    value: supportTicketsQueue
```

- Handle Incoming Events: The bound service routes tickets for processing:

```
from flask import Flask, request

app = Flask(__name__)

@app.route('/supportTicketsQueue', methods=['POST'])
def process_ticket():
    ticket = request.json
    print("Processing support ticket: ", ticket)
    # Business logic to handle the ticket
    return ('', 200)

app.run(port=5000)
```

- Output Bindings: Similarly, output bindings can send processed data back to a queue or another external system, streamlining asynchronous processing.

Effective event-driven architectures leverage key design patterns to optimize event flows, ensuring these systems meet scalability and resilience goals:

- Event Choreography: Each microservice reacts to events and may emit subsequent events as a result. This promotes loose coupling between services but requires meticulous design to avoid circular dependencies and to ensure reliability over large volumes of events.

- Event Sourcing and CQRS: Storing the state as a sequence of events rather than overwriting current states provides an immutable log of changes. Coupled with CQRS, which divides read and write operations, this pattern facilitates scalability and state reconstruction after failures.

Dapr simplifies implementing these patterns by abstracting state stores and enabling atomic transaction handling.

Visibility into event flows and application behavior is essential for diagnosing issues, optimizing performance, and improving fault tolerance in EDAs. Dapr enhances observability through integration with distributed tracing, logging, and metrics collection tools.

Implementing observability for Dapr-enabled EDAs may involve:

- Enable Distributed Tracing: Employing OpenTelemetry with tracing components like Zipkin or Jaeger can ensure trace collection across service boundaries. Configure tracing by defining components:

```
apiVersion: dapr.io/v1alpha1
kind: Component
metadata:
  name: tracing
  namespace: default
spec:
  type: tracing.zipkin
  version: v1
  metadata:
  - name: enabled
    value: "true"
  - name: exporterAddress
    value: "http://zipkin:9411/api/v2/spans"
```

- Aggregate Logging: Utilize centralized log services like Elasticsearch and Kibana to aggregate logs generated by distributed services running Dapr, enabling seamless log analysis.

- Monitor Real-Time Metrics: Leveraging Prometheus with Grafana dashboards helps visualize service health, latency, and event throughput, facilitating proactive resource management and alerting.

Imagine an e-commerce platform that handles order processing via an advanced event-driven system. Different microservices manage inventory, payment, and shipment. Leveraging Dapr, the architecture uses:

- Pub/Sub for Order Events: Orders placed trigger events routed to inventory and payment services.
- Choreography and Compensation Patterns: Inventory and payment failures lead to compensation actions, reinforcing system reliability.
- State Persistence for Event Sourcing: Each service maintains state independently, storing pertinent changes in state stores like CosmosDB, allowing flexible scaling and resilience.

Real-time monitoring with Grafana dashboards secures this architecture, delineating transaction flows, performance indicators, and congestion points, offering insights for continuous improvements.

By deploying Dapr for event-driven architectures, developers can streamline decoupled interactions and construct resilient, scalable applications that adapt rapidly to evolving business needs. As enterprises advance, Dapr remains a focal asset, simplifying orchestration amidst complex distributed systems.

9.6 Optimizing Performance with Dapr

Optimization of application performance is a critical consideration when employing Dapr for building microservices-based applications. The inherent distributed nature of these applications often introduces complexities related to latency, throughput, and resource utilization. Dapr's design provides several opportunities for enhancing performance while maintaining scalability and reliability. This section delves into key strategies and methodologies for optimizing performance with Dapr, exploring configurations, code-level adjustments, and architectural considerations.

Understanding Dapr's architecture and overheads is essential for effective optimization. Dapr is designed as a sidecar architecture, where each microservice instance communicates with a Dapr sidecar that provides access to Dapr's APIs and building blocks. This design introduces a certain amount of overhead due to interprocess communication and network hops, which can impact latency and resource usage. However, the structured abstraction Dapr offers outweighs these costs in numerous scenarios by simplifying service development and operation.

To effectively optimize performance with Dapr, it's essential to understand key architectural elements:

- **Service Invocation**: Facilitates communication between services over HTTP or gRPC. Choosing the optimal communication protocol based on expected payloads and latency requirements can yield performance gains.

- **State Management**: Handles distributed state persistence. Selecting appropriate state stores and strategies for state access patterns significantly impacts response times and scalability.

- **Pub/Sub**: Provides asynchronous message communication. The chosen message broker and configuration (e.g., batch processing, topic partitioning) play crucial roles in achieving throughput goals.

By strategically configuring these components and employing best practices, developers can enhance system-wide performance.

Optimizing Communication Protocols

The choice between HTTP and gRPC for service invocation is fundamental to optimizing network-related performance. gRPC generally provides more efficient communication with lower latency and higher throughput due to its use of HTTP/2 for transport, binary message encoding, and built-in support for multiplexing requests.

Consider a scenario where services need rapid communication with minimal latency. Opting for gRPC might look as follows:

```
from dapr.clients import DaprClient
with DaprClient() as client:
```

9.6. OPTIMIZING PERFORMANCE WITH DAPR

```
content = b'Hello from service A'
# Use gRPC for lower latency
response = client.invoke_method(
    app_id='service-b',
    method_name='MethodB',
    data=content,
    http_verb='POST',
    headers={'Content-Type': 'application/grpc'}
)
print(response.text())
```

For high throughput scenarios, especially when handling large data transfers, buffering and chunking techniques might also be employed. Furthermore, employing client-side and server-side request/response compressions can be beneficial.

Configuring Sidecar Resources

The Dapr sidecar process itself requires resource management to ensure optimal performance. Proper allocation of CPU and memory resources to the Dapr sidecar can prevent bottlenecks and ensure consistent performance, especially under high load conditions.

Resource limits and requests for the Dapr sidecar in Kubernetes can be set within deployment specifications to ensure adequate allocation as follows:

```
apiVersion: apps/v1
kind: Deployment
metadata:
  name: my-app
spec:
  replicas: 2
  template:
    metadata:
      labels:
        app: my-app
    spec:
      containers:
      - name: my-app
        image: my-app:latest
        resources:
          requests:
            cpu: "500m"
            memory: "256Mi"
          limits:
            cpu: "1"
            memory: "512Mi"
      - name: daprd
        image: daprio/dapr
        resources:
          requests:
            cpu: "200m"
```

```
      memory: "100Mi"
    limits:
      cpu: "500m"
      memory: "200Mi"
```

Careful management of these resources ensures that the Dapr sidecar delivers the required performance without starving the main application.

Enhancing State Management Strategies

State management in Dapr should be optimized based on the component's nature and data access patterns. Several strategies can help improve performance:

- **Choosing the Right State Store**: Various state stores (e.g., Redis, MongoDB, Cosmos DB) offer different performance characteristics. Selecting a store based on the application's consistency, latency, and throughput requirements is crucial.

- **Data Partitioning and Sharding**: For high-volume applications, partitioning data across multiple shards or partitions can increase parallelism and reduce load on individual data stores, improving performance metrics like query response times.

- **Read and Write Caching**: Utilizing local or near-cache mechanisms can reduce access latencies for frequently read data, decreasing the frequency of hitting persistent stores and improving response times.

In practice, caching can be implemented at the application or component level with techniques such as using in-memory databases (like Redis) or employing local caches within the microservice code itself.

Optimizing Pub/Sub Patterns

To optimize performance for applications relying heavily on pub/sub models, developers should consider aspects like broker choice, message formats, and subscription configurations:

- **Message Broker Selection**: Systems like Kafka or Azure Service Bus are designed for different load profiles and latency characteristics. The choice of message broker should align with the

9.6. OPTIMIZING PERFORMANCE WITH DAPR

specific requirements of message durability, order guarantees, and frequency.

- **Efficient Message Payloads**: Employ compact serialization formats like Protocol Buffers or Avro, reducing serialization/deserialization overhead and network transfer time.

- **Subscription Management**: Control consumer concurrency levels, employ message batching, and handle parallel processing to maximize throughput while maintaining manageable resource consumption.

Implementing pub/sub can be achieved through Dapr with precisely tuned configurations:

```
apiVersion: dapr.io/v1alpha1
kind: Component
metadata:
  name: kafka-pubsub
  namespace: default
spec:
  type: pubsub.kafka
  version: v1
  metadata:
  - name: brokers
    value: "kafka.default.svc.cluster.local:9092"
  - name: consumerGroup
    value: "performance-group"
  - name: authRequired
    value: "false"
  - name: maxMessageRetries
    value: "3"
```

Monitoring and Observability

Comprehensive monitoring is vital to understanding performance and driving optimization. Dapr provides capabilities to incorporate observability into microservices, enabling real-time performance tracking and anomaly detection.

Key monitoring practices include:

- **Logging**: Implement structured logging within services and Dapr sidecars to capture performance-related data points and transactional flows.

- **Metrics Collection**: Utilize Prometheus to gather metrics related to service response times, error rates, and resource utilization. Create Grafana dashboards to visualize these metrics dynamically, aiding in trend analysis.

- **Distributed Tracing**: Employ OpenTelemetry to achieve detailed tracing across service boundaries, revealing latency issues and helping pinpoint bottlenecks.

Typical configuration for dynamic observability:

```
apiVersion: dapr.io/v1alpha1
kind: Component
metadata:
  name: tracing
  namespace: default
spec:
  type: tracing.zipkin
  version: v1
  metadata:
  - name: enabled
    value: "true"
  - name: exporterAddress
    value: "http://zipkin:9411/api/v2/spans"
```

Case Study: Performance Optimization for Retail Platform

A retail platform implementing Dapr across its diverse services—catalog management, order processing, and shipment tracking—undertakes an optimization process focusing on:

- **Adopting gRPC for Service Communication**: Switching from REST APIs to gRPC enhanced response times for synchronous, intra-data center calls, particularly for latency-critical interactions like payment and inventory checks.

- **State Store Strategy**: Transition from a general-purpose state store to a highly-optimized, low-latency Redis setup enabled faster inventory updates and reduced downtime during high-transaction periods.

- **Enhanced Monitoring**: With Prometheus metrics and Grafana visualizations, the platform identified key congestion points in the order process, allowing informed scaling decisions, which in turn improved overall throughput by 25%.

Through tailored implementations of Dapr across its architectural landscape, the retail platform could meet customer demands, handle peak loads efficiently, and maintain competitive responsiveness.

Optimizing performance with Dapr entails careful consideration of multiple factors—ranging from communication protocols and resource allocations to caching strategies and message patterns. By applying these insights and continuously refining system design based on observability feedback, developers can leverage Dapr to build sophisticated, high-performing microservice applications that align with modern demands.

9.7 Case Studies and Real-World Integrations

The practical application of Dapr in real-world scenarios demonstrates its versatility and effectiveness in building scalable and reliable applications. This section explores various case studies and integrations where Dapr has been employed to solve complex problems, streamline development processes, and enhance operational efficiencies. By examining these case studies, we gain insights into how Dapr's abstractions and components are leveraged in diverse industries, offering best practices and tangible outcomes.

- **Case Study 1: Global E-Commerce Platform**

    One of the most illustrative examples of Dapr in action is a global e-commerce platform that faced challenges with scaling its services to accommodate fluctuating demand during peak shopping seasons. The platform needed a solution that could facilitate rapid scaling without sacrificing performance or reliability.

    - **Problem**: With traditional monolithic architectures, the platform struggled with slow deployment cycles, increased downtime during updates, and limited scalability. The infrastructure needed to constantly adapt to sudden traffic spikes during promotional sales, leading to bottlenecks and reduced customer satisfaction.
    - **Solution**: Leveraging Dapr, the platform rearchitected its systems into microservices spread across multiple cloud

CHAPTER 9. ADVANCED DAPR FEATURES AND INTEGRATIONS

regions. This redesign focused on enhancing flexibility through a combination of Dapr's building blocks—service invocation and pub/sub—to manage internal communications and processing.

– **Implementation**:

  * **Service Invocation**: Using Dapr's service invocation API, the platform decoupled service interactions between customer, inventory, and payment services, facilitating load distribution across regions.

```
import "github.com/dapr/go-sdk/client"

func invokeInventoryService(itemId string) {
    client, err := client.NewClient()
    if err != nil {
        panic(err)
    }
    defer client.Close()

    resp, err := client.InvokeServiceWithContent(context.
        Background(),
        "inventory-service",
        "checkAvailability",
        &client.DataContent{ContentType: "application/json", Data:
            []byte('{"itemId":"' + itemId + '"}')})

    if err != nil {
        panic(err)
    }
    fmt.Println("Inventory service response:", string(resp))
}
```

  * **Distributed Pub/Sub**: The application employed Kafka via Dapr's pub/sub components to manage order events, ensuring seamless communication between different services regardless of geographical location.

```
apiVersion: dapr.io/v1alpha1
kind: Component
metadata:
  name: orders
  namespace: platform
spec:
  type: pubsub.kafka
  version: v1
  metadata:
  - name: brokers
    value: kafka-broker1:9092,kafka-broker2:9092
  - name: topics
    value: inventory,notifications,billing
```

9.7. CASE STUDIES AND REAL-WORLD INTEGRATIONS

- **Outcomes and Benefits**:
  Implementing Dapr transformed the platform's performance, reducing latency by over 40% and achieving near-linear scalability. The deployment times improved significantly, with downtime during updates nearly eliminated due to the microservices architecture. Customer satisfaction increased with faster service, particularly noticeable during high-demand times.

- **Case Study 2: Financial Services Firm**

  A financial services firm focused on providing real-time investment insights leveraged Dapr to transition from a cumbersome on-premises infrastructure to an agile cloud-based solution.

  - **Problem**: The firm's legacy systems struggled with processing and delivering real-time data streams across its user base. Delays in data processing and service unavailability during peak times were prevalent, significantly impacting user experience.

  - **Solution**: By adopting Dapr, the firm modularized its architecture, using Dapr components for state management and service invocation, transforming its data pipeline into a robust, flexible system deployed across multiple cloud environments.

  - **Implementation**:
    * **State Management**: Key-value state management through Dapr's abstraction over Azure Cosmos DB ensured low-latency access to investment data.

```
apiVersion: dapr.io/v1alpha1
kind: Component
metadata:
  name: cosmosdb-state
  namespace: finance
spec:
  type: state.azure.cosmosdb
  version: v1
  metadata:
  - name: url
    value: https://<cosmosdb_account>.documents.azure.com:443/
  - name: masterKey
    value: <account-master-key>
  - name: database
```

```
      value: investments
    - name: collection
      value: portfolio
```

* **Real-Time Event Processing**: The use of a pub/sub pattern with RabbitMQ allowed the firm to handle real-time data feeds with higher throughput and reliability.

```
apiVersion: dapr.io/v1alpha1
kind: Component
metadata:
  name: rabbitmq-pubsub
  namespace: finance
spec:
  type: pubsub.rabbitmq
  version: v1
  metadata:
  - name: host
    value: amqp://guest:guest@rabbitmq:5672/
  - name: durable
    value: true
```

- **Outcomes and Benefits**:

  The Dapr-enabled architecture yielded remarkable improvements, including a 50% reduction in data processing times and a significant increase in system availability. The firm's ability to deliver real-time insights was enhanced, leading to a more dynamic interaction with clients.

- **Case Study 3: Healthcare Technology Integration**

  A healthcare provider aiming to integrate disparate healthcare records into a single, comprehensive view of patient history turned to Dapr to streamline its data integration capabilities.

  - **Problem**: Previous attempts to integrate healthcare data sources across multiple systems were hampered by inconsistencies in data formats and reliability issues in data exchanges.

  - **Solution**: The healthcare provider utilized Dapr bindings to connect with various data providers and APIs, while Dapr's state management abstracted data persistence.

  - **Implementation**:

    * **Data Integration Bindings**: Using bindings for Azure Blob Storage and REST APIs simplified

integration with existing electronic health record (EHR) systems.

```
apiVersion: dapr.io/v1alpha1
kind: Component
metadata:
  name: azureblob-binding
  namespace: healthcare
spec:
  type: bindings.azure.blobstorage
  version: v1
  metadata:
  - name: accountName
    value: healthcaredata
  - name: accountKey
    value: <storage-account-key>
  - name: container
    value: patient-records
```

* **Consistent State Persistence**: Persisting patient state across interactions using Redis supported the aggregation of multiple data formats into a unified schema.

```
apiVersion: dapr.io/v1alpha1
kind: Component
metadata:
  name: redis-statestore
  namespace: healthcare
spec:
  type: state.redis
  version: "v1"
  metadata:
  - name: redisHost
    value: my-redis:6379
```

– **Outcomes and Benefits**:

The integration streamlined data access, reducing discrepancies and improving diagnostics through a single patient view, ultimately enhancing patient care. The provider reported improved data accuracy and a reduction in processing delays, facilitating better-informed clinical decisions.

- **Insights from Real-World Integrations**

These case studies present a consistent pattern of improvement, indicating Dapr's positive impact on diverse applications. Their common themes reveal essential insights:

– **Scalability**: Dapr's support for microservices and seamless cloud deployment helps organizations scale horizontally, accommodating growth without performance degradation.

– **Interoperability**: By abstracting underlying complexities through standardized components, Dapr fosters interoperability across heterogeneous architectures.

– **Rapid Development and Deployment**: Dapr accelerates product development cycles by streamlining integration and reducing boilerplate code, encouraging innovation and a faster time-to-market.

The experiences shared herein underscore Dapr's value as a scalable, flexible, and robust platform for tackling modern development challenges and achieving transformative results.

Chapter 10

Deploying Dapr in Cloud-Native Environments

This chapter outlines deployment strategies for running Dapr in cloud-native environments, emphasizing alignment with cloud-native principles. It explains setting up cloud-based infrastructure, deploying Dapr on Kubernetes, and scaling applications to meet demand efficiently. Additionally, the chapter covers management of Dapr applications in production, leveraging cloud provider services, and implementing CI/CD pipelines to streamline deployment processes, ensuring robust and scalable application development in the cloud.

10.1 Understanding Cloud-Native Principles

The principles of cloud-native architecture are central to creating software systems that can fully leverage cloud computing's potential. At its core, cloud-native architecture emphasizes automation, scalability, and resilience, allowing developers to build and run applications that take full advantage of the cloud environment. Understanding these principles is crucial for deploying distributed systems in which elements can dynamically scale, recover from failures, and accelerate time-to-market.

One primary principle of cloud-native architecture is the concept of microservices. Microservices refer to the architectural style that structures an application as a collection of loosely coupled services, each of which represents a specific business function. This approach contrasts with traditional monolithic architectures, where all components are built into a single unit. Microservices enable independent deployment and scaling of application components, facilitating agility in both development and deployment processes.

Implementing microservices typically involves the usage of APIs (Application Programming Interfaces) for communication between services. An essential part of cloud-native systems is the reliance on lightweight communication protocols such as HTTP/REST or gRPC. These protocols ensure that services can communicate efficiently no matter the underlying infrastructure. Developers often use API gateways to manage, secure, and control the flow of traffic between services, offering benefits such as centralized authentication, load balancing, and rate limiting.

```
from flask import Flask, jsonify, request

app = Flask(__name__)

@app.route('/hello', methods=['GET'])
def hello_world():
    return jsonify({'message': 'Hello, World!'})

if __name__ == '__main__':
    app.run(host='0.0.0.0', port=5000)
```

The above code demonstrates a simple RESTful microservice implemented in Python using Flask. It serves the '/hello' endpoint, returning a JSON-formatted response. Such services epitomize cloud-native design's simplicity and ease of deployment.

Another fundamental principle is containerization, which provides a consistent environment to deploy applications irrespective of the host

10.1. UNDERSTANDING CLOUD-NATIVE PRINCIPLES

system's specific configurations. Containers encapsulate a microservice, along with dependencies and runtime, into a single deployable unit. Technologies like Docker and container orchestration platforms such as Kubernetes are pivotal in managing these entities.

Using Kubernetes significantly streamlines the deployment and scaling of cloud-native applications. Kubernetes enables automatic scaling, load balancing, and self-healing of applications through its native orchestration capabilities. A Kubernetes deployment can be scaled up or down based on real-time demand, optimizing resource usage and cost.

```
apiVersion: apps/v1
kind: Deployment
metadata:
  name: example-deployment
spec:
  replicas: 3
  selector:
    matchLabels:
      app: example
  template:
    metadata:
      labels:
        app: example
    spec:
      containers:
      - name: example-container
        image: example-image:v1
        ports:
        - containerPort: 80
```

This YAML file specifies a Kubernetes deployment for an application named 'example-deployment'. The 'replicas' field indicates that the application should run three instances, ensuring availability and enabling load balancing. Kubernetes manages resource distribution across nodes, automatically deploying and scaling these instances based on the defined strategy.

A key cloud-native principle involves adopting a stateless architecture wherever possible. Stateless services are not dependent on data stored locally, making them inherently more scalable and resilient. In scenarios where state is necessary, for instance, user sessions in an e-commerce application, distributed databases or caches are often employed to manage state externally from the service logic.

Cloud-native architecture also prescribes the usage of infrastructure as code (IaC), which involves managing and provisioning computing resources through machine-readable definition files, rather than physical hardware or interactive configuration tools. Popular IaC tools include Terraform and CloudFormation, which allow developers to describe infrastructure in version-controlled code repositories, enhancing maintainability and enabling automation.

```
provider "aws" {
  region = "us-west-2"
}

resource "aws_instance" "example" {
  ami = "ami-08d70e59c07c61a3a"
  instance_type = "t2.micro"

  tags = {
    Name = "ExampleInstance"
  }
}
```

This Terraform script deploys an AWS EC2 instance. The IaC approach supports dynamic scaling and seamless updates, aligning with cloud-native principles of automation and speed.

Additionally, the twelve-factor app methodology serves as a foundational guideline for developing cloud-native applications, focusing on best practices such as strict separation of build and run stages, treating logs as event streams, and executing processes as one or more stateless services. This methodology aids in crafting services that are portable and easily deployable in any cloud environment.

Security is another pillar of cloud-native architecture, crucial for safeguarding the distributed nature of microservices. Implementing security at multiple layers, commonly known as defense in depth, ensures robust protection against potential vulnerabilities. Cloud-native applications leverage secure communication channels, such as Transport Layer Security (TLS), and apply principles like least privilege and zero trust to enhance security posture.

Observability is critical to maintaining the health and performance of cloud-native applications. This involves capturing, storing, and analyzing logs, metrics, and traces, often utilizing logging frameworks like Elastic Stack or monitoring systems like Prometheus and Grafana. These tools facilitate real-time insights into application performance and user behavior, enabling rapid detection and resolution of issues.

Embracing cloud-native principles requires a shift in mindset and organizational processes, incorporating DevOps practices to bridge development and operations. Continuous Integration/Continuous Deployment (CI/CD) pipelines automate the testing and deployment processes, ensuring that new code is seamlessly delivered to production environments with minimal human intervention. This practice not only accelerates release cycles but also reduces the risk of human error, embodying the cloud-native ethos of agility and reliability.

Ultimately, cloud-native principles empower organizations to build systems that are highly adaptable, scalable, and resilient. These principles address the growing need for applications to handle increased complexity and demand, unlocking new opportunities for innovation in the rapidly evolving digital landscape.

10.2 Preparing Your Environment for Dapr

Preparing an environment for deploying Dapr (Distributed Application Runtime) involves a systematic approach to setting up infrastructure that supports cloud-native application development and deployment. This section details the prerequisite steps and considerations necessary for an optimal Dapr implementation, ensuring the environment is both performant and resilient.

Before delving into environment setup, it's crucial to understand the role of Dapr. Dapr is a portable, event-driven runtime that simplifies the development of resilient, microservices-based applications. It abstracts away infrastructure complexities, enabling developers to focus on business logic. Central to preparing an environment for Dapr is establishing a robust foundation that accommodates its architecture and leverages its capabilities.

The initial step in preparing an environment for Dapr involves setting up a local development environment. This is critical for efficient testing and validation of microservices before deployment to production environments. Developers often utilize Docker for containerization, ensuring a consistent development environment across diverse systems. Installing Docker Desktop offers quick access to Docker functionalities for Windows, macOS, and Linux systems.

```
sudo apt-get update
sudo apt-get install docker-ce docker-ce-cli containerd.io
```

The above commands demonstrate how to install Docker on an Ubuntu system. Ensuring Docker is correctly installed and running constitutes a preliminary step not only for Dapr applications but for microservices in general.

Subsequently, Kubernetes serves as the orchestration platform, managing the deployment and scaling of microservices in a cluster environment. Setting up a local Kubernetes environment using Minikube or KinD (Kubernetes in Docker) is an ideal way to emulate production-like conditions on a developer's machine. Minikube creates a virtual machine that hosts the Kubernetes nodes, while KinD operates inside Docker containers, offering lightweight alternatives as local testing environments.

```
curl -LO https://storage.googleapis.com/minikube/releases/latest/minikube-linux-
    amd64
sudo install minikube-linux-amd64 /usr/local/bin/minikube
minikube start
```

Executing these commands initializes Minikube and starts a local Kubernetes cluster. Validate the successful setup by confirming your nodes' status through the 'kubectl' command-line tool.

With Docker and Kubernetes in place, install the Dapr CLI, which facilitates the management and deployment of Dapr building blocks in applications. The CLI supports interaction with Dapr instances, simplifying various operations such as 'init', 'run', and 'stop'.

```
wget -q https://raw.githubusercontent.com/dapr/cli/master/install/install.sh -O - | /
    bin/bash
```

Running this script installs the Dapr CLI, preparing your environment for runtime interactions. After installation, confirm Dapr's version to ensure it's accessible from the terminal.

Once the local environment is established, proceed to deploy Dapr on your Kubernetes setup. Deploying Dapr involves installing its runtime components, which include Dapr sidecar, placement service, operator, and other critical services required for functionality.

10.2. PREPARING YOUR ENVIRONMENT FOR DAPR

```
dapr init --kubernetes
```

Executing this command deploys Dapr to the local Kubernetes cluster, initializing its components and establishing necessary configurations to run alongside your applications.

Dapr's building blocks, such as state management, pub/sub messaging, and service invocation, require further configuration. This necessitates connecting with backend systems for comprehensive functionality. For example, configuring state stores or message brokers aligns Dapr's abstracted operations with specific infrastructure services. Developers must provide configuration YAML files with component details representing the backend system connections used by Dapr.

```
apiVersion: dapr.io/v1alpha1
kind: Component
metadata:
  name: statestore
  namespace: default
spec:
  type: state.redis
  version: v1
  metadata:
  - name: redisHost
    value: "redis-master.default.svc.cluster.local:6379"
  - name: redisPassword
    value: ""
```

This YAML file specifies a Dapr-compliant Redis state store in a Kubernetes cluster. With this configuration, services can utilize Redis without embedding its specifics in the service code, adhering to the principle of loose coupling.

Understanding the network security implications within Kubernetes is another vital step. Configuring network policies and access controls ensures protection against unauthorized access. Network policies in Kubernetes can be applied via YAML files to enforce communication rules between pods.

```
apiVersion: networking.k8s.io/v1
kind: NetworkPolicy
metadata:
  name: allow-dapr-traffic
spec:
  podSelector:
    matchLabels:
      app: dapr
  policyTypes:
```

```
- Ingress
ingress:
- from:
  - podSelector:
      matchLabels:
        app: myapplication
```

This network policy permits incoming traffic from pods labeled 'myapplication' to those labeled 'dapr'. Defining such rules is critical in maintaining a secure microservices infrastructure.

Developers should also integrate Continuous Integration and Continuous Deployment (CI/CD) pipelines to streamline deploying and updating Dapr applications. CI/CD tools, such as Jenkins or GitLab CI, automate testing, building, and deploying microservices, enhancing reliability and efficiency. Essential to building a CI/CD pipeline is checking the application's source code into a version control system such as Git and using build configuration files that detail the build process.

```
stages:
  - build
  - deploy

build:
  stage: build
  script:
    - docker build -t myapp-image .

deploy:
  stage: deploy
  script:
    - kubectl apply -f k8s/deployment.yaml
```

This configuration specifies a two-stage GitLab CI/CD pipeline to build and deploy Docker images to a Kubernetes cluster, aligning with cloud-native practices ensuring rapid, automated delivery of Dapr applications.

As a culmination of the preparation process, conducting thorough testing within your environment is essential. Load-testing tools and simulation tests gauge the readiness of the environment, identifying potential bottlenecks and points of failure. Tools like Locust or Apache Jmeter can simulate real-world loads to validate if the setup meets expected operational demands.

Establishing a performance baseline through testing informs optimizations and adjustments necessary to comply with production standards.

Ensuring scope for scalability is indispensable when preparing environments to accommodate fluctuating demands on distributed systems.

Ultimately, a thorough preparatory process primes your environment for efficient Dapr deployment, aligning closely with cloud-native applications' dynamic and scalable nature. Embracing these steps reinforces the foundational aspects necessary for leveraging Dapr's features fully, paving the way for productive, resilient, and scalable microservices systems in development and production ecosystems.

10.3 Deploying Dapr on Kubernetes

Deploying Dapr on Kubernetes involves a series of detailed steps designed to seamlessly integrate the Distributed Application Runtime into a Kubernetes ecosystem. This section comprehensively explores the processes, considerations, and configurations required to successfully deploy Dapr within Kubernetes, facilitating the management and operation of cloud-native, microservices-based applications.

Dapr harnesses Kubernetes' capabilities to deploy microservices by providing helping abstractions for state management, service invocation, pub/sub messaging, and more. As Kubernetes orchestrates container deployment, scheduling, and scaling, it inherently complements Dapr's runtime model, enabling developers to focus on designing resilient services without delving into infrastructure complexities.

- Before deploying Dapr, ensure a Kubernetes cluster is present and operational. Kubernetes clusters can be provisioned through various services, such as Google Kubernetes Engine (GKE), Amazon Elastic Kubernetes Service (EKS), or Azure Kubernetes Service (AKS). Local environments using Minikube or docker-based KinD are valuable for development and initial testing purposes.

- To interact with your Kubernetes cluster, the 'kubectl' command-line interface must be configured. 'kubectl' serves as the primary tool for running commands against Kubernetes clusters.

```
gcloud container clusters get-credentials [CLUSTER_NAME]
```

CHAPTER 10. DEPLOYING DAPR IN CLOUD-NATIVE ENVIRONMENTS

The above command retrieves the credentials and configures 'kubectl' for interaction with a GKE cluster. Each cloud provider has analogous steps to achieve 'kubectl' connectivity.

- Deploying Dapr on Kubernetes necessitates setting up its control plane, comprising the necessary components to manage the runtime operations. This control plane includes the Dapr Sidecar Injector, Operator, Placement Service, Sentry, and Dashboard.

Begin by installing the Dapr CLI, which simplifies many deployment and management tasks.

```
wget -q https://raw.githubusercontent.com/dapr/cli/master/install/install.sh -O - | /bin/bash
```

With the Dapr CLI installed, the next step is initializing Dapr within your Kubernetes cluster. This can be done using the following command:

```
dapr init --kubernetes
```

This command automatically configures and installs the necessary Dapr components in the Kubernetes cluster. These components span across several namespaces, managing the aspect of service invocation, state, binding, pub/sub, and observability within the cluster environment.

- After initializing Dapr, verify that all components are deployed correctly using 'kubectl'.

```
kubectl get pods --namespace dapr-system
```

The command should display the list of Dapr control plane pods. Each pod, such as the Sidecar Injector and Placement Service, should be up and running. Should any issues arise, logs can be retrieved using 'kubectl logs' to facilitate troubleshooting.

```
kubectl logs [POD_NAME] --namespace dapr-system
```

- "Daprizing" an application refers to integrating Dapr capabilities and components within existing services. This involves adding

10.3. DEPLOYING DAPR ON KUBERNETES

Dapr sidecars to application pods, which manage service invocation, state storage, and message brokering without embedding these functionalities directly in service logic.

Convert a typical Kubernetes deployment into a Dapr-aware deployment by introducing annotations that signal to Dapr to inject its sidecar:

```
apiVersion: apps/v1
kind: Deployment
metadata:
  name: myapp
spec:
  replicas: 3
  selector:
    matchLabels:
      app: myapp
  template:
    metadata:
      labels:
        app: myapp
      annotations:
        dapr.io/enabled: "true"
        dapr.io/app-id: "myapp"
    spec:
      containers:
      - name: myapp
        image: myapp-image:v1
        ports:
        - containerPort: 80
```

With the above configuration, Dapr is enabled for the application via the 'dapr.io/enabled' annotation. The 'dapr.io/app-id' annotation specifies a unique identifier used by various Dapr components to interact with the service. Enabling Dapr provides the service with access to sidecar functionalities to manage inter-service communication securely.

- Once integrated, Dapr components such as state stores, pub/sub brokers, and secret stores need configuration. Define these component configurations using YAML files and deploy them to the cluster.

Here's an example configuration for utilizing Redis as a state store:

```
apiVersion: dapr.io/v1alpha1
kind: Component
metadata:
```

```
  name: redis-statestore
  namespace: default
spec:
  type: state.redis
  version: v1
  metadata:
  - name: redisHost
    value: "my-redis-master.default.svc.cluster.local:6379"
  - name: redisPassword
    value: ""
```

Deploy the configuration using 'kubectl':

```
kubectl apply -f redis-component.yaml
```

Dapr automatically leverages this configuration within its sidecar components, simplifying the integration of such backend services with deployed applications.

- Securing inter-service communication is crucial as microservices interact extensively across the network. When deploying Dapr, fostering secure protocols such as mTLS (mutual Transport Layer Security) ensures data encryption in transit. Dapr's built-in support for mTLS facilitates secure communication across sidecars.

- Additionally, network policies and role-based access control (RBAC) should be enforced to limit access and permissions, aligning with security best practices. Define network policies within Kubernetes to control traffic flow between pods.

```
apiVersion: networking.k8s.io/v1
kind: NetworkPolicy
metadata:
  name: allow-dapr
spec:
  podSelector:
    matchLabels:
      app: myapp
  policyTypes:
  - Ingress
  ingress:
  - from:
    - podSelector:
        matchLabels:
          dapr.io/app-id: "myapp"
```

10.3. DEPLOYING DAPR ON KUBERNETES

This policy exemplifies limiting traffic to pods labeled with the specific app-id, reducing unauthorized access.

- Observability components are integral to monitoring and troubleshooting the deployed applications and their interactions with Dapr. Dapr's runtime captures metrics and exposes endpoints that can be integrated with external monitoring systems.

Leverage systems such as Prometheus for metrics aggregation and Grafana for visualization. Ensure that Dapr components expose necessary metrics for detailed insights into service operations.

For example, deploy a Prometheus configuration to scrape Dapr metrics as follows:

```
scrape_configs:
 - job_name: 'dapr'
   metrics_path: '/metrics'
   static_configs:
   - targets: ['dapr-sidecar:9090']
```

Such configurations enable detailed observation of service performance and allow stakeholders to promptly detect any anomalies, ensuring the reliability of applications running in the Kubernetes environment.

- Deploying Dapr on Kubernetes is an iterative process that benefits from adhering to best practices, including:

    - Continuously updating Dapr components to leverage performance improvements and security fixes.

    - Emphasizing a declarative approach through infrastructure-as-code for reproducible environments.

    - Regularly auditing configurations to align with compliance and security standards.

    - Automating deployments via CI/CD pipelines for efficient and error-minimized rollouts.

Ultimately, deploying Dapr on Kubernetes augments microservices architectures by abstracting complex runtime tasks and facilitating robust, scalable applications that align with modern cloud-native deployment principles. Through careful planning, configuration, and adherence to best practices, Dapr empowers developers to build sophisticated services with minimal operational overhead, pushing the boundaries of what is achievable in distributed systems design.

10.4 Scaling Dapr Applications

Scaling Dapr applications involves strategic considerations and technical executions that align with both cloud-native principles and the operational realities of diverse workloads. Effectively scaling microservices with Dapr enhances their capacity to handle increasing demand, optimizing resource utilization while maintaining service reliability and performance.

Inherently, Dapr services are conducive to scalability, primarily due to their microservices-based architecture. However, ensuring this scalability necessitates thoughtful implementation of scaling strategies, resource management, and monitoring practices to provide a robust environment that can meet the fluctuating needs of modern applications.

- **Horizontal and Vertical Scaling:** Dapr applications can be scaled both horizontally and vertically, each method having distinct advantages and considerations.

    - **Horizontal Scaling** refers to adding more service instances to distribute load. This approach enhances redundancy and allows systems to manage more requests concurrently. Kubernetes facilitates horizontal scaling through its replication controller and autoscaling mechanism.

    - **Vertical Scaling** involves increasing the resources (CPU, memory) allocated to a service. While this can be effective in maximizing the capacity of a single instance, it introduces limitations based on individual resource availability and cost efficiency.

- For cloud-native environments, horizontal scaling is typically preferred due to its flexibility and fault tolerance.

10.4. SCALING DAPR APPLICATIONS

- **Horizontal Pod Autoscaling (HPA):** Kubernetes' Horizontal Pod Autoscaler (HPA) automates the scaling of the number of pod replicas for a deployment based on observed CPU utilization or other select metrics. This is a critical tool for maintaining performance under variable load conditions.

To utilize HPA for a Dapr application, the deployment must specify resource requests and limits.

```
apiVersion: apps/v1
kind: Deployment
metadata:
  name: dapr-app
spec:
  replicas: 2
  selector:
    matchLabels:
      app: dapr-app
  template:
    metadata:
      labels:
        app: dapr-app
    spec:
      containers:
      - name: dapr-container
        image: dapr-image:v1
        resources:
          requests:
            memory: "64Mi"
            cpu: "250m"
          limits:
            memory: "128Mi"
            cpu: "500m"
```

This deployment configuration defines resource requests and limits, setting the stage for HPA to make informed scaling decisions based on resource consumption.

Define the HPA policy using the following YAML configuration:

```
apiVersion: autoscaling/v1
kind: HorizontalPodAutoscaler
metadata:
  name: dapr-app-hpa
spec:
  scaleTargetRef:
    apiVersion: apps/v1
    kind: Deployment
    name: dapr-app
  minReplicas: 2
  maxReplicas: 10
  targetCPUUtilizationPercentage: 75
```

This configuration instructs Kubernetes to maintain CPU utilization at 75%, scaling the number of pods automatically between 2 and 10 replicas based on current load, thereby ensuring the system can adapt to demand fluctuations.

- **Advanced Metrics and Custom Metrics for Scaling:** Beyond basic resource metrics like CPU and memory, custom metrics can provide more granular control over autoscaling decisions. Metrics such as request latency or message queue length can be more indicative of service load and user-perceived performance.

Kubernetes supports custom metrics through adapters such as Prometheus Adapter, which exposes custom application metrics to HPA:

```
apiVersion: autoscaling/v2beta2
kind: HorizontalPodAutoscaler
metadata:
  name: dapr-app-hpa
spec:
  scaleTargetRef:
    apiVersion: apps/v1
    kind: Deployment
    name: dapr-app
  minReplicas: 2
  maxReplicas: 10
  metrics:
  - type: Pods
    pods:
      metric:
        name: requests_per_second
      target:
        type: AverageValue
        averageValue: 100
```

In this example, the HPA scales the pods based on the custom metric requests_per_second, maintaining it around an average value of 100. This dynamic adaptability can significantly enhance an application's responsiveness to real operational demands.

- **Service Invocation and Load Balancing:** Load balancing is a crucial aspect of scaling Dapr applications as it manages the distribution of traffic among service instances, ensuring even workloads. Dapr integrates with underlying cloud-native systems to support advanced load-balancing techniques.

10.4. SCALING DAPR APPLICATIONS

Kubernetes inherently provides a level of load balancing through services, which distribute requests across available pod replicas. You can enhance this by leveraging Dapr's service invocation API, which includes its own built-in service discovery and invocation logic for efficient inter-service communication.

Designing effective load balancing strategies ensures service health and performance while scaling out. You can specify custom routing rules and priorities based on business logic or performance assessments to optimize request distribution intelligently.

- **Stateful Services and Scaling:** Most microservices applications, while aiming to be stateless, often contend with stateful elements like databases or user sessions. Scaling stateful services requires careful consideration to ensure consistency and reliability across distributed systems.

Dapr facilitates state management via its state API, which abstracts backend state stores such as Redis, Azure Cosmos DB, or AWS DynamoDB. When scaling applications with stateful dependencies, architects should ensure that Dapr components are configured for multi-instance environments:

```
apiVersion: dapr.io/v1alpha1
kind: Component
metadata:
  name: statestore
  namespace: default
spec:
  type: state.redis
  version: v1
  metadata:
  - name: redisHost
    value: "redis-primary.default.svc.cluster.local:6379"
  - name: redisPassword
    value: ""
  - name: enablePartitioning
    value: "true"
```

Enabling partitioning and horizontal scaling of state backends underpins an application's capability to grow while preserving data integrity and performance across scale changes.

- **Monitoring and Observability:** To maintain application health during scale, a robust monitoring framework is essential.

Observability in Dapr encompasses collecting logs, metrics, and traces, which provide insights into how applications perform under various loads.

Prometheus and Grafana can be configured to track application-specific and Dapr-sidecar metrics, such as service response times and inter-service call latencies. Dapr includes support for OpenTelemetry, which can be integrated with systems to collect distributed traces that detail interactions between services.

Using these insights, you can identify bottlenecks or failures potentially induced by scaling and adjust strategy as needed.

- **Challenges and Considerations:** Scaling Dapr applications also requires diligence regarding:
    - **Cold Starts:** Rapid scaling events may introduce delays (cold starts) as new instances provision and initialize. Fine-tuning container images and resource requests can mitigate these effects.
    - **Cost Management:** Balancing resource allocation to avoid overprovisioning while maintaining service quality impacts costs. Continuous monitoring aids in identifying optimal scaling points.
    - **Latency Sensitivity:** Applications sensitive to network latency may require specific configuration or infrastructure adjustments, such as colocating services or optimizing communication paths.

- **Scaling Best Practices:** Implementing effective scaling strategies aligns with best practices in service design and architecture.
    - Employ asynchronous messaging patterns to decouple services, allowing them to scale independently.
    - Use circuit breaker and retry policies to handle intermittent failures gracefully.
    - Leverage service meshes alongside Dapr to manage network-level concerns such as retries, failovers, and congestion control.

Scaling Dapr applications in Kubernetes enhances the resilience and capacity to handle variances in demand, aligning with cloud-native development paradigms. This transformative capability supports a durable, customer-focused service delivery model that not only sustains current growth but also accommodates future expansions and enhancements in application ecosystems.

10.5 Managing Dapr in Production

Managing Dapr in a production environment involves a strategic approach to ensure operational efficiency, reliability, and scalability. While Dapr simplifies the intricacies of deploying microservices-based architectures, managing its runtime components in production settings requires attention to best practices, monitoring, security, and ongoing maintenance.

The transition from development to production encompasses several considerations unique to operating microservices in a cloud-native ecosystem. This section elaborates on these aspects, providing insight into effectively managing Dapr applications at scale in a production environment.

- **Ensuring Robust Deployment Practices:** Successful management of Dapr in production begins with robust deployment strategies. Utilizing infrastructure-as-code (IaC) tools such as Terraform or GitOps methodologies ensures environments are consistent, reproducible, and traceable across deployments.

  In production, the usage of Continuous Integration/Continuous Deployment (CI/CD) pipelines is crucial. A well-established pipeline automates the testing, validation, and release processes, minimizing human error and accelerating time-to-market for updates and new features.

  A typical GitOps workflow deploys changes using Git repositories as the source of truth for declarative infrastructure. Tools like Flux or Argo CD continuously sync the state between Git and the Kubernetes clusters, ensuring operations are consistent with the declared infrastructure.

```
apiVersion: argoproj.io/v1alpha1
kind: Application
metadata:
  name: my-dapr-app
spec:
  source:
    repoURL: 'https://github.com/myorg/my-dapr-app-gitops'
    targetRevision: HEAD
    path: 'k8s/'
  destination:
    server: 'https://kubernetes.default.svc'
    namespace: 'production'
  project: 'default'
```

This configuration encapsulates how Argo CD synchronizes Git repositories with Kubernetes, streamlining application deploys based on source repository changes.

- **Logging and Monitoring:** Dapr's production efficiency hinges on comprehensive logging and monitoring to oversee its runtime operations and service outputs. Implementing observability allows teams to proactively manage application health and swiftly diagnose issues.

    - **Centralized Logging:** Aggregate logs using platforms like the Elastic Stack (ELK), which includes Elasticsearch, Logstash, and Kibana. Centralized logging consolidates logs from multiple services into a single view, facilitating easier analysis and faster root-cause identification.
    - **Metrics Collection:** Tools like Prometheus can be utilized to gather performance metrics from both Dapr and application components. These metrics are invaluable in evaluating service health, resource usage, and client experience.

        A sample 'prometheus.yml' configuration for scraping Dapr metrics:
        ```
        scrape_configs:
        - job_name: 'dapr'
          static_configs:
            - targets: ['dapr-sidecar.myapp.svc.cluster.local:9090']
        ```
    - **Distributed Tracing:** Employ OpenTelemetry to deploy instrumentation into your services, capturing traces across distributed systems. Traces provide deep insight into service calls, dependencies, and performance bottlenecks, es-

sential for understanding user workflows and optimizing operations.

- **Configuration Management:** In production environments, configuration management becomes pivotal to adapt services swiftly without necessitating code changes. Dapr supports dynamic configuration of its components through Kubernetes ConfigMaps and Secrets, which can include settings for state stores, pub/sub brokers, or custom functionality.

  Example of a Dapr component configuration using a ConfigMap:

  ```
  apiVersion: dapr.io/v1alpha1
  kind: Component
  metadata:
    name: pubsub-component
    namespace: production
  spec:
    type: pubsub.redis
    version: v1
    metadata:
    - name: redisHost
      valueFrom:
        configMapKeyRef:
          name: redis-configmap
          key: host
  ```

  Utilizing such configurations encapsulates environment-specific values, allowing varying configurations across development, testing, and production.

- **Security and Compliance:** Protecting microservices in a production environment requires diligent application of security best practices, ensuring both compliance and risk mitigation.

  - **Secure Communication:** Dapr supports mutual TLS (mTLS) by default, encrypting data in transit between services and preventing unauthorized access. Standardizing mTLS within production ensures secure service-to-service communication.

    In Kubernetes, augment security measures using network policies that restrict traffic based on namespace, labels, or IP addresses. These policies can prohibit unauthorized entities from accessing sensitive application data.

    Example of a Kubernetes Network Policy for service isolation:

```yaml
apiVersion: networking.k8s.io/v1
kind: NetworkPolicy
metadata:
  name: restrict-access
  namespace: production
spec:
  podSelector:
    matchLabels:
      app: my-dapr-app
  policyTypes:
  - Ingress
  ingress:
  - from:
    - namespaceSelector:
        matchLabels:
          project: myproject
```

- **Role-Based Access Control (RBAC):** Enforce security by defining precise role-based access control (RBAC) policies within Kubernetes. RBAC ensures personnel have only the permissions necessary to perform their roles, mitigating the risk of accidental or malicious changes.

```yaml
apiVersion: rbac.authorization.k8s.io/v1
kind: Role
metadata:
  namespace: production
  name: pod-reader
rules:
- apiGroups: [""]
  resources: ["pods"]
  verbs: ["get", "watch", "list"]

apiVersion: rbac.authorization.k8s.io/v1
kind: RoleBinding
metadata:
  name: read-pods
  namespace: production
subjects:
- kind: User
  name: jane-doe
  apiGroup: rbac.authorization.k8s.io
roleRef:
  kind: Role
  name: pod-reader
  apiGroup: rbac.authorization.k8s.io
```

- **Performance Optimization:** Production environments must be configured for optimal resource use to prevent performance degradation under load.

    - Pod Density: Evaluate the appropriate density of pods per

node, balancing network latency, storage access times, and CPU constraints.

- Resource Requests and Limits: Configure resource requests and limits tailored to actual consumption patterns, boosting efficiency while preventing resource starvation.
- Caching: Leverage Dapr's building blocks for caching, strategically storing results or computations to relieve pressure on upstream services and databases during high-load periods.

- **Handling Failures and Resiliency:** No system is immune to failure, though Dapr's runtime adds inherent resiliency through design patterns like retries, timeouts, and circuit breakers. Implement these patterns using Dapr's APIs and middleware to enhance system robustness.

  - Retries and Circuit Breakers: Configure Dapr service invocation to automatically retry failed requests and activate circuit breakers when thresholds cross a limit.
  - Backoff Strategies: Use exponential backoff strategies, limiting instant retries after failures, thereby preserving both network and system resources.

- **Continual Testing and Load Balancing:** Post-deployment success demands ongoing validation of system capabilities. Implement strategies for:

  - Load Testing: Integrate tools such as Apache JMeter or Locust to simulate varied load intensities, identifying circuit pressure points and resource constraints.
  - Chaos Engineering: Apply chaos engineering principles, intentionally introducing faults to assess system behavior and failure response strategies.

Managing Dapr in a production setting revolves around aligning operational practices with cloud-native principles. Through robust deployment methodologies, observability integrations, and security rigor, organizations can leverage Dapr's capabilities to consistently and effectively operate microservices, meeting both user needs and business goals. This structured approach ensures the reliability and resilience necessary for modern agile development environments.

10.6 Leveraging Cloud Provider Services

In modern computational landscapes, cloud providers such as AWS, Azure, and Google Cloud Platform offer a plethora of services that can be harnessed to enhance the functionality, scalability, and resilience of Dapr applications. By leveraging these cloud-native services, developers and operations teams can streamline deployments, reduce maintenance overhead, and focus on core business objectives while benefiting from the infrastructure and services provided by cloud vendors.

The integration of Dapr with these cloud services allows for a seamless enhancement of application capabilities by abstracting away underlying complexities and promoting a more agile development environment. This section explores the effective use of cloud provider services alongside Dapr, providing detailed insights into various service integrations and configurations that maximize performance and reliability.

- **Cloud Storage Services**

Cloud storage services are essential for Dapr applications that require scalable and reliable data backends. Services such as Amazon S3, Azure Blob Storage, and Google Cloud Storage provide a sandbox for persisting application data, supporting different consistency, availability, and access models.

- **Example Integration: Azure Blob Storage**

Integrating Azure Blob Storage with a Dapr application allows services to store and retrieve data objects efficiently. This is achieved through Dapr's state management APIs, which can abstract access to Azure Blob Storage.

```
# Azure Blob Storage as a component in Dapr
apiVersion: dapr.io/v1alpha1
kind: Component
```

10.6. LEVERAGING CLOUD PROVIDER SERVICES

```
metadata:
  name: azureblob
  namespace: default
spec:
  type: state.azure.blobstorage
  version: v1
  metadata:
    - name: accountName
      value: "your_storage_account"
    - name: accountKey
      value: "your_account_key"
    - name: containerName
      value: "your_container_name"
```

The above configuration sets up Azure Blob Storage as a persistent state store in a Dapr-enabled Kubernetes environment. This enables Dapr applications to perform operations on Azure Blob Storage without embedding SDK-specific or storage access logic into the application codebase.

- **Cloud Database Services**

Offloading database management to cloud database services like Amazon RDS, Azure SQL Database, or Google Cloud SQL can simplify data handling by delegating backup, replication, scaling, and patching responsibilities to the cloud provider.

- **Example Integration: Google Cloud Firestore**

Firestore, a NoSQL document database, can be used as a backend state store or pub/sub component in Dapr.

```
# Firestore state store configuration for Dapr
apiVersion: dapr.io/v1alpha1
kind: Component
metadata:
  name: firestoredemo
  namespace: default
spec:
  type: state.firestore
  version: v1
  metadata:
    - name: projectId
      value: "your_project_id"
    - name: clientEmail
      value: "your_service_account_email"
    - name: privateKey
      value: "your_private_key"
```

This configuration enables a connection to Google Cloud Firestore that can be used to manage application state or persist data for Dapr-enabled services, providing resilience and scalability from Google's global infrastructure.

- **Messaging and Event Services**

Dapr's pub/sub capability can be seamlessly integrated with cloud messaging services, enabling robust and scalable event-driven architectures. Leveraging services such as AWS SNS/SQS, Azure Service Bus, or Google Pub/Sub offers distributed systems durable, asynchronous communication channels.

- **Example Integration: AWS SNS and SQS**

Integrating AWS SNS and SQS with Dapr provides a powerful, decoupled message ingestion and processing pipeline.

```
# AWS SNS and SQS configuration for Dapr pub/sub
apiVersion: dapr.io/v1alpha1
kind: Component
metadata:
  name: messagebus
  namespace: default
spec:
  type: pubsub.aws.sns.sqs
  version: v1
  metadata:
    - name: accessKey
      value: "your_access_key"
    - name: secretKey
      value: "your_secret_key"
    - name: region
      value: "your_region"
    - name: snsTopicArn
      value: "arn:aws:sns:your_region:your_account:your_topic"
    - name: sqsQueueUrl
      value: "https://sqs.your_region.amazonaws.com/your_account/your_queue"
```

Here, AWS SNS is used to publish messages to a topic, and SQS handles the message queueing, allowing Dapr applications to process these messages as part of reactive workflows.

- **Security and Identity Services**

10.6. LEVERAGING CLOUD PROVIDER SERVICES

Cloud provider-managed security services offer enhanced security levels with integrated identification and access management tools. Leveraging services like AWS IAM, Azure AD, and Google IAM ensures secure access configurations.

- **Example Integration: Azure Key Vault**

Azure Key Vault can be integrated into Dapr applications to manage service secrets, tokens, and certificate management.

```
# Azure Key Vault as a Dapr component
apiVersion: dapr.io/v1alpha1
kind: Component
metadata:
  name: azurekeyvault
  namespace: default
spec:
  type: secretstores.azure.keyvault
  version: v1
  metadata:
  - name: vaultName
    value: "your_vault_name"
  - name: spnClientId
    value: "your_client_id"
  - name: spnClientSecret
    value: "your_client_secret"
```

This integration allows Dapr applications to retrieve secrets securely without hardcoding sensitive information in application code, reducing vulnerability risk.

- **Computing and Machine Learning Services**

Cloud providers' computing services, such as AWS Lambda, Azure Functions, or Google Cloud Functions, offer event-driven compute capabilities that enhance scalability. Additionally, incorporating machine learning services such as Amazon SageMaker or Google AI Platform empowers Dapr applications with predictive analytics and intelligent features.

- **Example Integration: Google Cloud Functions**

Using Google Cloud Functions in conjunction with Dapr holds potential for scaling compute workloads dynamically where some service logic can be offloaded to these serverless components.

```python
# Invoking Google Cloud Functions from Dapr Service
import os
import requests

def invoke_cloud_function(data):
    url = f"https://your_region-your_project.cloudfunctions.net/your_function_name"

    response = requests.post(url, json=data)
    return response.json()
```

This Python snippet demonstrates calling an external cloud function from within a Dapr service, extending compute operations while maintaining separation of concerns.

- **Monitoring and Logging Services**

Leveraging cloud-native monitoring services like AWS CloudWatch, Azure Monitor, or Google Cloud Operations enhances observability in Dapr applications. These services provide seamless integration for log collection, metric tracking, and alerting, aiding operational insights.

- **Example Integration: AWS CloudWatch**

Integrate AWS CloudWatch into the monitoring stack of a Dapr-enabled application to capture logs, metrics, or custom events.

```yaml
# CloudWatch logging configuration with Fluentd in Dapr
apiVersion: v1
kind: ConfigMap
metadata:
  name: fluentd-config
data:
  fluentd.conf: |
    <source>
      @type forward
      bind 0.0.0.0
      port 24224
    </source>
    <match **>
      @type cloudwatch_logs
      log_group_name fluentd
      log_stream_name {instance_id}
      aws_key_id YOUR_AWS_KEY
      aws_sec_key YOUR_AWS_SEC_KEY
      region YOUR_AWS_REGION
    </match>
```

By exporting logs to CloudWatch, Dapr applications gain integrated log management capabilities with extensive querying, visualizing, and alerting features.

- **Conclusion**

Leveraging cloud provider services in conjunction with Dapr enriches applications with robustness, scalability, and performance efficiency. By embedding cloud-native tools, Dapr-enabled applications gain the necessary agility and resilience for modern computing demands, aligning development practices with industry scaling and reliability standards. This synergy results in applications that not only meet but exceed user expectations by delivering seamless, performant, and innovative digital experiences.

10.7 CI/CD for Dapr Applications

Implementing Continuous Integration and Continuous Deployment (CI/CD) pipelines for Dapr applications is essential for maintaining agility and ensuring rapid, reliable delivery of microservice functionalities in cloud-native environments. CI/CD bridges the gap between development and operations by automating testing, building, and deployment processes, enhancing software quality and accelerating release cycles. For Dapr applications, embedding CI/CD processes aligns with the microservices architecture's dynamic nature, where applications consist of distributed, decoupled components that require synchronized updates and efficient management.

This section delves into best practices and tools for integrating CI/CD pipelines tailored to Dapr-enhanced microservices, ensuring seamless deployments that leverage Dapr's runtime benefits while maintaining operational stability and security.

Setting Up a CI/CD Workflow

A robust CI/CD pipeline incorporates numerous stages, each serving a specific purpose in validating, integrating, deploying, and monitoring microservices. Setting up this workflow involves selecting appropriate tools and defining processes suited to a Dapr-powered microservices architecture.

The CI/CD Pipeline Stages

- **Source Code Management (SCM)**:
    - Use a version control system like Git to host your application's source code, enabling collaboration and change tracking. Platforms such as GitHub, GitLab, or Bitbucket can serve as the SCM state repository.

- **Automated Testing**:
    - Implement unit tests using frameworks like pytest, JUnit, or Mocha to verify the correctness of functionality.
    - Integrate linting and style checkers to ensure code quality standards. Linters such as ESLint for JavaScript or Pylint for Python are common choices.

- **Build**:
    - Incorporate Docker for building containers, encapsulating microservices with their dependencies. This step enhances consistency across environments by packaging applications into standardized units.
    - Use Dockerfiles to define build instructions, ensuring images reflect the correct application and runtime versions.

- **Continuous Integration**:
    - Employ automation servers like Jenkins, Travis CI, or GitHub Actions to automate tests and build processes with each code commit.
    - Configuration files, like .travis.yml or Jenkinsfile, outline stages and execution environments.

- **Deployment**:
    - Use deployment tools or services such as Kubernetes, Helm, or Flux to manage application deployment on Kubernetes clusters.

10.7. CI/CD FOR DAPR APPLICATIONS

– Implement Helm charts to define, install, and upgrade complex Kubernetes applications using templates for managing Dapr configurations.

- **Continuous Deployment**:

    – Extend CI/CD to automate full deployments to test or production environments after successful build and test stages, ensuring every update reaches users without manual intervention.

    – Gate deployments using feature toggle tools like LaunchDarkly or Harness, enabling gradual exposure based on user roles or conditions.

- **Monitoring and Feedback**:

    – Incorporate monitoring and feedback loops to provide real-time insights into deployed application performance.

    – Utilize monitoring services like Prometheus and Grafana to visualize metrics and trends, supporting proactive incident response.

Example CI/CD Configuration Using GitHub Actions

GitHub Actions can automate deployment workflows for Dapr applications by defining a series of executable steps in a YAML file within the repository.

```yaml
# GitHub Actions workflow file: .github/workflows/dapr-ci-cd.yml
name: Dapr CI/CD

on:
  push:
    branches: [ main ]
  pull_request:
    branches: [ main ]

jobs:
  build:
    runs-on: ubuntu-latest

    steps:
    - name: Checkout code
      uses: actions/checkout@v2

    - name: Set up Docker Buildx
      uses: docker/setup-buildx-action@v1
```

```
    - name: Log in to Docker Hub
      uses: docker/login-action@v1
      with:
        username: ${{ secrets.DOCKER_USERNAME }}
        password: ${{ secrets.DOCKER_PASSWORD }}

    - name: Build and push Docker images
      uses: docker/build-push-action@v2
      with:
        context: .
        push: true
        tags: ${{ secrets.DOCKER_USERNAME }}/dapr-app:latest

  deploy:
    runs-on: ubuntu-latest
    needs: build

    steps:
    - name: Checkout code
      uses: actions/checkout@v2

    - name: Deploy to Kubernetes
      uses: azure/k8s-deploy@v3
      with:
        namespace: dapr-app
        manifests: |
          k8s/deployment.yaml
        images: ${{ secrets.DOCKER_USERNAME }}/dapr-app:latest
```

This configuration automates building Docker images from the repository, then deploying the Kubernetes resources upon changes to the main branch, ensuring an updated application in the cluster.

Implementing Dapr-Specific Considerations

In cloud-native environments, Dapr's runtime components like pub/sub, state management, or binding services require specific configurations and deployments:

- **Versioned Components**: Ensure Dapr components like configurations for state stores or pub/sub brokers are version-controlled and updated with the application code. This practice minimizes compatibility issues during deployment and updates.

- **Sidecar Injection**: Utilize annotations like dapr.io/enabled: "true" in Kubernetes manifests to automate Dapr sidecar container injection during deployments, simplifying microservices-to-Dapr integrations.

10.7. CI/CD FOR DAPR APPLICATIONS

```
# Kubernetes deployment with Dapr sidecar annotations
apiVersion: apps/v1
kind: Deployment
metadata:
  name: dapr-app
spec:
  replicas: 3
  selector:
    matchLabels:
      app: dapr-app
  template:
    metadata:
      labels:
        app: dapr-app
      annotations:
        dapr.io/enabled: "true"
        dapr.io/app-id: "dapr-app"
    spec:
      containers:
      - name: dapr-container
        image: dapr-app-image:latest
        ports:
        - containerPort: 80
```

Security and Compliance in CI/CD

CI/CD pipelines must implement security best practices to safeguard application integrity and data privacy:

- **Credentials Management**: Store credentials securely using environment secrets provided by CI/CD platforms. Secrets management services like AWS Secrets Manager or Azure Key Vault can enhance security and compliance by encrypting sensitive data.

- **Secure Dependencies**: Regularly audit application and container dependencies for vulnerabilities using tools like Snyk or Dependabot to prompt patches and updates.

- **Isolation**: Ensure build agents or runners execute in isolated environments to minimize shared resource risks and comply with organizational security standards.

Continuous Improvement and Iteration

CI/CD pipelines for Dapr applications should be adaptable, allowing for continuous improvement based on feedback and real-world application performance:

- **Metrics Review Sessions**: Schedule regular review sessions to assess pipeline metrics, such as build times or deployment frequencies, identifying bottlenecks and areas for process optimization.

- **Experimentation with Feature Flags**: Implement feature flags for A/B testing and phased rollouts, collecting user feedback and metrics to drive iterative improvements.

- **Post-Deployment Observability**: Monitor application health post-deployment through logging and analytics dashboards, iterating upon feedback loops to mitigate issues before they impact users.

Conclusion

CI/CD for Dapr applications encapsulates a holistic approach to managing microservices, enabling teams to deliver innovative solutions with speed and precision. By incorporating tailored strategies that align with Dapr's microservice architecture, CI/CD pipelines facilitate an efficient, resilient, and scalable deployment process that supports modern application demands. Integrating these methodologies within development workflows ensures robust, future-proof applications capable of evolving with technological advancements and consumer expectations.

10.7. CI/CD FOR DAPR APPLICATIONS

www.ingramcontent.com/pod-product-compliance
Lightning Source LLC
Chambersburg PA
CBHW052141220526
45471CB00004B/1468